PATTERNS
— on —
PARCHMENT

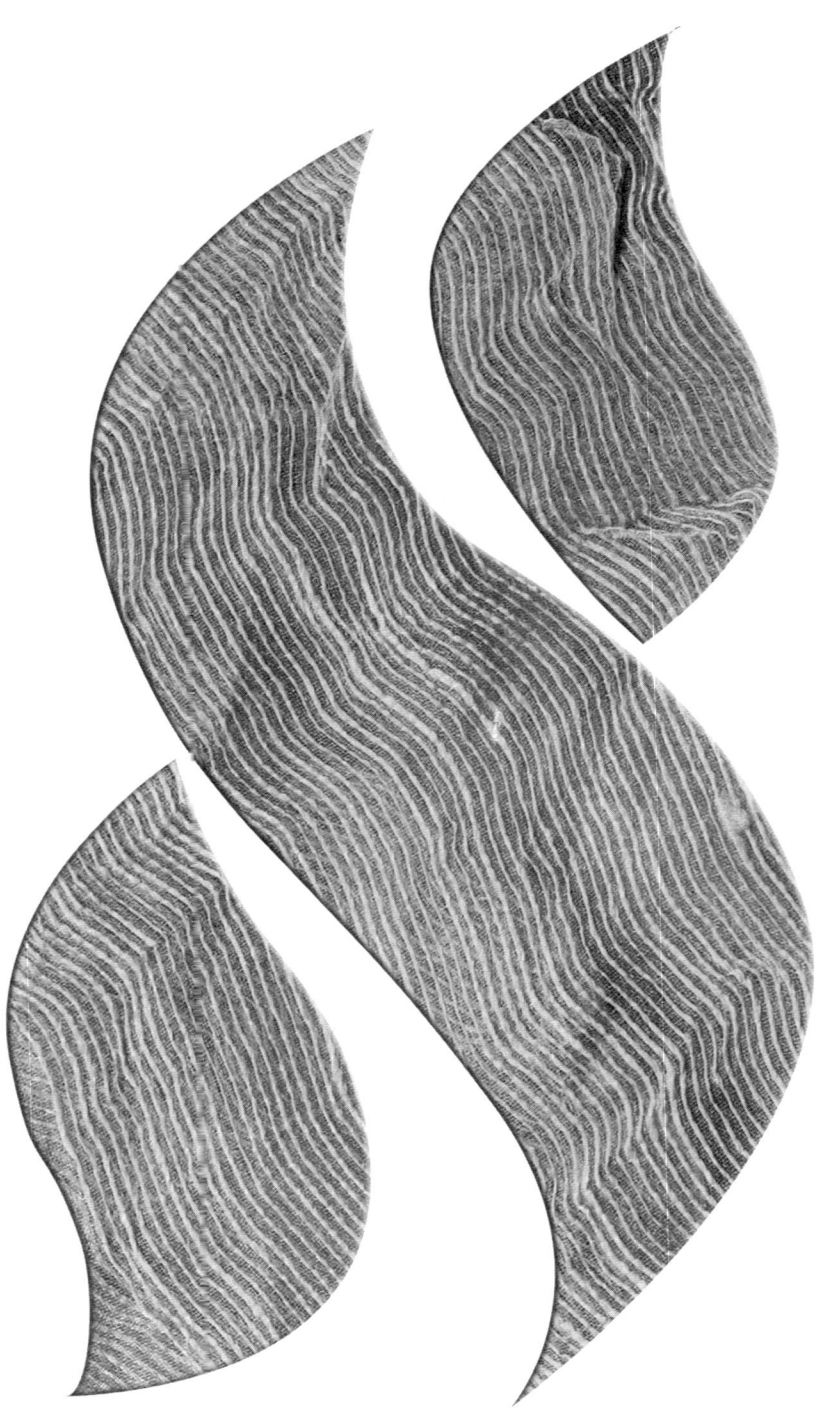

PATTERNS on PARCHMENT

The Structural Unity of the Five Books of Moses

DR. ROBERT APPLESON

MOSAICA PRESS

Mosaica Press, Inc.

© 2016 by Mosaica Press

Typeset by Rayzel Broyde

All rights reserved

ISBN-10: 1-937887-68-5   ISBN-13: 978-1-937887-68-1

No part of this publication may be translated, reproduced, stored in a retrieval system or transmitted in any form or by any means, electronic, mechanical, photocopying, recording, or otherwise, without prior permission in writing from both the copyright holder and the publisher.

Published and distributed by:

Mosaica Press, Inc.

www.mosaicapress.com

info@mosaicapress.com

Rabbi Gedalia Dov Schwartz
3001 West Chase Avenue
Chicago, Illinois 60645

ג' תמוז תשע"א, ג' פרשת בלק
July 5, 2011

Dr. Robert Appleson
9136 North Crawford Avenue
Skokie, Illinois 60076

Dear Dr. Appleson,

    After reading various parts of your scholarly work "Patterns on Parchment," I have been greatly impressed by the methodology of your research and analysis. Besides the background use of the basic Midrashic texts, your novel use of mathematics in establishing patterns and interpretations truly support the integrity of the Torah as a divine document. Your work is a worthy addition to the Torah literature of this genre.

Sincerely,

Rabbi Gedalia Dov Schwartz

GDS/sm

In Memory of

HaRav Ephraim Greenblatt, ZT"L

How blessed were we to live in Memphis during Rabbi Greenblatt's many years of teaching, scholarship, Torah initiative, and moral guidance. His glow touched so many of us so deeply that words cannot describe the lessons still carried in our hearts. These lessons are no less the Rivevot Ephraim *— the myriads of Ephraim — than the outstanding volumes of Jewish legal responsa by which he is known to Torah scholars around the world. May the pages that follow attest to his inspiration of an entire community, and may the memory of this righteous man be for a blessing.*

Table of Contents

Acknowledgments 9
Foreword by Rabbi Yitzchak Breitowitz 11
Introduction 13

Stage 1: Apparent Randomness in the Five Books/ Enter the Shared Principles

Section 1: Seeming Imperfection in the Text and
　　　　　How It Reflects on Authorship 25

Section 2: Torah Paragraphs and the Shared Principles 35

Section 3: Shared Principles and the
　　　　　Order of the Five Books 50

Section 4: Division of a Book into Five Parts and a Part into
　　　　　Five Subparts 59

Stage 2: Sizing Up the Pattern, Checking It in Genesis, and Developing a Strategy

Section 5: Analyzing the Pattern 83

Section 6: Checking Genesis 100

Section 7: Strategy for Testing the Pattern 122

Stage 3: Applying the Strategy and Analyzing the Results

Section 8: Testing the Pattern in Exodus 143

Section 9: Testing the Pattern in Leviticus 169

Section 10: Testing the Pattern in Numbers 190

Section 11: Concluding Evaluation and
　　　　　Broader Implications 212

ELABORATION ON STAGE I

Section 12: The Wellhausen Hypothesis: Origins, Development,
　　　　　and Points of Opposition 241

Section 13: Textual Integrity and Role of the Ten
　　　　　Commandments 263

Section 14: Mastery and Failure with the Shared Principles and
　　　　　Deuteronomy's Pattern 272

SUPPLEMENT to STAGES II AND III

Section 15: Supplement to the Test in Genesis 301

Section 16: Supplement to the Test in Exodus 314

Section 17: Supplement on Matching Division Points 327

APPENDICES

Appendix a: Location of *P'tuchot* in the
　　　　　Five Books of Moses 339

Appendix b: Spelling and Spacing Differences in
　　　　　Torah Scrolls 342

Appendix c: List of Remaining Parts in First Four Books
　　　　　Subdivided into Subparts 344

Appendix d: Glossary 352

About the Author 360

Acknowledgments

Though this book bears my name as author, many people helped bring it to fruition. My thanks go to Rabbis Doron Kornbluth and Yaacov Haber and their staff at Mosaica Press for turning my manuscript into a finished product. Their efforts to allow less known writers a fitting audience deserve ample recognition. Rabbi Kornbluth's painstaking and insightful editorial work improved the manuscript in many ways. Rayzel Broyde's responsive design also merits high praise.

I am especially indebted to Rabbis Gedalia Dov Schwartz *shlita*, Rosh Bet Din of the Chicago Rabbinical Council, and Yitzchak Breitowitz *shlita*, Senior Lecturer at Ohr Somayach. Taking time from their vital work, they reviewed my manuscript and wrote the approbation and foreword for this book in a most generous way. Thanks to my friend Dr. Justin Gordon for connecting me with Rabbi Breitowitz.

In just a few pages, you will encounter the ideas of Rabbi Yehoshua Honigwachs on the organizational structure of the Five Books of Moses. Not only do I rely here on these ideas (which merit much broader awareness), but also Rabbi Honigwachs liberally consulted with me many times, thus allowing me to build on his work. Particular gratitude is due my friend Rabbi Moshe Englander for guiding me to Rabbi Honigwachs' book *The Unity of Torah*.

Rabbis Aron Rosenberg and Kalman Worch of Skokie, Illinois, have given me more than I can describe — both as teachers and as models for behavior. Rabbi Rosenberg has led me through the writings of the Maharal of Prague, whose original structural thought has brought me understanding beyond any previous study. Rabbi Worch's logical insights and pinpoint memory of Talmudic and Midrashic sources have often allowed me to navigate challenges in the Torah's structure. Thanks also to Rabbi Yaakov Kreisman for providing a more systematic background in Ramban's commentary.

Three individuals from my years in Cincinnati gave regularly of their time to fill the gaps in what was an uneven background at best: Rabbis Jacob Lustig, Stuart Lavenda, and Yaakov Dovid Homnick. But for their efforts, and the unique motivation from Rabbi Homnick, I could not have gained nearly as much in Skokie. And I could not have reached even my level in Cincinnati without the inspiration of Rabbi Juda Mintz in Atlanta and the encouragement of Rabbi Mendel Lewitin in Nashville to bring me back to Jewish study. For all those teachers who invested in me, but most of all for my Rebbe, Rabbi Ephraim Greenblatt *zt"l*, who taught me growing up in Memphis, I hope this book provides some measure of return.

While the debt to my teachers can never be repaid, I owe my wife Charlene even more. My loving companion and the caring mother of our children, she has promoted my learning, often taking over chores to allow me more study time. Her own dedicated study and noble character constantly inspire me, and she richly deserves equal credit in this work.

My two study partners and friends, Dr. Elliott Ostro and Howard Weiss, have acted as valuable sounding boards as the manuscript progressed. Many other friends and family members have also given welcome encouragement. I especially want to recognize and express gratitude to several of them who have joined me in underwriting this book to fulfill the mitzvah of spreading and supporting Torah. Their names and dedications follow.

Roxanne and Ross Abrams

In honor of the memory of their parents, Rhoda and Philip Katz and Harriet and Joseph Abrams, who transmitted Jewish values and the importance of maintaining the chain of Jewish tradition.

Dr. and Mrs. Avrum and Rita Epstein

In loving memory of Linda Schlanger Stiegel, Harvey and Ruth Epstein, William and Ester Schlanger, and Frida Landau.

All of these acknowledgments reflect the truth that even help from others takes Divine Providence. Thus, I thank our Creator for giving me such a wonderful wife and family, along with supportive teachers and friends, and for allowing me a role in building up His Torah.

Robert Appleson
September 7, 2015
Skokie, Illinois

Foreword

by Rabbi Yitzchak Breitowitz, Senior Lecturer, Ohr Somayach

For centuries, people have been perplexed over the apparent randomness and abrupt transitions in the narratives and laws contained in the Torah. While the Talmud, Midrash, and later commentaries such as Rashi and Ramban offer sporadic explanations for a number of these instances, many remain unexplained. The failure to discern an intelligible pattern in the Five Books of Moses is not simply a literary concern; some scholars have used this apparent lack of coherent organization as proof of multiple patchwork authorship, thereby undermining the fundamental principle of the Divine origin of the Torah and the binding nature of mitzvot.

In a pathbreaking study published more than twenty years ago, Rabbi Yehoshua Honigwachs[1] claimed to have discovered a pattern of organization based on the fundamental principles of the Ten Commandments. Matching each of the first five "Person to God" laws with its respective counterpart in the "Interpersonal" column, Honigwachs discerned five organizing principles and endeavored to show that each Book's primary and dominant focus was on one of these principles. He then attempted to show that secondary and tertiary divisions (based on the rarely studied traditional and authoritative paragraph divisions of *p'tuchot* and *s'tumot*) within each Book proceeded to address (in minor key as it were) all the other principles as well. Each Book of the Torah therefore becomes a reiteration of the fundamentals of the Decalogue; each Part, while retaining the uniqueness of its dominant emphasis, becomes a microcosm of the whole. The totality of God's revelation is thus reflected in each discrete segment, much as the entire human genome can be found within the structure of a single somatic cell. Rabbi Honigwachs' work sadly did not receive the attention it deserved. More importantly, while the book ably articulated the general thesis, the actual details were only worked out for the Book of Genesis. The promised volumes on the remaining Books have not appeared.

Robert Appleson, Ph.D., has taken up the gauntlet and has laboriously and methodically applied the Honigwachs model to the entire Five Books. Dr. Appleson is uniquely qualified for this daunting task. First, he approached this hypothesis with a skeptical eye — he needed to be convinced and would not move forward until he was. He thus meticulously examines all possible flaws in the Honigwachs' argument. Second, his doctoral experience in mathematical pattern recognition gives him the tools to discern which patterns are likely to be deliberate and planned and which could be assigned to randomness and chance. Third, as a *baal korei* (professional Torah reader), he is well-positioned to see the profound organizational significance of the Torah's paragraph divisions. Essential to the appreciation of the Torah's deep structures, these divisions are simply ignored by most readers, and those reading translations will not be aware of them at all.

While solidly grounded in Rabbi Honigwachs' pioneering work, Dr. Appleson contributes many new ideas, modifications, nuances, and improvements of his own, based on his familiarity with mathematics, statistics, probability, and classical Biblical commentary. His writing is lucid, well-organized, (relatively) easy to follow, and enjoyable. He leads the reader by the hand gently and methodically. This is certainly a work that a nonprofessional (like myself!) can read and enjoy.

If I had to sum up my view in one sentence, it is this: the attentive reader who carefully studies and digests the ideas in this book will walk away with a deeper and more profound appreciation of the infinite wisdom of the Creator that is embodied in His holy Torah. There is surely no higher praise that can be bestowed.

Introduction

The work commonly known in English as the Five Books of Moses also goes by its Greek name, the Pentateuch, and by its original Hebrew name, the Torah. By whatever name, this text forms the bedrock of Judaism. It is also the basis of Christianity and surfaces often in disputes between religion and secularism. Despite the US Supreme Court's rulings on using public grounds to display the Ten Commandments (part of the Torah),[2] arguments over separation of church and state still fill the media. Does such a display constitute "legislation respecting an establishment of religion," thus violating the First Amendment to the Constitution? Are the Commandments so basic to our culture as to transcend designation as a religious doctrine?

Yet, beyond the dueling Constitutional interpretations lies a crucial question even more daunting: how much of the Five Books came from God? No party — and surely not the Court — can hope to settle this question of origin with broad assent in our society. At the same time, one's belief about origin can drive his stance on public display of the Commandments as much as how the First Amendment is construed. At a deeper level, it can affect one's whole life.

Take the two most divergent positions on the origin of the Five Books. Total deniers of Divine origin see Torah values as reflecting past agendas and prejudice, which should preclude government recognition of the Commandments, even as a cultural proxy. In contrast, proponents of purely Divine authorship (myself among them) agree on the lasting authority of the Commandments.[3] Accordingly, efforts to bar display on public grounds, especially in a country founded on Biblical principles, seem misguided and often arrogant.

This rift over moral philosophy between affirmers and deniers of Divine authorship only widens for issues of personal lifestyle like homosexuality and recreational drug use. The stakes and passions in these issues dwarf those for symbolic displays on government property.

Thus, it is no surprise that debate over the Torah's origin extends to venues well beyond the judicial bench — venues where the accuracy and credibility of the text can be examined with the tools of current scholarship. For example, some have joined the dispute in archaeology over whether evidence from excavations supports or discredits Biblical accounts.[4]

Others have engaged in sophisticated statistical study of the so-called "Bible Codes." According to proponents of the codes, analysis of the Hebrew text reveals encoded words formed from letters at prescribed intervals, words that prophetically suggest events occurring long after Biblical times. If true, the codes demonstrate the Torah's credibility through its prediction of the future. However, detractors argue that "encoded" words can also be generated from other common texts by the same methods, so the Bible Codes prove nothing.[5]

And we cannot forget the clash over the Torah's perceived lack of conformity to modern science, especially regarding evolution and the age of the earth. Views on this issue range so broadly as to defy neat classification. One approach, which maintains the Divine origin of the text while accepting modern science, argues that there is no contradiction in the account of Creation between Torah and science when both are correctly understood.[6]

The foregoing aspects of the debate are important if only to provide a sense of its scope. However, we will examine the text of the Torah without the influence of archaeology, coding studies, cell biology, or astrophysics. Setting aside these other factors may be understood through the metaphor of a person watching a movie in a fully lit theater.[7] While this person can see the screen, the action projected on it is actually obscured by the ambient light. Here, too, conflicting claims outside the text can detract from the clarity within.

Thus we focus on one point only: does the character of the text indicate a single author (Divine or otherwise) or more than one? The question of Divine origin clearly lurks nearby, for the idea of direct transcription (by Moses) of God's word does not mesh easily with a sense of several authors. This book therefore does not dwell on arguments for

God's existence, communication with mankind, or intervention in our world.

Those espousing multiple (human) authorship of the Five Books are commonly known as Source Critics. Their view of authorship rose to prominence in the nineteenth century and now dominates Biblical Criticism, the literary approach to the Bible taught in most colleges and universities. So pervasive is Source Criticism that many see it as a necessary ingredient in any literary analysis of the Bible, i.e., in Biblical Criticism generally. Thus, even when a Biblical literary study (say, about poetic technique) need not involve multiple authorship of the Torah, an analyst may still refer to several hypothesized authors. Such references can lead one to confuse Biblical Criticism with Source Criticism, though Bible Critics need not be Source Critics.

To justify their view of multiple authorship, Source Critics point to seeming randomness and inconsistency in the text, such as sequences of unrelated topics and discrepant versions of the same law. This randomness and inconsistency preclude, they say, any chance the Five Books are a unified document, so the full text must have been compiled over time from different sources. As Bible scholar Martin Noth put it (when speaking about the Book of Numbers): "There can be no question of...its originating from the hand of a single author. This is already clear from the confusion and lack of order in its contents."[8]

Thus, Source Critics dismiss Divine dictation of the Five Books through a single channel, leaving at most a compromised opening for Divine influence on the text through several perceived authors. This influence must, at most, take the form of less definitive or less transparent guidance (what some call "Divine inspiration") that allows for many textual imperfections. Of course, accepting that level of imperfection means abandoning the broad and lasting authority of the Five Books — even if they are seen as Divinely influenced. After all, given such imperfection, how do we decide which Biblical laws retain authority (having come from God alone) and which do not (having the influence of human limitations)?

Until recently, advocates of single authorship and defenders of broad and lasting authority could but challenge Source Critics on specific cases of perceived randomness and inconsistency, essentially explaining why any particular case of randomness and inconsistency is neither random nor inconsistent. While these challengers have explained such individual cases well enough to uphold the integrity of the text, skepticism over a unified document remains. This sense of textual fragmentation persists largely because there has been little sign of a more encompassing pattern.[9]

However, such a pattern does exist. I, too, was skeptical of it at first, but, as we will see, there is indeed a clear pattern that unifies the Torah through a parallel progression of themes found in each Book. I did not find this pattern. It was proposed by Rabbi Yehoshua Honigwachs in *The Unity of Torah*,[10] which, sadly, received very little exposure. The difficulty in attracting more readers stemmed largely from the complexity of textual analysis and from the background needed to fully grasp its details.

However, this pattern, with its potential impact on the authorship debate, deserves broad attention. Thus, the pursuit of a larger audience has prompted the new approach found here — an approach refined through presentations to groups with a wide range of textual background.

One key feature of this approach is to put essential information close at hand and to provide graphic illustrations and other visual prompts (such as the framing of key analyses). A second feature is to separate the major features of the pattern from more intricate background information to avoid distraction. Finally, I try to remind the reader at frequent intervals 'where we are" in the overall development. Along the way, we will see how the Torah has been reformatted in its translation from Hebrew and how this reformatting could obscure such a pattern.

This book is intended for those interested in the structure and organization of the Five Books of Moses. Anyone, whether religiously observant or not, whether Jewish or not, with at least a modest grasp of the Five Books is invited — with or without some knowledge of Hebrew. All I ask is an open mind and a willingness to engage with the text of the Five Books.

In line with my heritage and study, I take my guidance from classic Hebrew sources. In particular, two medieval authorities are especially basic in understanding the text of the Torah, known by their Hebrew acronyms as Rashi and Ramban. As you will see, these two commentaries address many questions of order and organization. Notwithstanding the key role of Rashi and Ramban, I also recognize material contributions of other scholars, whether Jewish or not, and explicitly acknowledge their work in this book. The meaning of a pattern in the Five Books goes beyond Judaism.

While I come to our subject without a formal degree in Biblical studies, I do bring a decent grasp of classic structural commentary, as well as two credentials beyond those held by most writers. The first is training as a *baal korei* — one who reads from a Torah scroll on behalf of a Jewish congregation. This function demands an intimacy with the Hebrew text that allows one to chant it without using vowels, punctuation, or melodic cues. The second credential is training in mathematics, with my doctoral work involving pattern recognition. Rest assured, you will not find any high-powered formulas here, but my background has made me extremely sensitive to changes in focus and tone in the text, changes that can be seen to mark structural boundaries. This is a sensitivity I hope to share with the reader as we test and confirm the pattern together.

And, now, on to the task.

Our approach includes three main stages:

> **The Three Stages of Understanding the Structure of the Torah**
>
> Stage I explains the issue of authorship and describes the pattern of Shared Principles. The special case of Deuteronomy is noted, followed by examples of the pattern in the other books.
>
> Stage II weighs the pattern's ability to explain sequences of topics, but also projects factors likely to invalidate the pattern. After the pattern is checked in Genesis, a protocol is developed to test the pattern in Exodus, Leviticus, and Numbers.
>
> Stage III uses the protocol from Stage II to challenge the pattern in Exodus, Leviticus, and Numbers and shows the results in each of those Books. A comprehensive analysis then follows.

These three stages constitute the main body of the approach, include the relevant information for most readers, and should be read in order. However, there are two further components, as well:

> Elaboration treats more fully subjects introduced in Stage I — the approach to authorship of the text known as Source Criticism, the integrity of the Torah's paragraph structure, broader textual reflections of the Ten Commandments, and the relationship of Deuteronomy to the other Books.
>
> Supplement adds details of the pattern in Genesis and Exodus from Stages II and III and explains more specifically how the progression of the pattern is reliably detected.

Stages I–III and these two further components are partitioned into numbered Sections (1–17), thus reserving the word "Chapter" for a chapter in the Torah. Endnotes will be found at the end of each Stage and at the end of the Elaboration and Supplement. The reader may find it useful to reread the concluding evaluation in Section 11 of Stage III in light of the Elaboration.

In dealing with issues in the text, we will sometimes encounter concepts or wording in which the normal English counterpart of the original Hebrew does not adequately capture a feature or distinction. In such cases, I have rendered the Hebrew into italicized transliteration with the translation in square brackets. Where Hebrew words have come into common English usage (e.g., "Torah") or where they identify the name of a person or place, I do not italicize them. Also, where common English usage differs from the technically correct transliteration (e.g., Isaac versus Yitzchak), I have chosen the former. In translating the different Divine names, I have opted for simplicity by generally ignoring the differences and using the common translation "God" though the distinctions are discussed in more detail in Stage II. The following guide to transliteration will help in pronouncing transliterated Hebrew words.

1. Consonants are generally pronounced as in English, including the normal sounds of the paired *sh* (as in "ship") and *tz* (as in "glitzy"). The transliterated letter *y* is always treated as a consonant, and the transliterated letter *c* is always pronounced as a hard "c" (as in "can"). In addition, there are two consonant combinations *ch* and *kh*, which are both pronounced as the guttural ending of the expression of distaste "yech." All remaining cases of successive consonants (other than *sh*, *tz*, *ch*, and *kh*) signal a break in syllables.
2. Vowels are pronounced according to the following table for each transliterated symbol:

Symbol	Pronunciation	Symbol	Pronunciation
a	ah (as in "ma")	*o*	oh (as in "doe")
e	eh (as in "red")	*u*	oo (as in "nu")
i	ee (as in "bee")	*ai*	igh (as in "Thai")
‘	i (as in "bit")	*ei*	ay (as in "rein")

   All remaining vowel combinations (other than *ai* and *ei*) signal a break in syllables.

Using this transliteration guide, I can now explain my departure from a common naming convention. English books discussing the Five Books often refer to the Jewish people of that era as "Israelites." This terminology agrees with the predominant Hebrew name used in the text itself: *b'nei Yisrael* [the children of Israel]. In fact, the first use of the Hebrew name for "Jews" [*Y'hudim*] in the Bible occurs in the Book of Esther, written centuries after the Five Books.[11] However, the term "Israelites" sometimes masks signs of the pattern when a Hebrew term other than *b'nei Yisrael* dominates. Thus, I use "Jewish people" instead of "Israelites."

We close this introduction with a brief look at textual sources, their relationship to each other, and how they are cited. Naturally, our main source is the Torah, which, along with the Prophets and Writings, forms the Jewish Bible — known in Hebrew as *Tanakh* and by Christians as the Old Testament. Passages from the Jewish Bible are cited by book with the standard notation of (chapter:verse).

Within the Jewish legal tradition, the Torah stands as "the written law." Within the same tradition, "the oral law," which accompanied and informed the written law but which passed from generation to generation by word of mouth, is accorded equal standing. Though originating at Mount Sinai with the written law, the oral law was first written down in the second century, with this redaction extended with rabbinic analysis through the sixth century, resulting in the sixty-three-tractate compendium known as the Talmud. We will cite the more common version, the Babylonian Talmud, by tractate followed by folio number and "a" or "b" (depending on the side of the folio).

Finally, the Talmud often quotes from two types of passages within recognized collections that were first transmitted by word of mouth but were redacted at the same time as the Talmud. The first type, called a *baraita*, is a legal pronouncement not originally included in the redaction of the oral law. The second type, called a *midrash*, is an explanation or illustrative story. We will cite both types of passages by the name of the collection followed by the notation of (chapter, paragraph number). A glossary of these and other terms can be found at the very end of the book, in the last of the appendices.

Notes

1. In the interest of full disclosure, Rabbi Honigwachs is a friend and colleague of mine from our days in the Ner Israel Rabbinical College almost forty years ago. While I greatly admire him and his work, he was not consulted in the writing of this essay.
2. In June 2005, the US Supreme Court ruled on two cases, *Van Orden v. Perry* and *McCreary County v. ACLU*, with the first ruling allowing use of government property for display and the second prohibiting such use. Two characteristics cited in allowing the display in Van Orden were that this display had (1) been donated with a civic (presumably non-religious) intent: publicizing values to help reduce juvenile delinquency; and (2) stood without drawing complaint for a number of years. Cf. S. Wilf, "The Ten Commandments Cases: A View from Within," *40 Connecticut Law Review*, 2008, pp. 1329–1345.
3. While differing in Sabbath practices, traditional Jews and Christians refrain from work as a reminder of God resting on the seventh day of Creation. Outside the Commandments, more pronounced variation can occur in interpreting the Five Books. For example, traditional Judaism calls for abortion when a woman's life is endangered by pregnancy, while traditional Catholicism favors survival of the fetus and bars an abortion. Much of this discrepancy can be traced to different readings of Exodus 21:22–23.
4. See K. Kitchen's broad analysis, *On the Reliability of the Old Testament*, (Grand Rapids, MI: Eerdmans, 2003).
5. For more details, see J. Satinover, *Breaking the Bible Code* (New York: Morrow and Co, 1997).
6. Cf. G. Schroeder, *The Science of God* (New York: Simon and Schuster, 1997).
7. This metaphor is a variant of an illustration shared by Rabbi Aron Rosenberg, former head of the Skokie Community Kollel, and attributed to the late Rabbi Yehudah Leib Chasman.
8. M. Noth, *Numbers: a Commentary* (London: SCM Press, 1968), p. 4.
9. Notable exceptions can be found in the work of Mary Douglas. See especially *In the Wilderness* (Oxford: Oxford University Press, 2001), which argues that contrary to Noth's position cited in the note above, the Book of Numbers had a single author.
10. Rabbi Yehoshua Honigwachs, *The Unity of Torah* (New York: Feldheim Publishers, 1991).

11   The Book of Esther recounts events in the Persian Empire, whose conquest of Babylonia had followed Babylonia's exile of the Jewish people with the destruction of the First Temple. There are differences of opinion on when that destruction occurred (fifth or sixth century before the Common Era), but all agree that an earlier attack by the Assyrians had already resulted in the dispersion of ten of the original twelve Tribes of Israel. Because Judah was the dominant tribe of the two remaining before the Babylonian exile, it became natural to make Judah synonymous with the Jewish people. Judah was then shortened to "Jew."

STAGE I

Apparent Randomness in the Five Books

Enter the Shared Principles

Section 1
Seeming Imperfection in the Text and How It Reflects on Authorship

Even when we approach the Torah as believers, the text presents an enigma: there is little sign of an overall pattern. This patchwork character stands out especially in Exodus, Leviticus, and Numbers, where historical narrative mixes with law, often with no clear connection between the two. Even within some legal subtexts, the transition from one group of laws to the next group of laws does not always flow naturally. And though Genesis consists of narrative mainly in chronological order, the joining of certain events seems strained. We will soon explore specific transition imperfections that cover each of these situations.

Beyond these transition concerns are issues over points of division. Deuteronomy, with its primary content being Moses' final addresses, stands naturally as a separate book, but why should the prior text (i.e., the entire Bible before Deuteronomy) be split into four books? In particular, why place the description and building of the Tabernacle at the end of Exodus, rather than in Leviticus (where they would seem to fit better) with sacrifices and other priestly duties? These specific questions are addressed in Section 3. I will label seeming imperfections in transition or in division of topics as **order challenges**.

To attempt to determine a possible pattern, we will focus on textual organization, hence order challenges. However, besides cases of seeming disorder, there are also perceived discrepancies in the text, which we term **consistency challenges**. One major class of consistency challenges, i.e., those over discrepant laws, usually involves a version in Deuteronomy that differs in details from an earlier version (e.g., keeping the Sabbath in Deuteronomy 5 vs. Exodus 20). A second major class of consistency challenges draws on the different names of God, with two names appearing predominately over any others. We will address these two major classes later, as well as other types of consistency challenges.[1]

> In summary, there are two types of challenges in the Torah's text:
> 1. Order challenges — including both difficult transitions and arbitrary grouping of topics.
> 2. Consistency challenges — with seeming discrepancies between different parts of the text.

In terms of order challenges, we look at concrete examples of difficult transitions. To understand them requires knowing what makes the transition troublesome in each case. We should also know how classical Jewish sources have addressed such challenges. Conveniently for this purpose, we need only consult the authoritative eleventh century commentary of Rabbi Sh'lomo ben Yitzchak, better known by his Hebrew acronym Rashi. Rashi's phrase-specific comments regularly deal with consecutive topics whose logical connection is not obvious.

Five notable cases of such comments by Rashi appear in Display 1.1. You will see that each type of transitional challenge described at the outset is represented:

- transition from law to narrative and vice versa (Cases 3 and 5).
- transition from one legal subtext to another without an apparent link (Cases 2 and 4).
- transition from one narrative subtext to another without an apparent link (Case 1).

In each case, the first line identifies both the specific transition that drew Rashi's comment, as well as the point where the topics shift. In the parenthetical sentence beginning on the second line, we see why Rashi thought the transition needed to be explained. After that sentence, we say how Rashi connected the topics to justify the transition.

DISPLAY 1.1: Difficult Transitions and Rashi's Explanations

1. Sale of Joseph followed by affair of Judah and Tamar; shift after Genesis 37:36.
   (This transition is troubling in interrupting the focus on Joseph, which resumes after the affair.) Rashi explains that Judah, who made Jacob think Joseph had been killed by an animal rather than sold, was then deceived through Tamar's disguise as a harlot. Insertion of the affair after the sale of Joseph thus signifies measure-for-measure punishment.
2. Laws of altars followed by civil laws; shift after Exodus 20:23.
   (The ritual matters addressed in the first topic do not seem connected to civil law, thus raising the question of why the Torah presented them together.) Rashi explains that this juxtaposition indicates that the highest court of law is to be located immediately adjacent to the Temple and its altar.[2]
3. Death of Aaron's sons followed by conditions on priestly service; shift after Leviticus 10:7.
   (The death of the sons is attributed in the text to their bringing "a strange fire," but not to any conditions that would have rendered the sons ineligible.) Rashi notes the first of these conditions prohibits intoxication, thus reflecting the cause that a strange fire was brought.
4. Laws of a suspected adulteress followed by laws of Nazirite; shift after Numbers 5:31.

   (The suspected adulteress undergoes a trial enforced by a jealous husband, while the Nazirite takes on restrictions voluntarily through an oath.) Rashi explains that seeing the disgrace of the suspected adulteress may bring someone to become a Nazirite by swearing off wine, which loosens inhibitions.
5. Inheritance laws followed by bar on Moses' entry to Canaan; shift after Numbers 27:11.
   (This transition from law to narrative is complicated by an earlier account of God denying Moses' entry in Num. 20:12, leading us to ask why a restatement should occur here.) Rashi explains that the inheritance laws were told to Moses with the intensive wording *naton titen* [you shall surely give (the inheritance)], so he might have assumed he alone was to apportion the land in Canaan, i.e., he was to enter Canaan after all, despite the earlier decree.

These cases show that difficult transitions were not ignored by classical commentary and were, in fact, explained clearly. Yet only the explanations for Cases 3 and 4 bear any relation to each other. And because the explanations treat only the adjoined topics at hand and do not place the transitions into any broader context, no sense of overall organization emerges.

The Wellhausen Hypothesis and Source Criticism

For Jews and Christians with the most traditional beliefs, this lack of an underlying order merely signals the inability of human intellect to recognize a Divinely guided pattern. For many others, the absence of an obvious organizing principle is more troubling. Against this background, in the late nineteenth century, German academic Julius Wellhausen propounded the Wellhausen Hypothesis as an alternative to the traditional notion of Divine authorship. His influential book *Prolegomena to the History of Ancient Israel* effectively melded and popularized previous ideas on the subject.[3]

According to the Wellhausen Hypothesis, the Torah was compiled with fragments of four different documents by different authors. This accounted for the lack of an overall pattern and for the perceived textual inconsistencies. Among these perceived inconsistencies, the use of different names for God plays a special role in the Wellhausen Hypothesis in determining how to attribute a particular subtext to one of the four "source" documents.

Beyond rejecting single authorship of the Torah, Wellhausen explicitly derided ritual portions of the text as later additions by priests bent on strengthening their control of religious practice. Thus, some Christian leaders welcomed the Wellhausen Hypothesis (and what became known as Source Criticism) because it reinforced Christianity's break with the Jewish ritual (e.g., the dietary laws in Leviticus 11) that survived the destruction of the Second Temple in 70 CE. Theologian W. Robertson Smith, who served as editor of the *Encyclopedia Britannica*, followed this approach in his preface to the 1885 translation of Wellhausen's work.

Opposition to the Wellhausen Hypothesis and Source Criticism

Yet other churchmen saw Source Criticism as an unjustified assault on Divine authority. In line with that objection, influential scholars like Norman Snaith of Methodist Theological College held that attacking Judaism would also harm Christianity because of the ties between the religions. Snaith identified key concepts in the Jewish Bible as critical to the New Testament.[4]

Beyond raising primarily theological arguments, traditional scholars of both faiths also rose to challenge the assumptions and methods of Source Criticism, especially after Wellhausen reached English readers. For example, the Wellhausen Hypothesis claimed the detailed ritual laws in Leviticus were written much later than other parts of the text. This claim relied on the premise that humanly devised structures always grow more complex with time, so Leviticus' complex sacrificial ritual must have developed much later than the voluntary sacrifice reported in Genesis. Oxford Professor Reverend George Rawlinson countered that premise with examples in cultural development. For example, the English language is simpler than its precursor Anglo-Saxon, and Italian is simpler than Latin.[5]

In addition, as pointed out by German thinker Rabbi David Tzvi Hoffman, Wellhausen's claims of textual inconsistency often derived from blindness to context or from errors in Hebrew translation or Biblical syntax. A critical case involves Exodus 20:21, which was mistakenly read by Wellhausen to allow for altars being placed anywhere (and not just during the wanderings in the Wilderness). This misreading created an unwarranted discrepancy with respect to the centralized worship implied in Deuteronomy 16:16.[6] The objections of Rawlinson and Hoffman, along with those of other traditionally oriented scholars, were prominently featured in the Hertz Pentateuch, which was completed in 1936 and served until recently as the standard printed Torah text for English-speaking synagogues.[7]

Limited Success of the Opposition

As time went on, more and more problems (see Section 12 for details) came to light in Wellhausen's work, and Source Critics increasingly described their position with a more generic term "Documentary Hypothesis." While even non-believers conceded the effectiveness of the counterattack,[8] and the inherent weakness in the Wellhausen Hypothesis itself, Source Criticism nonetheless entrenched itself in academia, pushing Judaism and Christianity away from their customary views of the text. In the end, Wellhausen's opponents exposed enough flaws to undermine his particular approach, but still failed (outside the traditional camp) to stem the presumptive denial of single authorship of the Torah.

At the heart of this failure lies the inability of traditionalists to offer an overall organizing principle for the Torah. Of course, the presence of such a principle would not, by itself, establish Divine authorship — or even inspiration — of the text. The text could have, theoretically, been written by one human being. Still, the existence of a single clear and comprehensive organizing principle would give room for Divine authorship.

In fact, traditionalists have often tacitly conceded the absence of an overall pattern. Even a stalwart adversary of the Documentary Hypothesis, Rabbi Dr. Umberto Cassuto (d. 1951), acknowledged some non-uniformity in the text, which occurred, he speculated, in the melding of variant cultural traditions at the single point when the Torah was written.[9] Such indirect concessions of the lack of overall unity in the text have left advocates of Divine authorship on the defensive in public debate.

A Clear and Comprehensive Organizing Principle

But there is no need for continued concession. Rabbi Yehoshua Honigwachs, in *The Unity of Torah*, proposed an organizing principle based on five thematic links within the Ten Commandments. These links, which I call Shared Principles, were first identified in a recognized source, the *Mekhilta*,[10] almost 2,000 years old. For example, the Commandment barring idolatry and the Commandment barring adultery share the principle of loyalty to a primary relationship. We describe the five Shared Principles fully later on.

While the *Mekhilta*'s Shared Principles have been known since the late first century, no one before Rabbi Honigwachs had suggested a pattern for the entire Torah using them. In *The Unity of Torah*, he presented

- a thematic progression of each whole Book through the five Shared Principles A-B-C-D-E;
- a repeated progression of A-B-C-D-E within Genesis itself into components called Parts;
- a subdivision of each Part of Genesis into Subparts according to the same progression A-B-C-D-E.

This three-level pattern of repeated progressions is illustrated below.

DISPLAY 1.2: Progression of Shared Principles through Five Books and within Genesis

1st Level

Shared Principle A	Shared Principle B	Shared Principle C	Shared Principle D	Shared Principle E
Genesis	Exodus	Leviticus	Numbers	Deuteronomy

2nd Level 3rd Level

Genesis Divides Into:
Part A (Principle A)   subdivides into Subpart A (Prin. A), Subpart B (Prin. B), Subpart C (Prin. C)...
Part B (Principle B)   subdivides into Subpart A (Prin. A), Subpart B (Prin. B), Subpart C (Prin. C)...
Part C (Principle C)   subdivides into Subpart A (Prin. A), Subpart B (Prin. B), Subpart C (Prin. C)...
Part D (Principle D)   subdivides into Subpart A (Prin. A), Subpart B (Prin. B), Subpart C (Prin. C)...
Part E (Principle E)   subdivides into Subpart A (Prin. A), Subpart B (Prin. B), Subpart C (Prin. C)...

Rabbi Honigwachs indicated that subsequent volumes of his work would show the same kind of structure within Exodus, Leviticus, Numbers, and Deuteronomy, with all of the divisions and subdivisions coinciding with the Hebrew paragraph structure presented on a Torah scroll. If this highly synchronized structure were verified, one could hardly argue that pieces of the Five Books were written at different times by different authors and then combined. Such a compilation, predating the advent of modern software, would defy human capacity in integrating the complexity of the pattern. Yet, because most people with the necessary background for *The Unity of Torah* did not grasp the impact on the authorship debate, the book found few readers, even among its intended audience. The subsequent volumes intended by Rabbi Honigwachs were never published, and thus the pattern of Shared Principles remains hardly known.

Initial Skepticism and Gradual Acceptance

For me, as an observant Jew, no validation of faith through a unifying structure in the Torah was or is needed. Yet, because of my background in mathematical pattern recognition, *The Unity of Torah* piqued both special interest and extreme skepticism. Given the historic debate over the Torah's authorship, it seemed highly unlikely that such an overall pattern (if it truly existed) would have remained undiscovered for so long.

In fact, I suspected that despite Rabbi Honigwachs' clear dedication to intellectual honesty, there lay something in his approach akin to purported models of the Golden Ratio in the Egyptian pyramids and in various classic paintings. The Golden Ratio is a mathematical proportion of width to length in a rectangle that is considered most pleasing to the eye and that occurs repeatedly in nature. In the models in the pyramids and the paintings, if one studies them closely, it always turns out that the alleged occurrence of the Golden Ratio depends on some forced visualization.[11] In other words, those looking for the Golden Ratio tend to find it, whether deserving or not.

So, too, I believed that should someone reasonably familiar with the Torah (as it appears in Hebrew on a scroll) try independently to divide the text based on the Shared Principles, there would be extensive differences with the divisions of Rabbi Honigwachs. The extent of these differences would then confirm the presence of some forced organization, even though not intentionally applied.

This was my sense of *The Unity of Torah* when I first read it in 2001. So sure I was of some forced organization that I could not imagine investing the time myself to attempt the divisions. Two years later, however, I found a passage in the *Midrash Rabbah* on Song of Songs that changed my mind (more on that source later). From then on, I gradually, and often grudgingly, came to accept the pattern presented by Rabbi Honigwachs. Now I offer, through my own journey, a popular account of the momentous pattern of Shared Principles.

Roadmap for First Leg of the Journey

The journey begins with the source and definition of the pattern, followed by selected applications and explanation as outlined below.

Section 2. The paragraph structure on a Hebrew Torah scroll is usually missed in translation. According to the *Mekhilta*, five shared principles mark the Ten Commandments on two tablets side by side: Shared Principle A for the 1st and 6th Commandments, Shared Principle B for the 2nd and 7th, etc. Another ancient source can be read to suggest the Torah's paragraphs are ordered through these Shared Principles.

Section 3. The context of each whole Book aligns in order with the Shared Principles: Principle A for Genesis, Principle B for Exodus, etc. However, unlike the first four books, Deuteronomy has no dominant theme matching the Shared Principle of its context. This disparity can be understood through the need in Deuteronomy for elaboration of a broad range of previous laws to avoid the failures in Numbers.

Section 4. There is a parallel progression through the Shared Principles within each book, i.e., each Book splits into five Parts whose context/dominant themes align in order with the Shared Principles. Most Parts themselves subdivide likewise in order into five Sections with the same parallel progression.

This book relies extensively on Rabbi Honigwachs' work. However, three new features provide easier access for the reader and a clearer motivation for the role of the Shared Principles:

1. an expanded view of paragraphs on a Torah scroll and reformulation of the Shared Principles;
2. identification of a recognized source for using the Shared Principles to organize the text;
3. a linkage of variance in the two versions of the Ten Commandments to the Shared Principles.

Within these sections, there are occasional variations from the structural interpretation of specific subtexts in *The Unity of Torah*. These variations partly reflect the heavy focus of that book on Genesis, with textual divisions for the latter books treated only briefly. Variations also occur occasionally in Sections 6, 8, 9, and 10, where the validity of the pattern is tested within individual Books, and in later sections that supplement those sections. In checking the pattern in Genesis (see Sections 6 and 15), there is the most complete basis for comparison with *The Unity of Torah*. The burden of any errors, particularly as they relate to such variations, is mine to bear, not that of Rabbi Honigwachs.

Section 2
Torah Paragraphs and the Shared Principles

i. Paragraphs on a Torah Scroll

In seeking an organizing principle for any document, one must look for relationships among easily recognized subunits of the text. For English documents, those recognized subunits would generally be paragraphs, whose beginning points are often indicated by left indentation. For Torah text, a similar convention delineates the counterpart of a paragraph, known in Hebrew as a **parshah** [plural: **parshiyot**], of which there are a total of 295. Instead of opening with a blank space on the left, however, a *parshah* ends with a blank space on the left.

Parshah vs. Parshah

To gain a working sense of the Torah's paragraph structure will take some further details of the actual scroll format. In grasping these details, and in identifying a source for an overall pattern, the word *parshah* and its precise meaning as a single paragraph will be essential. Thus, we must distinguish this meaning from a related (but discrepant) usage that occurs in informal Jewish parlance. In that informal usage, *parshah* refers to one of the fifty-four weekly portions read on the Sabbath that together comprise the whole Torah. In fact, people often speak of "the *parshah* of the week," though the actual Hebrew word for such a portion is "*sidrah*."[12] This distinction matters because a single weekly portion generally contains many paragraphs.

Basic Features of the Scroll Format

Now back to the scroll format. A trained scribe writes a Torah scroll in Hebrew (read right to left) on pieces of parchment sewn together as one continuous sheet. The actual text appears in columns justified on both the left and right with (typically) forty-two lines in each column. The count of characters on individual lines on one scroll varies with the two-sided justification, as well as with two other key factors: differences in letter width within the Hebrew alphabet and limitations on letters to begin a column.[13] Taking spaces between words as single characters, I have counted as few as thirty and as many as forty-two characters on different lines of the same scroll.

In this format, there will often be 245 columns of text in which the 295 *parshiyot* [paragraphs] occur. Display 2.1 below provides a miniature view of five columns on a scroll (with the columns of text shaded for illustrative contrast only).

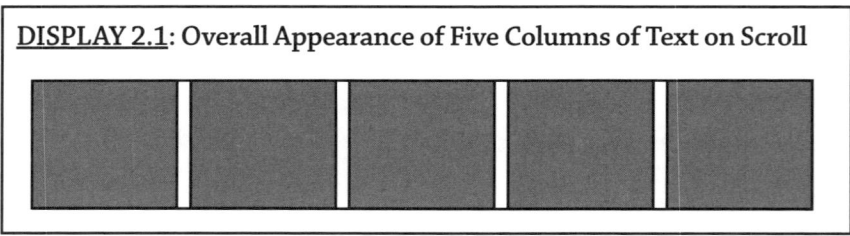

DISPLAY 2.1: Overall Appearance of Five Columns of Text on Scroll

Spacing within the Text

We will now look more closely within the columns of text to describe the spacing. Each *parshah* ends with a blank space extending to the left edge of the column. Such a space, called a **p'tuchah** [plural: **p'tuchot**], may be as wide as the entire column, but must be open on the left. Many *parshiyot* are further divided into subparagraphs by uniformly short blank spaces called *s'tumot* in the middle of lines. Appendix a lists the location of all *p'tuchot* in the Torah according to both the Ashkenazic (northern European and Russian) and Sephardic (Mediterranean) traditions, while Section 13 explains how we assert with confidence that these locations have not changed from the original document.

Display 2.2 now illustrates in greater detail two columns of text with several *parshiyot*. In this model, the letters a, b, c, d. and e mark where a new *parshah* begins. For example, the last *parshah* starting on the right column begins at point c and runs onto the left column, ending on the line above d. Note that *s'tumot* [spaces closed to the left] occur twice on the first *parshah* in the first column and once in the last *parshah* on the left column. In a printed Torah, *p'tuchot* and *s'tumot* are symbolized by a פ and ס respectively. The character "x" in the body of the model text below represents a Hebrew letter or a single blank space between words. *(Display 2.2 on opposite page.)*

As shown here, the scroll offers no overt signs of structure other than spacing, and, most striking, there are no visible counterparts of periods or of commas. In fact, as a result of this absence, our placement of end of verses and our grouping of words rely solely on the Masoretic tradition (see Section 13). This absence of other visible punctuation lends added weight to *parshiyot* in addressing the structure of the text.

Moreover, since a single *parshah* generally treats only law[14] or only narrative, our initial sense of randomness in transitions between law and narrative comes from disparities between consecutive *parshiyot*, i.e., before and after a *p'tuchah*. A few questions arise in topical connections within paragraphs, but such internal connections are generally more transparent. Thus, when we find difficult transitions between two legal topics or between two narrative accounts, such transitions also generally occur at *p'tuchot*. In particular, the points of shift identified for the five difficult transitions in Display 1.1 above are all *p'tuchot*.

Missing the Paragraph Structure in Translation

A key to the previous failure to identify an overall pattern of the Torah text is the fact that the whole concept of *p'tuchot* (and therefore any sense of *parshiyot*) gets omitted in translation. In other words, as vital as the paragraph structure is to the text, bibles printed in languages other than Hebrew typically do not show that structure at all. This omission draws on a common academic view that spacing on scrolls came only well after the written text and is no more intrinsic than the (much) later chapter framework.

DISPLAY 2.2: Model of Torah Text with *Parshiyot* Beginning at Points a, b, c, d, and e

```
xxxxxxxxxxxxxxxxxxxxxxxxxxxxxxxx       xxxxxxxxxxxxxxxxxxxxxxxxxxxxxxxx
xxxxxxxxxxxxxxxxxxxxxxxxxxxxxxxx       xxxxxxxxxxxxxxxxxxxxxxxxxxxxxxxx
xxxxxxxxxxxxxxxxxxxxxxxxxxxxxxxx       xxxxxxxxxxxxxxxxxxxxxxxxxxxxxxxx
xxxxxxxxxxxxxxxxxxxxxxxxxxxxxxxx                 xxxxxxxxxxxxxxxxxxxx
xxxxxxxxxxxxxxxxxxxxxxxxxxxxxxxx       xxxxxxxxxxxxxxxxxxxxxxxxxxxxxxxx<a
xxxxxxxxxxxxxxxxxxxxxxxxxxxxxxxx       xxxxxxxxxxxxxxxxxxxxxxxxxxxxxxxx
xxxxxxxxxxxxxxxxxxxxxxxxxxxxxxxx       xxxxxxxxxxxxxxxxxxxxxxxxxxxxxxxx
xxxxxxxxxxxxxxxxxxxxxxxxxxxxxxxx       xxxxxxxxxxxxxxxxxxxxxxxxxxxxxxxx
xxxxxxxxxxxxxxxxxxxxxxxxxxxxxxxx       xxxxxxxxxxxxxxxxxxxxxxxxxxxxxxxx
          xxxxxxxxxxxxxxxxxx           xxxxxxxxxx           xxxxxxxxx
xxxxxxxxxxxxxxxxxxxxxxxxxxxxxxxx<d     xxxxxxxxxxxxxxxxxxxxxxxxxxxxxxxx
xxxxxxxxxxxxxxxxxxxxxxxxxxxxxxxx       xxxxxxxxxxxxxxxxxxxxxxxxxxxxxxxx
xxxxxxxxxxxxxxxxxxxxxxxxxxxxxxxx       xxxxxxxxxxxxxxxxxxxxxxxxxxxxxxxx
xxxxxxxxxxxxxxxxxxxxxxxxxxxxxxxx       xxxxxxxxxxxxxxxxxxxxxxxxxxxxxxxx
xxxxxxxxxxxxxxxxxxxxxxxxxxxxxxxx       xxxxxxxxxxxxxxxxxxxxxxxxxxxxxxxx
xxxxxxxxxxxxxxxxxxxxxxxxxxxxxxxx       xxxxxxxxxxxxxxxxxxxxxxxxxxxxxxxx
xxxxxxxxxxxxxxxxxxxxxxxxxxxxxxxx       xxxxxxxxxxxxxxxxxxxxxxxxxxxxxxxx
xxxxxxxxxxxxxxxxxxxxxxxxxxxxxxxx       xxxxxxxx             xxxxxxxxxxx
xxxxxxxxxxxxxxxxxxxxxxxxxxxxxxxx       xxxxxxxxxxxxxxxxxxxxxxxxxxxxxxxx
          xxxxxxxxxxxxx                                    xxxxxxxxxxx
xxxxxxxxxxxxxxxxxxxxxxxxxxxxxxxx<e     xxxxxxxxxxxxxxxxxxxxxxxxxxxxxxxx <b
xxxxxxxxxxxxxxxxxxxxxxxxxxxxxxxx       xxxxxxxxxxxxxxxxxxxxxxxxxxxxxxxx
xxxxxxxxxxxxxxxxxxxxxxxxxxxxxxxx       xxxxxxxxxxxxxxxxxxxxxxxxxxxxxxxx
xxxxxxxxxxxxxxxxxxxxxxxxxxxxxxxx       xxxxxxxxxxxxxxxxxxxxxxxxxxxxxxxx
xxxxxxxxxxxxxxxxxxxxxxxxxxxxxxxx       xxxxxxxxxxxxxxxxxxxxxxxxxxxxxxxx
xxxxxxxxxxxxxxxxxxxxxxxxxxxxxxxx       xxxxxxxxxxxxxxxxxxxxxxxxxxxxxxxx
xxxxxxxxxxxxxxxxxxxxxxxxxxxxxxxx       xxxxxxxxxxxxxxxxxxxxxxxxxxxxxxxx
xxxxxxxxxxxxxxxxxxxxxxxxxxxxxxxx       xxxxxxxxxxxxxxxxxxxxxxxxxxxxxxxx
xxxxxxxxxxxxxxxxxxxxxxxxxxxxxxxx       xxxxxxxxxxxxxxxxxxxxxxxxxxxxxxxx
xxxxxxxxxx          xxxxxxxxxx         xxxxxxxxxxxxxxxxxxxxxxxxxxxxxxxx
xxxxxxxxxxxxxxxxxxxxxxxxxxxxxxxx       xxxxxxxxxxxxxxxxxxxxxxxxxxxxxxxx
xxxxxxxxxxxxxxxxxxxxxxxxxxxxxxxx       xxxxxxxxxxxxxxxxxxxxxxxxxxxxxxxx
xxxxxxxxxxxxxxxxxxxxxxxxxxxxxxxx       xxxxxxxxxxxxxxxxxxxxxxxxxxxxxxxx
xxxxxxxxxxxxxxxxxxxxxxxxxxxxxxxx       xxxxxxxxxxxxxxxxxxxxxxxxxxxxxxxx
xxxxxxxxxxxxxxxxxxxxxxxxxxxxxxxx                             xxxxxxxxx
xxxxxxxxxxxxxxxxxxxxxxxxxxxxxxxx       xxxxxxxxxxxxxxxxxxxxxxxxxxxxxxxx<c
xxxxxxxxxxxxxxxxxxxxxxxxxxxxxxxx       xxxxxxxxxxxxxxxxxxxxxxxxxxxxxxxx
```

The academic view relies on some variances between spacing on current Torah scrolls and spacing on the oldest known Biblical manuscripts — i.e., those found among the Dead Sea Scrolls in eleven arid caves in Qumran from 1947 to 1956. In 1994–5, the University of Arizona used accelerator mass spectrometry to carbon-date some of these manuscripts. Among them was a manuscript labeled 4Q22 (Document 22 from the 4th Qumran cave), which includes almost all of Exodus. With 95% confidence, the Carbon-14 content of this manuscript placed it within the years 164 BCE and 48 CE.[15] In contrast, the earliest known manuscript whose *p'tuchot* generally match today's Torah scrolls is the Aleppo Codex of the tenth century.[16]

If we consider only the comparative age of two discovered documents, variances between those documents in the placement of *p'tuchot* imply that spacing conventions were not well established until after the earlier one was written. In other words, since there are variations in spacing between the earlier Dead Sea Scrolls and the much later Aleppo Codex, it seems as if spacing itself is not intrinsic to the Torah or its overall structure. It is this implication on which the common academic view relies in dating spacing conventions after the Dead Sea Scrolls.[17]

Problems with the Common Academic View

However, there is a vital question beyond the comparative age of the documents: are the Dead Sea Scrolls likely to reflect authentic Jewish textual tradition? To answer this question, we must involve ourselves (a bit!) with the archaeology of Qumran (though this subject is largely outside of our main area of interest). Here, however, the likelihood of authentic textual tradition in the Dead Sea Scrolls depends on how the people of Qumran related to the Judaism of their time — an issue that naturally falls to archaeologists. Among them, there are three main camps on this issue:[18]

- According to what has been the predominant school of thought, the Dead Sea Scrolls belonged to the Essenes, an isolated sect that broke away from mainstream Judaism and ultimately disappeared.
- More recently, a different school has emerged in which the

inhabitants of Qumran are seen as the elite originators of Christian thought.
- There are also those (smaller in number) who see Qumran primarily as a haven for refugees from other parts of Israel in those times, without as much focus on a particular philosophy.

In the first two perspectives (encompassing the vast majority of archaeological thought), the people of Qumran purposely withdrew from mainstream Judaism. Once outside the norms of society, losing the self-policing of a historical rabbinic community that (most) carefully preserved its sacred Scriptures, their scrolls would be more susceptible to copying errors or even to intentional adjustments, such as can be found today in the Torah scrolls of the tiny remaining Samaritan sect. For one thing, smaller groups are much more prone to error than the larger mainstream society because only a critical mass can "catch errors" in minority text before they become majority text. The same susceptibility would therefore apply to the manuscripts of Qumran in regard to the placement of *p'tuchot*.

However, the susceptibility to error of Qumran versions of the Torah goes well beyond having fewer people checking copies for accuracy. Many scrolls found at Qumran testify to the community's fixation on an imminent "End of Days." In fact, this fixation appears not only in scrolls seen as holy artifacts of Qumran beliefs, but also in scrolls dictating ritual and communal behavior, often at great odds with Jewish practice set forth in the Torah.[19] In this light, we see the likelihood that the accuracy of Qumran scrolls involving Torah passages was compromised.

But there is something else wrong in comparing the age of the Dead Sea Scrolls to that of the Aleppo Codex in order to judge the relative antiquity of the spacing [*p'tuchot*]. The location of *p'tuchot* was fixed long before the Aleppo Codex, as the Talmud indicates clearly in *B'rakhot* 12b. There, in discussing the scope of Torah passages that may be inserted in the liturgy, the Talmud says that such excerpts must be whole *parshiyot*. The exact language of the Talmud is: "Where Moses ended *parshiyot*, so do we (in the liturgy), and where he did not, we do not." This means that the location of *p'tuchot* must have been fixed before that statement was made in the fourth century. (Incidentally, there is no such rule for passages in the liturgy from the Prophets or from the Writings — only for those from Moses, i.e., from the Torah.)

Now, one may rightly point out that just because an event occurred by the fourth century or earlier does not prove it occurred before the writing of the Dead Sea Scrolls (164 BCE to 48 CE). Do bear in mind though that, in keeping with Jewish Law, Torah scrolls and manuscripts would normally be buried in the ground (not placed in arid caves) when they become worn with use. The moisture of the earth would wholly degrade the parchment or other material, leaving no artifact (like the Dead Sea Scrolls) behind. That fact would explain why no Torah scroll or manuscript (with the current positioning of *p'tuchot*) has survived from earlier times. Thus, the survival of the Dead Sea Scrolls attests not to a faithful copy of the Torah used in Jewish practice, but only to their irregular resting place. In other words, the evidence of the Dead Sea Scrolls does not negate the plausibility of today's *p'tuchot* predating the Qumran community.

Textual Integrity and the Role of Sof'rim

This plausibility is boosted by the Talmud's description of the role of *sof'rim* [scribes] in *Kiddushin* 30a, which specifies their practice of counting all the letters of the Torah. From the context, "counting" actually means a detailed accounting.[20] Indeed, Rashi, writing in the eleventh century, says this role also applied to the *sof'rim* cited in I Chronicles 2:55, preceding the Dead Sea Scrolls by many centuries. As discussed in Section 13, Jewish tradition views these *sof'rim* as the forerunners of the Masoretes to whom the Aleppo Codex is attributed.

Part of the task of the *sof'rim* included checking proper placement of *p'tuchot*, in line with another ancient work (but of less certain vintage) called *Masekhet Sof'rim*, which invalidates Torah scrolls with any *p'tuchah* missing or out of place. This work normally appears as an appendix in the volume of the Babylonian Talmud with *Avodah Zorah*, and includes many rules concerning the Mosaic Text that appeared later in Maimonides' *Mishneh Torah*, written in the twelfth century, which codifies the standards for Torah scrolls.[21]

It is most plausible that the paragraph structure of the Torah has not changed over time, and that the spacing of the Dead Sea Scrolls deviated from Jewish norms in the same way that the Qumran sect's beliefs and practices deviated.

Modern Bibles and Chapters

What non-Hebrew bibles generally show instead of *p'tuchot* are the customary chapter and verse numbers, which were first devised by the Archbishop of Canterbury, Stephen Langton (d. 1228). Because his system provided an efficient way to locate passages of interest (and indeed we use his system here!), it became standard notation within several generations and was incorporated into early printed bibles in the fifteenth century. Medieval Jewish leaders, responding to Christian authorities in religious disputations, also found themselves referring to chapters and verses in such responses. In this way, *p'tuchot* came to be supplanted as points of reference.

To grasp how much the use of chapters obscures the paragraph structure of the text, just consider the book of Genesis using Appendix a. Genesis contains fifty chapters and forty-four *parshiyot* [paragraphs], with only nineteen of the *p'tuchot* coinciding with the end of chapters. This means that most of the chapters we refer to today do *not* correspond to the historic spacing of the Torah itself. Yet this limited agreement still grossly understates the true disparity. Since six *parshiyot* fall within the first chapter and five fall within the forty-ninth, only thirty-three *parshiyot* remain for the other forty-eight chapters. Among those thirty-three, only four match with a single chapter, while eleven dominate two or more chapters and thirteen comprise less than half a chapter. A pattern involving *p'tuchot* would be difficult to find in this environment (which uses only chapters and verses in organization), since it ignores the historic paragraph structure of the Torah. Continued disregard cannot be justified by the academic view that grants authority to the Dead Sea Scrolls in setting the Torah's structure.

ii. The Five Shared Principles of the Ten Commandments

While *p'tuchot* may have been supplanted as points of reference in the common reading of the Mosaic text, the essential standard by which we must judge the efficacy of an overall pattern cannot ignore them.

Any unified and comprehensive pattern must provide a meaningful framework through which *parshiyot* proceed one to another.

In fact, were there such a pattern, we might have expected some recognized and venerable source to allude to the organization of the *parshiyot*. This reinforced my skepticism in finding no such citation in *The Unity of Torah*.

Possible Source Involving the Ten Commandments

Many months after reading *The Unity of Torah*, however, a source emerged in a piece of Talmud (*B'rakhot* 11b–12a) dealing with whether the Ten Commandments should be recited in daily prayer. One argument obligating such recitation contends that other portions of the Torah in the standard prayers already reflect the Ten Commandments. In that vein, an English commentary[22] cited the text *Midrash Rabbah* (circa. 500 CE) on the Song of Songs. The passage 5:14 reads, in part:

> From Commandment to Commandment, the Torah's **parshiyot** and **dikduk** were written.

Thus, the commentary used this Midrash as proof that the Ten Commandments are represented in prayer passages drawn from the Torah outside the Commandments. In this interpretation, the word *parshiyot* was read as derived from the word *peirush* [explanation], and *dikduk* was understood as "specifics." Put differently, the commentary read the Midrash to say the rest of the Torah can be explained through the Ten Commandments, and the specifics of other Torah passages accord with the Commandments. A bit of research confirmed that this interpretation follows traditional Jewish thought.

However, it struck me that the Midrash could also mean that the order of *parshiyot* involves the Ten Commandments,[23] where the word *parshiyot* would be understood literally, as we normally use the word, as paragraphs on a scroll. The word *dikduk* might then mean the specific places where each *parshah* starts and stops (in Modern Hebrew, *dikduk* means "grammar"). In fact, though we translate the initial phrase in the Midrash as "from Commandment to Commandment," we would render it more literally as "between each Commandment and (another) Commandment."[24] This peculiar construction (stressing what is between Commandments) suggests a meaning beyond that of the whole of the Commandments as the source of the rest of the Torah. Though I still strongly doubted the existence of an overall pattern, here in the *Midrash Rabbah* was at least a possible source for the ordering claimed by Rabbi Honigwachs. I decided to test it myself.

Comparing Jewish and Christian Ten Commandments

This required looking more carefully at the Shared Principles as stated in relation to the Jewish listing of the Decalogue in Exodus 20. Because this listing is vital, we must distinguish it from the Catholic and Protestant listings[25] familiar to the public. While the Christian listings differ mainly in combining or dividing a few Jewish Commandments, rather than in actual meaning, the Shared Principles make sense only for the classic Jewish listing as seen below.

The listing and wording of the Commandments can be compared among faiths as follows:

- Catholics combine Jewish Commandments 1 (belief in God) and 2 (not to believe in other gods) into their Commandment 1 and divide Jewish Commandment 10 into Catholic Commandments 9 (not to covet another person's wife) and 10 (not to covet another's goods).
- Protestants typically list Jewish Commandment 2 as their Commandment 1, with Jewish Commandment 1 considered a preface. The Protestant Commandment 2 bars making an idol, which Jewish Commandment 2 includes as a detail within not believing in other gods.
- Jews and Christians list the other Commandments in essentially the same language.

In their Sabbath practices, traditional Jews and Christians differ in both the designated time during the week (from sundown Friday to nightfall Saturday[26] versus Sunday) and the activities forgone during that time (thirty-nine creative acts linked to the Tabernacle[27] versus physical or paid labor). With regard to the rest of the Decalogue, however, there are only relatively slight distinctions between Jewish and Christian observance.[28] Despite this shared sense of the Commandments as a whole by Judaism and Christianity, the *Mekhilta*'s Shared Principles require a feature present only in the classic Jewish listing. That feature is the division of the Commandments into the first five and the second five, with a defined relationship between the two groups. This then informs the content of the two tablets.[29]

Framework of the Shared Principles

In this side-by-side format, the first five Commandments (on the first tablet) concern Man's relationship to God, and the second five (on the second tablet) concern Man's relationship to Man. This division reflects a fact vital to the Jewish listing: for each of the first five Commandments, God is mentioned somewhere in the associated verses, though not mentioned in the last five.[30] (This can be verified by examining Exodus 20: 2–14.)

Consider Display 2.3. For each Commandment on the first tablet and its adjacent neighbor on the second, (i.e., the 1st and 6th, the 2nd and 7th, and so on), there is a Shared Principle in the third column (see endnote for origin of the Shared Principles stated below).[31]

DISPLAY 2.3: Adjacent Commandments and Shared Principles		
First Tablet (Man & God)	Second Tablet (Man & Man)	Shared Principle
1. To believe in God	6. Not to murder	A. Respecting Creation
2. Not to believe in other gods	7. Not to commit adultery	B. Loyalty to Primary Relationship
3. Not to take God's name in vain	8. Not to steal	C. Limited Access to Spiritual/Physical Resources

| 4. To remember the Sabbath | 9. Not to bear false witness | D. Duties of Community (*edut*) |
| 5. To honor parents (with promise of future benefit) | 10. Not to covet | E. Accepting One's Place/Status |

Because the proposed pattern depends on the Shared Principles, we must grasp them fully. To gain that grasp, we now examine how each of the Shared Principles embodies the two Commandments that it connects in the *Mekhilta*'s framework.

Shared Principle A in the Ten Commandments

Commandment 1 (to believe in God) fits Shared Principle A (respecting Creation) because denying God's existence means the world materialized on its own, thus reflecting a lack of respect for Creation. By the same token, one who violates Commandment 6 (not to murder) denies respect to Creation by destroying another human being who was formed in God's image (see Genesis 1:27).

Shared Principle B in the Ten Commandments

As for Shared Principle B (loyalty to a primary relationship), linking Commandment 2 (not to believe in other gods) and Commandment 7 (not to commit adultery) seems plain enough.

Shared Principle C in the Ten Commandments

While Shared Principle C (limited access to spiritual and physical resources) clearly fits Commandment 8 (not to steal), how it connects with Commandment 3 (not to take God's name in vain) may be less intuitive. Some people understand Commandment 3 as simply prohibiting blasphemy or, in more common speech, irreverence (notably, cursing) using God's name. What, you may ask, does cursing have to with limited access to resources?

In Jewish tradition, the ban on irreverence captures only part of this Commandment. It also bans making use of God's name in promises unnecessarily — literally, taking God's name in vain. Some authorities even interpret this Commandment to prohibit invoking God's name in support of a self-serving action.³² In line with its broader interpretations, it should now be clear why Commandment 3 fits Shared Principle C (limited access to spiritual and physical resources).

Shared Principle D in the Ten Commandments

If any Commandment seems unrelated to its Shared Principle, it is Commandment 4 (to remember the Sabbath), which in no obvious way links to Shared Principle D (duties of testimony). Quite the opposite! When understood properly, the Sabbath is *all about* testimony. In fact, to fulfill this Commandment, the Oral Law demands Friday evening that Jews recite the passage Genesis 2:1–3 (see *Shabbat* 119b), which describes the first Sabbath. In line with the inclusion of the Sabbath among *edot* [testimonial observances], this recitation bears witness to God's creation of the world.³³ Of course, then, Commandment 9 deals with testimony.

Shared Principle E in the Ten Commandments

That brings us to Shared Principle E (accepting one's place/status), which links Commandment 5 (to honor one's parents) and Commandment 10 (not to covet). The link to Commandment 10 is immediate, but the link to Commandment 5 takes further thought. The Talmud in *Kiddushin* 30b describes the phenomenon of bringing a child into the world as a partnership between God and the child's parents. As a result, the child is expected to accept his parents' authority and his obligation to care for their needs. Thus, a child who does not honor his parents in either respect does not accept (or appreciate) what they have given him unselfishly through a Divine relationship.³⁴ This lack of acceptance of behavioral limitation and obligation parallels a lack of acceptance of one's material possessions in the act of coveting.

Moral Progression and Broader Meaning

Before we apply the Shared Principles, there are two other features within them that we should recognize:

- First, Rabbi Honigwachs, following the thirteenth century

commentator Chizkuni on Exodus 20, sees parallel progressions in the first five Commandments (increasing sensitivity to God) and in the second five (increasing sensitivity to Man). In the second progression, forgoing adultery (Commandment Seven) reflects greater sensitivity than forgoing murder (Six); forgoing stealing (Eight) reflects a higher level than forgoing adultery (Seven); and so on. This insight especially applies to Commandment Nine: *Lo taaneh b'reakha ed shaker* [Do not testify against your associate as a false witness]. In the prior commandments, no extra-familial connection between persons is cited. Yet here the word *rea* [associate] implies a community beyond one's family.[35] Thus, Shared Principle D extends to "duties of testimony/community." The word *edut* [testimony] also shares the same root as *edah* [congregation], a communal form.

- Second, through the allusion to the land and the future in Commandment Five ("that your time will be lengthened on the land"), Shared Principle E acquires a broader association. It may be associated with laws or situations that would first apply in the promised land of Canaan and with various topics that look forward in time. Such topics include treaties affecting coming generations, blessings and curses, and interpretations of dreams.

In this light, we can now restate the Shared Principles both in full and in shorthand form. While the shorthand form will be used more frequently to avoid unnecessary length, we will still sometimes refer to the full statement to assist with certain details.

Shared Principle	Full Statement	Shorthand
A	Respecting Creation	Creation
B	Loyalty to primary relationship	Loyalty
C	Limited access to spiritual and physical resources	Limits
D	Duties of testimony/ community	Community
E	Accepting one's place/status (with ties to land/future)	Acceptance

Section 3
Shared Principles and the Order of the Five Books

At the outset, we cited two types of problems with the Torah text that have prompted the questioning of single authorship. The first type, termed **order challenges**, included the Torah's division into five Books, when only the last Book (Deuteronomy) seems, on its face, to have an obvious rationale to stand separately. In *The Unity of Torah*, however, the Shared Principles (as presented in Display 2.3) align with the initial context of each whole book as follows:

> <u>DISPLAY 3.1</u>: Shared Principles and the Order of the Five Books
>
> Creation: context of Genesis via Creation itself and violence before the Flood.
>
> Loyalty: context of Exodus via enslavement (to master other than God).
>
> Limits: context of Leviticus via *korbanot* [offerings to bring one close to God] and the priestly service.
>
> Community: context of Numbers via preparations for conquest.
>
> Acceptance: context of Deuteronomy via Moses' addresses to the Jewish people before entering Canaan to fulfill their destiny.

Dominant Themes in First Four Books

In the first four books, the dominant themes (not just the initial contexts) also align in order with the Shared Principles as shown below:

a. Genesis not only opens with the context of creation and murder — aligning with Principle A (Creation) — but also exhibits Principle A throughout the entire Book, with murder or planned murder recurring throughout Genesis, even after the Flood, occupying a central role, for example, in the life of Joseph and his brothers who sought to kill him.

b. The opening theme of slavery in Exodus, reflecting Principle B (Loyalty), continues well into the Book. In addition, the references to the gods of Egypt bespeak the practice of idolatry that also fits this Shared Principle. The Covenant at Sinai (especially the oath "we will do and we will understand..." in Exodus 24:7), and the Sin of the Golden Calf (in Chapter 32 — once again idolatry) reinforce Loyalty as a theme.

c. The first two-thirds of Leviticus heavily involve *korbanot* [offerings to bring one close to God] and the priestly service in keeping with Principle C (Limits), especially with respect to spiritual resources. The remainder of the book often deals with limits on physical resources — such as regarding land ownership and cultivation (see Chapter 25).

d. Numbers begins with a census in preparation for the conquest of Canaan, along with the layout of the camp, while substantial parts of the Book also treat the various wars fought to get into the land. Clearly, these topics fit Principle D (Community), and the communal practices and failures, notably the Incident of the Spies (involving improper testimony in Chapters 13–14), cement the connection with this Shared Principle.

Lack of a Dominant Theme in Deuteronomy

Deuteronomy does not follow this pattern of alignment of a dominant theme with the same Shared Principle as that of its initial context — in this case, Principle E (Acceptance). Instead, Deuteronomy ranges over much of the previous Torah legislation without having a true dominant theme. Rabbi Honigwachs seeks to reconcile this disparity in Deuteronomy (relative to the other Books) using the Jewish people's failure to correct their repeated transgression in Numbers. As a result of this failure, Deuteronomy focuses on providing more guidance through additional laws and through more details and more explanation for laws given earlier. And that, says Rabbi Honigwachs, is why Deuteronomy ranges over different Shared Principles.

Let us understand his explanation more fully:

With the rising expectations of sensitivity in the Shared Principles, the task of the Jewish people in each Book was to master the Shared Principle associated with that Book.

Thus, the people were expected to master Principle A (Creation) in Genesis, Principle B (Loyalty) in Exodus, etc. The people would demonstrate such mastery by overcoming sin linked to the respective Shared Principle, allowing them to move to the next Shared Principle in the next Book.

Applying this framework first in Genesis, murder (Principle A) had been the dominant transgression until the time of Joseph. At that time, despite his brothers' enmity towards him, they eschewed bloodshed (Chapter 37), selling him instead into slavery.

This learned respect for Creation thus allowed the Jewish people to confront Principle B (Loyalty) in Exodus. While the Golden Calf showed unfaithfulness to their primary relationship with God, the building of the Tabernacle at the end of Exodus represented correction through dedication to Him alone. Likewise in Leviticus 24, the people recognized and did not tolerate the sin of blasphemy, which violated Principle C (Limits). That brings us to Numbers, where progress through the Shared Principles was arrested.

So far, once the Jews "mastered" one Shared Principle, they moved on to the next.

Arrested Development

More specifically, because the Jewish people met the expectations linked to the first three Books, fulfillment of Shared Principle D (Community) would be the expectation and dominant theme of Numbers. However, as recounted in the text, the Incident of the Spies (Chapters 13 and 14) displayed, through improper testimony, failure to live up to that Shared Principle. (Remember that the full statement of Principle D refers to "testimony/community.")

This testimony then led to massive apprehension over the conquest of Canaan and a further failure to exercise communal responsibility to wage war as expected.

These failures proved more damaging to the nation's progress towards the promised land of Canaan than had the Sin of the Golden Calf in Exodus. The gravity of the Golden Calf notwithstanding, only a limited group was involved in that transgression, and forgiveness came almost immediately through repentance and completion of the Tabernacle. In contrast, the Incident of the Spies led to thirty-nine more years of wandering, with the death of all but two of the men of that generation. Also, in the wake of that improper testimony, the Rebellion of Korach in Numbers 16 marked the refusal to accept exclusion from the status and prerogatives of priesthood, a failure under Principle E (Acceptance). A plague growing out of the rebellion took many lives. As Numbers ends, the Jewish people had fulfilled neither Principle D nor E.[36]

In truth, while this rationale for the division into five Books and for the differences in Deuteronomy made sense, I sought a more direct indication in the text before fully accepting the initial alignment between the Five Books and the Shared Principles. This indication would need to signal some clear difference involving Principles D (Community) and E (Acceptance). Further, the indication should occur at the end of Numbers or in Deuteronomy to suggest something still amiss with these two Principles. While seeking such an indication, it seemed prudent to withhold judgment on the initial alignment before trying to partition individual Books.

Different Versions of the Ten Commandments

An explicit indication of something still amiss with Principles D (Community) and E (Acceptance) occurs in the second version of the Ten Commandments in Deuteronomy 5. The key to this indication, which supports Rabbi Honigwachs' idea of arrested development, emerges in seeing how the second version differs from the first version in Exodus 20. The main variations involve wording in the following four Commandments:

| the Fourth (to observe the Sabbath) | the Ninth (not to testify improperly) |
| the Fifth (to honor parents) | the Tenth (not to covet) |

Notice that the Fourth and Ninth Commandments are those linked by Principle D (Community), while the Fifth and Tenth are linked by Principle E (Acceptance). In other words, the variations involve precisely the Shared Principles seen by Rabbi Honigwachs as being unfulfilled at the end of Numbers. This striking coincidence raises the question of whether the transgressions in Numbers may actually correspond to the major variations in the Ten Commandments.

If so, this correspondence would support the idea of arrested development in Numbers. It would also buttress Rabbi Honigwachs' sense of why Deuteronomy, unlike the other Books, reflects no single dominant Shared Principle; Deuteronomy comes to address failures spanning more than a single theme. Moreover, the correspondence would corroborate Nachmanides' thirteenth century introduction to Deuteronomy that broadly explains the variance between laws in that Book and preceding versions in the Torah. Nachmanides attributed such variance to the need for more details or explanations in response to failings in the Wilderness or in response to new or more difficult circumstances to be encountered in Canaan.[37]

Group Transgressions in the Book of Numbers

These implications provide a context for looking at the communal transgressions in Numbers. Those transgressions, as opposed to ones committed in a more private context, would seem most deserving of explicit attention in the law. Thus we enumerate four key failures in the Wilderness in Display 3.2:

> **DISPLAY 3.2**: **Key Group Transgressions in Numbers**
>
> 1. Incident of the Spies (Chapters 13–14), in which most of the group sent by Moses to evaluate the Land of Canaan for conquest came back with a discouraging report.
> 2. Korach's Rebellion (Chapters 16–17), in which Korach the Levite led a mutiny designed to gain a share in the priesthood for those not descended from Aaron.
> 3. Improper sexual relations with Midianite women (Chapter 25).
> 4. The request by the tribes of Reuben and Gad to settle outside Canaan (Chapter 32), so as to have more and better pasturage for their cattle and flocks than they expected to get in Canaan.

To these transgressions committed by a group, rather than by one or two individuals, one might also add the episodic murmurings against Moses over food and water (cf. Numbers 20:2–5). Yet, because those murmurings were partly grounded in real need, they do not, on the whole, stand out as much as the four transgressions cited above do.

Variant Wording in Commandments Linked to Group Transgressions

In any event, the four transgressions in Display 3.2 do suggest specific variations in the Commandments. Because we are considering a link to transgressions committed in a group, we focus on Commandments 9 and 10 on the second tablet (involving relations between Man and Man).[38] As shown below in Display 3.3, there are four chief differences.

> **DISPLAY 3.3: Chief Differences in Commandments 9 and 10**
>
> 1. In Commandment 9, the Exodus version speaks of an *ed shaker* [false witness], while the version in Deuteronomy speaks of an *ed shav* [vain witness].
> 2. In Commandment 10, Exodus uses the verb *lo tachmod* [do not covet] twice, while Deuteronomy replaces the second occurrence with *lo titaveh* [do not desire].
> 3. In Commandment 10, the object connected in Exodus with the first *lo tachmod* is *bet reekha* [your associate's house], while the object connected in Deuteronomy with *lo tachmod* is *eshet reekha* [your associate's wife].
> 4. Only in Deuteronomy, Commandment 10 includes *sadehu* [his (your associate's) field].

We can check the correspondence between each of the differences (1) through (4) in Display 3.3 and each of the communal transgressions 1 through 4 in Display 3.2.

In particular, shift (1) in Commandment 9 from *ed shaker* [false witness] to *ed shav* [vain witness] fits the Incident of the Spies (Item 1 in Display 3.2). The Spies' testimony was not actually a lie, but rather vain. They reported how the inhabitants saw them (see 13:33), which they could not possibly have known.

Similarly, change (2) in Commandment 10 from *lo tachmod* [not to covet] to *lo titaveh* [not to desire] fits the Rebellion of Korach. Korach did not violate *lo tachmod*, as he argued only for a share in the priesthood, not for sole possession, which is a technical requirement for violation.

Similarly change (3), by first mentioning another person's wife as ᴛhat is forbidden to covet, reflects the episode with the Midianite ˙omen, while the two tribes' desire for more pasturage suggests the clusion of another person's field in (4) as an object of desire.

This completes the correspondence between group transgressions Numbers and the variance in the two versions of Commandments nd 10. (Section 14 connects individual transgressions in Numbers ᴧariance in the two versions of Commandments 4 and 5, though variance in the first word in Commandment 4 is traditionally attributed to something other than transgression.[39]) We can now review our progress in understanding how the Five Books align with the five Shared Principles. Here is what we have seen:

- Within all five Books, initial contexts link to the Shared Principles in order: context of Genesis to Principle A (Genesis), context of Exodus to Principle B (Loyalty), and so on.
- Within the first four Books, dominant themes also link to the Shared Principles in order, but this link does not apply to Deuteronomy, which lacks a single dominant theme.
- Rabbi Honigwachs explains this difference through arrested development of the Jewish people after mastering Principles A–C in the first three Books. This success prepared them for themes in Numbers linked to Principle D (Community), but sins in the Wilderness led to further law in Deuteronomy, covering a range of Shared Principles.
- The explanation of arrested development is corroborated by changes in the second version of the Commandments and their correspondence with group transgressions of Principles D (Community) and E (Acceptance) in the Book of Numbers.

Through these considerations, it is now appropriate to accept the alignment of the Five Books with the Shared Principles.

Before proceeding to partition the individual books according to the Shared Principles, we should now deal with two remaining challenges mentioned in Section 1:

- the seeming misplacement of the instructions for and the building of the Tabernacle in Exodus (as opposed to Leviticus), and
- the inconsistency between the statement of laws in Deuteronomy and in the preceding books.

The Building of the Tabernacle

We begin with the seeming misplacement of the instructions for and the building of the Tabernacle. Nachmanides, also known by his

Hebrew acronym Ramban (Rabbi Moshe ben Nachman), implies a resolution of this challenge in his introduction to Exodus. There, he writes that the overall function of Exodus is to show the redemption of the Jewish people, both physically and spiritually, from their enslavement. In particular, the spiritual redemption would not be complete until they returned to the level of the special relationship the Patriarchs had with God, a return evident in the heavenly cloud settling over the Tabernacle. Inasmuch as that event is recorded in Exodus 40:34, the redemption, as well as the Book of Exodus, concludes there.[40] Note how well the association of Principle B (Loyalty) with Exodus fits Ramban's approach to this order challenge.

Inconsistency of Legal Statements

As for the inconsistency of legal statements, we have already mentioned Ramban's explanation of differences between laws stated in Deuteronomy and versions found earlier in the Torah. That explanation also deals directly with the latter remaining challenge by attributing such differences to the need to address failings in the Wilderness or to address special challenges in Canaan. Ramban's approach, on its own and quite apart from the Shared Principles, provides a clear alternative to the Wellhausen Hypothesis, which views Deuteronomy as having been written at the time of King Josiah, centuries later than the narrative portions in the earlier books.

Apart from consistency challenges focusing on law per se (such as the perceived discrepancy between Deuteronomy and the preceding text), one can point to other forms of inconsistency. Such additional challenges were also used by the Wellhausen Hypothesis to promote the view of the Torah as a compilation from different authors at different times. However, as already noted in Section 1 and as further detailed in Section 12, Wellhausen's specific use of purported inconsistencies has not fared well under serious scrutiny. In Section 6, we will see how the Shared Principles shed light on the most basic of these purported inconsistencies, i.e., the use of different names for God.

Section 4

Division of a Book into Five Parts and a Part into Five Subparts

In light of the considerations in Section 3, I became comfortable with the notion that the Torah's division into five Books aligns with the Shared Principles. Yet, no matter how interesting this alignment, it would still not provide a pervasive pattern that unifies the entire text. For such unification, the pattern must demonstrate, within individual Books (at least those before Deuteronomy), that it

- helps resolve order challenges, i.e., the adjoining of topics lacking a clear connection (recall that the lack of clear connection between consecutive topics can occur where one is narrative and one legal, where both are narrative, or where both are legal), and
- shows itself in a convincing and unforced way that reflects validity.

We will make our initial analysis of the pattern on both these points in Stage II.

To prepare for that analysis, we will describe the pattern of the Shared Principles within each Book (see Item i below) and give a tangible sense of textual partitions based on the pattern (see Items ii and iii below). These latter subsections delve into the text more deeply and as a result give the present unit much greater detail than any of the previous Sections. This level of detail will, however, make the reader familiar enough with the pattern to make the remainder of the book (not just the initial analysis) flow more naturally.

i. Description of the Pattern

Through two primary claims, Rabbi Honigwachs essentially defines the pattern:

> (1) Each Book can be divided through the Shared Principles (in order) into five Parts, each made up of consecutive *parshiyot*.

In other words, Part A links to Shared Principle A, Part B to Shared Principle B, etc. I will refer to this claim as **the Parts Claim**, which is illustrated below. In practice, a book would occupy many more columns of text and would include many more *p'tuchot* than shown here, but the figure does illustrate how a book might be partitioned (with gray indicating text and dotted lines the end of Parts). No *s'tumot* are shown. Keep in mind that Hebrew is read right to left.

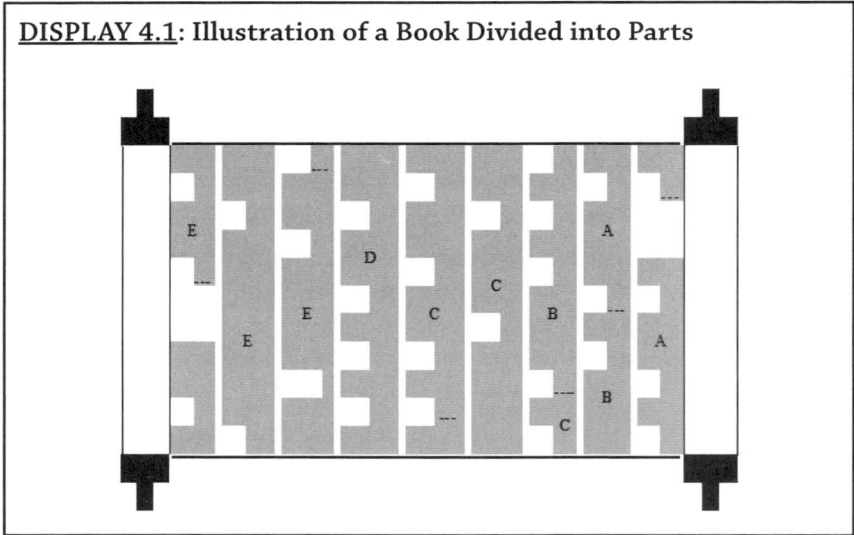

DISPLAY 4.1: Illustration of a Book Divided into Parts

> (2) Each Part with at least five *parshiyot* can then be subdivided in order through the Shared Principles into five Subparts, each made up of consecutive *parshiyot*.

In other words, Subpart A links to Principle A, Subpart B links to Principle B, etc. I will refer to this claim as **the Subparts Claim**. Since each Part is associated overall with a particular Shared Principle, the Subparts Claim means that a Part is also layered with each of the Shared Principles in order. This layering is shown below in Display 4.2, giving an expanded view of the three columns in Display 4.1 containing Part C.

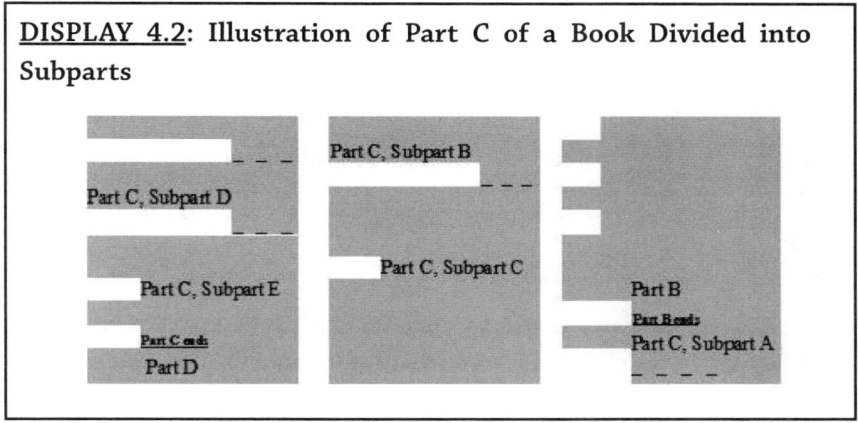

DISPLAY 4.2: Illustration of Part C of a Book Divided into Subparts

As shown in Display 4.2, each Subpart ends with a *p'tuchah*. In addition, Part C, Subpart A begins right after Part B, and Part C, Subpart E ends just before Part D. For this particular illustration, Subparts A, B, and D contain one *parshah* each, while Subparts C and E contain two *parshiyot* each. In actuality, a Subpart may contain many more *parshiyot*.

Rabbi Honigwachs asserts that some Subparts can themselves be divided into subunits called Segments. However, because many Subparts include fewer than five *parshiyot*, such Subparts cannot be subdivided into Segments. Moreover, we do not need such subdivisions to grasp the overall organization of the text. Consequently, I deal with subdivision of Subparts less extensively. Finally, recall that (as we saw previously in Section 3) the Book of Deuteronomy differs in structure from the other books. Even so, the last Book can be roughly divided into Parts (see Section 14), but we will not attempt subdivisions of these Parts into Subparts.

ii. Partition of Each of the First Four Books into Parts

At this point, we have not decided whether the Shared Principles actually help resolve order challenges involving apparently illogical or arbitrary transitions from one topic to another. Neither have we examined any of the reasons to doubt the validity of the pattern. Though I actually weighed some of those reasons before making my own partitions, it seems most logical here, just after defining the pattern, to give both a tangible sense of the proposed structure, as well as a preview of some particular issues.

In the frameworks below, I will show the partition of a Book into five Parts, each labeled with a capital letter corresponding to the five Shared Principles introduced in Display 2.3. To track these frameworks, the reader may use Appendix a, which lists all *p'tuchot* [open spacing] in the Torah. Alternatively, a Pentateuch that shows the spacing on a scroll may prove helpful.[41]

Genesis

DISPLAY 4.3: Genesis Divided According to the Shared Principles		
Part	Verses	Features Related to Shared Principle
A (Creation)	1:1–11:32	Universal History — Creation/ violence before Flood.
B (Loyalty)	12:1–21:34	Focus on Abraham — monotheism introduced/ threats of Sarah's violation/ special relationship with Abraham's offspring via the Covenant between the Parts
C (Limits)	22:1–25:18	Focus on Isaac — the Binding (how to approach God)/ Eliezer's mission (mention of God in his oath and need for Rebecca's agreement so as not to kidnap).
D (Community)	25:19–35:22	Focus on Jacob — birthright testimony and Laban's false promises.
E (Acceptance)	35:22–50:26	Focus on Tribes — Joseph's dreams of ruling/ his brothers' early rejection of that primary role/ Jacob foretelling future roles for his sons.

In this presentation of a partition of the Book of Genesis and in the other breakdowns provided in this Section, only a few features will be mentioned in order to illustrate how the Shared Principles relate to the text and where problems may lie. We will also alert the reader, as we go, to places in the Book with further analysis. Thus, the present examples give only a basic sense of the pattern, and the reader should not expect until later to systematically grapple with its validity.

Note the connection between themes cited in each of Part of Genesis and its respective Principle. In Part A, the recurring violence before the Flood relates to murder, the subject of the Sixth Commandment covered by Principle A (Respecting Creation). In Part B, each of the three themes cited (introduction of monotheism, threats of Sarah's violation, and a special relationship with Abraham's offspring) involves loyalty to a primary relationship (Principle B). However, it should be noted, specifically for Part B, that one of the themes (monotheism) is inferred but does not actually occur explicitly in the text. We will take up this problem in Section 6.

Another issue stands out in Part C, where the mission of Eliezer could be associated with a Principle other than C (Limits), such as B (Loyalty), since the mission involved both loyalty to Abraham and the goal of finding Isaac a wife. Such ambiguity of association is addressed more fully in Section 5. In Part D, the frequent themes of testimony and deceit clearly reflect Principle D (Duties of Testimony/Community). Finally, the recurrent dreams in Part E link it to the future, as addressed in the Fifth Commandment, thus marking Principle E (Acceptance).

Points of Division between Parts

In partitioning a single Book into five Parts, there will always be four points of division between successive Parts: between A and B, between B and C, between C and D, and between D and E. For Genesis, each of my four points of division matched those of Rabbi Honigwachs. In Exodus and Leviticus, however, there was not an exact match, and I have noted in the partitions that follow (which are mine) where variations occur in five cases: after Parts A, C, and D in Exodus and after Parts A and D in Leviticus. Citing these variations does not mean I am right and Rabbi

Honigwachs is wrong; rather, my independent partition simply did not replicate his.

With four of the variations, the distances between our respective points of division in the text are in fact fairly small. However, in Exodus, there is a large gap between my end of Part A (6:30) and where Rabbi Honigwachs ended it (17:16). This pronounced gap raises the question of how much points of division can differ before we lose confidence in the pattern's reliability. In Section 8, we will explore this specific discrepancy, and in Section 5 we will consider the general challenge, given the number of *parshiyot* in the Torah, in matching points of division.

Exodus

DISPLAY 4.4: Exodus Divided According to the Shared Principles		
Part	Verses	Features Related to Shared Principle
A (Creation)	1:1–6:30*	Egyptian oppression of Jewish people with infanticide/ midwives' belief in God/ revelation to Moses and Aaron.
B (Loyalty)	7:1*– 18:27	God's unique power shown in Plagues and Splitting of Sea/ Jews' sacrificing of Pascal Lamb showing break with Egyptian idolatry.
C (Limits)	19:1– 23:33*	Giving of Ten Commandments/ more detailed laws largely involving property obligations.
D (Community)	24:1*– 33:23*	Declaration to do and understand/ communal instructions for building/funding the Tabernacle with repeated mention of Sabbath and Tent of Meeting/ Sin of Golden Calf.
E (Acceptance)	34:1*– 40:38	Revelation to Moses fulfilled/ Tabernacle built by chosen artisans/ Priesthood given special duties — others accept lesser roles.

* Rabbi Honigwachs ends Part A after 17:16, Part C after 24:18, and Part D after 35:3.

In Part A, infanticide, belief in God, and revelation fit Principle A (Respecting Creation). Part B aligns with Principle B (Loyalty) in removing the domination of the Egyptians. The first Part in the Torah dealing mainly with law, Part C fits Principle C (Limits) very well, since property law sets limits. Also, Principle E (Acceptance) marks Part E, since fulfilling God's promise of revelation ties to the future. Choices for special roles suggest Acceptance (as chosen or not).

However, with Part D, we encounter a problem already noted in Genesis with Eliezer's mission — namely, that it could be reasonably associated with more than one Principle. The same problem would apply in Exodus with the Golden Calf. It is true that sin reflected a particular failure of the community in overwhelming the leadership, a failure that can arguably be associated with Principle D (Community). Yet, a more immediate connection might also be made with Principle B (Loyalty) on account of the element of idolatry or something close to it.

Leviticus

DISPLAY 4.5: Leviticus Divided According to the Shared Principles		
Part	Verses	Features Related to Shared Principle
A (Creation)	1:1– 14:57*	A person's wish to approach God as motivation for offerings/ categories of offerings and their laws.
B (Loyalty)	15:1*– 16:34	Laws of genital/vaginal discharge (affecting intimate relations)/ atonement on Yom Kippur (restoring relationship with God).
C (Limits)	17:1– 21:24	Laws of forbidden use of sanctified animals/ widely ranging laws, many associated with God's name and with holiness.
D (Community)	22:1– 26:2*	Laws of holidays and Sabbaticals/ Jubilee (communal obligation).
E (Acceptance)	26:3*– 27:34	Blessings and curses for future/ future dedication to religious service or use.

* Rabbi Honigwachs ends Part A after 15:33 and Part D after 26:46.

Outside of Part E, Leviticus consists primarily of law. In Parts A, B, and D, the legal subjects focus on matters associated with the respective Shared Principle: offerings (coming close to God) in Part A, primary relationships in Part B, and testimonial/communal obligations in Part D.

However, the law in Part C, especially in Chapter 19, covers many topics, exhibiting no real dominant subject. Yet, the repeated mention of God's name following many of these legal requirements intimates that their violation also involves taking God's name in vain. In other words, Part C aligns with Principle C (limited access to sanctity/resources).

As clear from Display 4.5, Part A makes up about half of Leviticus. While offerings do overlay this entire Part, other topics are present, some possibly linked to other Principles. For example, the death of two of Aaron's sons in bringing a strange fire in Chapter 10 suggests either Principle B involving a primary relationship or C involving limits on access to sanctity. There is also the topic of Biblical leprosy, whose sufferers must leave the community (Principle D).

Numbers

Part	Verses	Features Related to Shared Principle
DISPLAY 4.6: Numbers Divided According to the Shared Principles		
A (Creation)	1:1–10:36	Census (count of lives)/ laws of Nazirite (dedication to God)/ offerings brought for dedication of Tabernacle/ laws of "second" Passover involving people in contact with corpses.
B (Loyalty)	11:1– 18:32	Gossip over Moses' marital situation/ Incident of Spies and Rebellion of Korach (as failures of loyalty).
C (Limits)	19:1– 19:22	Laws of Red Heifer (access to purity).
D (Community)	20:1–26:1*	Communal strife in last year of wandering/ wars before Canaan entry.
E (Acceptance)	26:1*– 36:13	Inheritance/ settlement/ borders of Canaan/ tribal land allocation.

* There is a *p'tuchah* in the middle of 26:1.

As shown above, Parts C, D, and E of Numbers align well with their corresponding Shared Principles, but Parts A and B present real issues. First, Part A of Numbers, unlike Part A in each of the prior Books, offers only a few explicit connections with belief in God or sanctity of human life. Specifically, while the common thread of dedication can be tied to Principle A, dedication does not fit Principle A as directly as universal history in Genesis, murder and revelation in Exodus, and *korbanot* in Leviticus. One may argue that dedication fits Principle B (Loyalty) just as well or better.

Second, we can grant that Part B may properly include the gossip about Moses' marital situation reflecting Principle B (Loyalty). Yet, that Part also includes the Incident of the Spies and the Rebellion of Korach, which we have already linked to Principles D (Community) and E (Acceptance), respectively. While we can say the Incident of the Spies and the Rebellion of Korach reflect disloyalty in line with Principle B, it still seems we are simply choosing what fits.

iii. Examples of Parts Subdivided into Subparts

While each of the partitions of the (first four) Books results in five Parts, not all of those Parts can be subdivided into Subparts. This is because several Parts (i.e., Parts B and E of Leviticus and Part C of Numbers) contain fewer than five *parshiyot*, the minimum for subdivision. One of the outstanding questions is what significance or rationale, if any, can be attached to the fact that these three Parts differ from the seventeen others in the first four books.

Among the Parts that do subdivide, I have chosen to explain six (roughly one third of the seventeen), with at least one from each of the first four Books of the Bible. These choices, whose subdivisions follow, show alignments with the Shared Principles for one exclusively narrative Part, for one exclusively legal Part, and for four Parts treating both narrative and law. Most important, these choices cover the points of shift in the five difficult transitions presented in Display 1.1 (to which we will return in the next Section). The Parts not subdivided here (the eleven left in the first four Books) are all shown in Appendix c.

In his book, Rabbi Honigwachs did not fully treat subdivisions of Parts into Subparts, especially those not in Genesis. Thus I cannot say in subdividing Parts (as I could in dividing Books), how well my points of division match Rabbi Honigwachs' points. Where I could compare such points in these six cases, most were exact matches, and the rest were not far apart.

Genesis

DISPLAY 4.7: Part E of Genesis Subdivided According to the Shared Principles

Part	Verses	Features Related to Shared Principle
A (Creation)	35:23–37:36	Descendants of murderous Esau/ planned murder of Joseph, the dreamer, who is sold as slave.
B (Loyalty)	38:1–39:23	Judah's affair with daughter-in-law Tamar/ Potiphar's wife's designs on Joseph.
C (Limits)	40:1–40:23	Dreams of chief butler and baker on regaining access to Pharaoh/ interpretation of dreams by Joseph.
D (Community)	41:1–47:31	Pharaoh's dreams of communal plenty and famine/ Joseph placed over communal resources/ his brothers' testimony seeking grain/ test of brothers' care for Benjamin/ separate community for tribes.
E (Acceptance)	48:1–50:26	Jacob blessing his children/ Joseph's will to be reburied in Canaan.

Note that dreams guide the overall character of Part E of Genesis in line with Principle E (Acceptance), which includes a future orientation. Dreams actually occur in Subparts A, C, and D of Part E, where the subject or function of the dreams determines the Subpart. Specifically, in Subpart A, Joseph's dreams of ruling over the family motivate his brothers to kill him, with murder linked to Principle A (Creation). Meanwhile, the dreams in Subparts C and D focus, respectively, on individual access for Principle C (Limits) and on communal resources for Principle D (Community). Thus the Shared Principles are layered in order on top of Principle E.

Exodus

DISPLAY 4.8: Part C of Exodus Subdivided According to the Shared Principles

Part	Verses	Features Related to Shared Principle
A (Creation)	19:1–20:14	Revelation in giving the Ten Commandments.
B (Loyalty)	20:15–20:23	Banned images and altars revealing nakedness — like illicit union.
C (Limits)	21:1–22:12	Laws involving damages to persons and to property.
D (Community)	22:13–23:19	Duty to support poor, not to oppress weak or take false testimony/ holidays as testimonial occasions [*moadim*] and times to assemble.
E (Acceptance)	23:20–24:18	Blessing of bread/ promise of military victory/ Moses' ascent without Elders (exclusivity of role).

In contrast to Part E of Genesis, which is concerned entirely with narrative, Part C of Exodus deals mainly with law, with only a bit of narrative. Recall that this Part is tied to Principle C because law in general, especially with laws involving damages, reflects limits. Within the overlay of law, Subpart A is of key interest with the placement of the Ten Commandments, as well as the associated revelation reflecting Principle A (Creation). The next three Subparts (B, C, and D) are legal, and each respective topic fits its corresponding Principle. In particular, the subject in Subpart D is holidays, suggesting testimony (and hence Principle D) through the use of the word *moadim* [testimonial occasions], as well as times of assembly. Here again, we have a basic overlay, this time of Principle C in Part C, with a progression within that Part through the Shared Principles.

Leviticus

DISPLAY 4.9: Part A of Leviticus Subdivided According to the Shared Principles

Part	Verses	Features Related to Shared Principle
A (Creation)	1:1–7:38	Laws of *korbanot* [offerings], by which people get closer to God.
B (Loyalty)	8:1–10:7	Consecration of Priests, marking special relationship with them/ Aaron's sons die in bringing "strange fire" (violating relationship).
C (Limits)	10:8–12:8	Conditions on priestly service/ dietary laws.
D (Community)	13:1–14:32	Laws of the leper, who is sent outside camp, i.e., separated from community (Biblical leprosy punished speaking ill of others).
E (Acceptance)	14:33–14:57	Laws of "leprous" houses that will take effect in Canaan.

In Part A of Leviticus, each Subpart has *korbanot* associated with it. For example, in Subpart D (which deals with Biblical leprosy), a person whose disease has healed must bring a *korban* before returning to the camp. In Subpart A, however, the text is dealing generally with *korbanot* and their classifications, as opposed to specific circumstances that cause them to be brought. The notion of *korban* is rooted in the Hebrew word *karov* [near], thus suggesting the purpose of an offering: to bring one closer to God. Because this notion first comes in the second verse of Subpart A, it ties most directly to belief in God and Principle A.

The other four Subparts of Part A progress through Principles B–E, with the circumstances of the offerings in each Subpart tied to the respective Principle. For example, Subpart D presents laws of the Biblical leper who is punished for speaking ill of others (testimony) and is separated from the camp (community), thereby suggesting

Principle D. Yet, one might ask whether bringing a strange fire in Subpart B could be regarded as a violation of Principle C (Limits) instead of Principle B (Loyalty), since the strange fire transgressed limited access to sanctity. Still, we can see the overlay of *korbanot* and Principle A, along with the progression of all the Shared Principles in order.

DISPLAY 4.10: Part C of Leviticus Subdivided According to the Shared Principles

Part	Verses	Features Related to Shared Principle
A (Creation)	17:1–17:16	Eating forbidden blood / duty to cover blood of dead animal.
B (Loyalty)	18:1–18:30	Listing of illicit sexual relations resulting in expulsion of inhabitants of Canaan.
C (Limits)	19:1–19:37	Diverse laws often followed by the phrase "I am God" or "I am the Lord, your God," ending in rule for fair weights and measures.
D (Community)	20:1–20:27	Punishments carried out by communal judicial system for idolatry and illicit sexual unions.
E (Acceptance)	21:1–21:24	Special rules for priests involving burial of relatives, marriage, and physical fitness for service in the Tabernacle.

Part C of Leviticus presents only laws. It also differs from the other cases treated here in that it contains very few *parshiyot*, six to be exact — only one more than the minimum needed for subdivision. Subpart C includes Chapter 19, which was cited earlier in Subsection ii regarding its diverse legal topics. The present breakdown seems to confirm that this chapter fits with Shared Principle C through the repeated mentioning of God's Name. Note that both Subparts B and D discuss forbidden sexual activity (with D also treating idolatry), a theme associated with Principle B (Loyalty). The difference is that Subpart D treats punishments, which are enforced communally and thus linked to Shared Principle D (Community). Subpart E involves Principle E (Acceptance) in setting special rules for priests generally and for the High Priest in particular. For example, it goes with the role of a priest that he cannot go to the burial of anyone except a very close relative. This restriction also encompasses Principle C (Limits), which comes from Part C itself.

Numbers

DISPLAY 4.11: Part A of Numbers Subdivided According to the Shared Principles

Part	Verses	Features Related to Shared Principle
A (Creation)	1:1–3:4	Census (count of lives)/ camp arranged by flags (recalling revelation at Mount Sinai).
B (Loyalty)	3:5–4:49	Roles of Levites who have assumed spiritual mantle (primary relationship) of firstborn.
C (Limits)	5:1–7:89	Laws of misused consecrated property, suspected adulteress, and Nazirite/ priestly blessing in God's Name/ tribal leaders' offerings.
D (Community)	8:1–10:10	Levites represent community in Tabernacle/ Second Passover/ Clouds of Glory in camp travel/ trumpets in war and testimonial occasion.
E (Acceptance)	10:11–10:36	Future of Moses' father-in-law (renamed Chovav).

We noted in relation to Part A of Numbers (see the discussion concerning Display 4.6) that the connection with Principle A (Creation) is more difficult than with Parts A of Genesis, Exodus, and Leviticus. When we subdivide Part A of Numbers into Subparts as shown above, there is slightly more connection to Principle A in evidence, for example, in the dependence on the Clouds of Glory for movement of the camp, thus marking belief in God.

Still, the census and camp layout in Subpart A seem to only modestly reflect Principle A in comparison with Principle D (Community). Other Subparts of Part A align fairly well with the Shared Principles, though the suspected adulteress in Subpart C does raise a question. Part of the trial of this individual involves erasing God's name, which does fit Principle C (limited access to sanctity/resources). However, one may argue that Principle B (Loyalty) is a better fit.

One other structural point concerns the end of Part A of Numbers. On a Torah scroll, there is at that point (following Verse 10:36) the first of two large inverted Hebrew letters (each a *nun*), which is recognized traditionally as dividing the initial text of Numbers from the remaining text in which so many transgressions take place.[42]

DISPLAY 4.12: Part E of Numbers Subdivided According to the Shared Principles

Part	Verses	Features Related to Shared Principle
A (Creation)	26:1–27:5	Eligibility and census (count of lives) for military service/ Moses asks God about the daughters of Zelophehad inheriting land.
B (Loyalty)	27:6–27:11	Laws of inheritance based on familial relationship.
C (Limits)	27:12–30:17	Moses denied entry to Canaan/ laws of additional holiday offerings/ nullification of vows (using God's Name).
D (Community)	31:1–33:49	War with Midianites/ communal duty of Tribes of Reuben and Gad to assist in conquest of Canaan.
E (Acceptance)	33:50–36:13	Settlement and borders of Canaan/ land allocation among tribes.

Part E of Numbers concerns Canaan, including the guidance to conquer, settle, and inherit it. This fits accordingly with the Fifth Commandment's reference to the land: that honoring one's parents will grant prosperity there. Thus, Part E aligns with Principle E (Acceptance), which covers the Fifth Commandment. In identifying Subpart A of Part E, we are required, as we did in subdividing Part A, to identify a census with Principle A (Creation) — presumably since a census is a count of lives. However, in Part E, Subpart A also includes Moses' audience with God over inheritance, an instance of revelation that fits Principle A more smoothly.

Outside of Subpart A, the progress through the Shared Principles continues to align with the other Subparts. One of the most striking combination of topics occurs in Subpart C, where we have the bar on Moses' entry into Canaan, additional holiday offerings, and nullification of vows associated with Principle C (limited access to sanctity/resources). Note that the holidays also reflect Principle D (duties of testimony/community) in that they are termed *moadim* [testimonial occasions]. This association with Principle D agrees with Numbers as a whole. Thus, we have three layers of association in Subpart C:

- Shared Principle D for Numbers and the holidays;
- Shared Principle E for the land;
- Shared Principle C for limited access (ban on Moses' entry and nullification of vows).

As we said, more subdivisions of Parts can be found in Appendix c.

Summary and a Look Ahead

Let us review our progress as we conclude Stage 1:

- We saw how the debate over authorship of the Five Books hinges on whether or not there is an overall pattern in the text.
- We saw further that any such pattern must resolve Order Challenges in the text, and especially those involving the adjoining of apparently unconnected topics.
- We came to understand an overall pattern proposed by Rabbi Yehoshua Honigwachs based on five Shared Principles in the Ten Commandments.
- We were exposed to both major features and possible problems in the proposed pattern. This exposure involved dividing each of the first four Books into five Parts and in subdividing some of those Parts into five Subparts.

Taken together, all the divisions and subdivisions (including those highlighted in Section 4 above) represent my own independent attempt to structure the text against Rabbi Honigwachs' framework. I use the word "against" on purpose because I tried (unsuccessfully, as you will see) to make that framework fail. In the end, whether you embrace my partitions (or those of Rabbi Honigwachs) or not, you will not miss a genuine effort to disprove the pattern. That effort failed, and I now accept the pattern. With this acceptance, I profess single authorship of the Torah, not just from faith, but from reason: the near impossibility that such a highly synchronized text could have been compiled over time from more than one source — especially without today's software.

We are now ready to enter Stage II, which consists of three Sections that proceed as follows:

- Section 5 presents a preliminary analysis of the pattern and identifies particularly questionable aspects of the pattern, along with where failures in the pattern would most likely occur;
- Section 6 checks whether the pattern holds in Genesis; and
- Section 7 gives strategies, based on Sections 5 and 6, to test the pattern in the other books.

Notes

1. Other types of consistency challenges include, for example, variations in narrative accounts and linguistic style. These are discussed in Section 12.
2. Though Rashi's telegraphic comments, when taken literally, deal with the geographic proximity of the Court and the altars of the Temple, it seems natural to understand this proximity as making justice a pre-condition for worship, as articulated in Isaiah I 1:11–17.
3. Translated by Black and Menzies (Edinburgh: A & C Black, 1885). The original German version, entitled *Geschichte Israels*, was published in 1878.
4. N. Snaith, *The Distinctive Ideas of the Old Testament* (New York: Schocken Books, 1964).
5. J. H. Hertz (ed.), *Pentateuch and Haftorahs*, Second Edition (London: Soncino Press, 1981), pp. 557–9; which quotes Rawlinson directly, explaining his position in the context of the "evolution of sacrifice" promoted by Source Critics.
6. D. T. Hoffman, *Die Wichtigsten Instanzen gegen die Graf-Wellhausensche Hypothese*, (Berlin: Poppenlauer, 1904). Further details of Rabbi Hoffman's argument over centralized worship are provided in the Elaboration through a private partial translation by H. Weiss.
7. J. H. Hertz (ed.), *Pentateuch and Haftorahs*, five volumes (London: Oxford University Press, 1929–36). Rabbi Hertz, then Chief Rabbi of the British Empire, included his own extensive essays as "Additional Notes" following each of the Five Books. Much of this writing is directed against Source Criticism.
8. B. Katz, "The jig is up! And we're dancing to it!" *The American Rationalist*, Jan–Feb online issue (2003), pp. 2478–2479. Katz celebrates Conservative congregations replacing the Hertz Pentateuch.
9. U. Cassuto, *The Documentary Hypothesis and the Composition of the Pentateuch*, tr. (from Hebrew) Abrahams, (Jerusalem: Shalem Press, 2006), pp. 121–122.
10. The *Mekhilta* (also spelled *Mechilta*) is a compilation of traditional oral explanations of legal passages in Exodus. Rabbi Yishmael, whose name appears frequently in the Talmud, redacted the standard version of the *Mekhilta*. The explanation of five linked principles within the Ten Commandments occurs in this version of the *Mekhilta* in the section on Yitro [Jethro], Chapter 8.

11 An excellent treatment of forced visualization appears in M. Livio, *The Golden Ratio*, (New York: Broadway Books, 2002), pp. 47–61, 160–168.
12 The terms *parshah* and *sidrah* are used in the Talmud with the respective meanings of "paragraph" and "weekly portion" set forth here. Some choose to avoid the popular but mistaken connection of *parshah* to a weekly portion by distinguishing between the words *parshah* and *par-**a**shah* and by then speaking of "the *parashah* of the week." However, this approach requires more aural acuity than many people have.
13 Maimonides' classic code *Mishneh Torah*, in *Hilkhot Sefer Torah* 7:10, sets the size of letters on a line and also provides a range of 48–60 lines per column, rather than 42. These specifications are termed matters of "practice" for which a scroll would not be invalidated by non-compliance with them (*Hilkhot Sefer Torah* 7:11), as opposed to absolute specifications of word order. The limitation is based on Psalms 68:5, which speaks of rising to the highest edge in God's name. The Hebrew letters in the phrase "in God's name" are (in order) *bet*, *yud*, *hei*, *shin*, *mem*, and *vav*, which are those that may begin a column.
14 Included within "law" are explanations/justifications and accounts of laws' transmission/acceptance.
15 For a more complete account that also includes dating of manuscripts through paleography (analysis of script characteristics), see J. VanderKam and P. Flint, *The Meaning of the Dead Sea Scrolls: Their Significance for Understanding the Bible, Judaism, Jesus, and Christianity* (New York: HarperCollins, 2004), pp. 22–30.
16 Almost all of the Aleppo Codex was destroyed in 1947, but not before several scholars had studied it carefully. As part of this study, the location of each *p'tuchah* was checked.
17 This argument is offered by M. Brettler, *How to Read the Jewish Bible* (New York: Oxford University Press, 2007), pp. 29–30.
18 For each of the three main camps on the identity of the people of Qumran, the following sources advocate each respective position.
Essenes: J. VanderKam, *The Dead Sea Scrolls Today* (Grand Rapids, MI: Eerdman's, 1996). VanderKam also discusses a variation: the possibility of a Jewish sectarian group other than the Essenes.
Originators of Christianity: R. Eisenman, *The Dead Sea Scrolls and the First Christians* (Edison, NJ: Castle Books, 2006).
Refugees: N. Golb, *Who Wrote the Dead Sea Scrolls?: The Search for the Secret of Qumran* (New York: Simon & Schuster, 1996).

19 A great number of the messianic/end of days scrolls found in Cave 4 are described by Eisenman and M. Wise, *The Dead Sea Scrolls Uncovered* (New York: Barnes & Noble, 2004). Eisenman and Wise show how the content of these scrolls influences the key Community Rule Scroll (1QS). See also H. Eshel, *The Dead Sea Scrolls and the Hasmonean State* (Grand Rapids, MI: Eerdman's and Jerusalem: Yad Ben-Zvi, 2008) on the scroll 4QMMT, which explicitly rejects established Jewish ritual laws.

20 In other words, the word *sof'rim* does not mean scribes in the way we would normally use that English word, i.e., those whose task is simply to copy texts by hand. Rather, *sof'rim* were a special group charged with maintaining the integrity of the text.

21 For example, the rule in *Mishneh Torah, Hilkhot Sefer Torah* 8:11 invalidating a scroll with a *s'tumah* where there should be a *p'tuchah* and vice-versa can be found in *Masekhet Sof'rim* 1:14. There is, however, at least one place where the original *Mishneh Torah* manuscript differs from *Masekhet Sof'rim* — in the number of lines occupied by the poetic passage Deuteronomy 32:1–43. That difference may have been eliminated in many printed versions of the *Mishneh Torah* by a typesetter who "corrected" the manuscript to agree with *Masekhet Sof'rim*.

22 See the left sidebar commentary on page 246 in *B'rakhot*, Volume One of the El-'Am Talmud, ed. A. Z. Ehrman (Jerusalem/Tel Aviv: El-'Am — Hotza'a Leor Israel, 1982).

23 This source did not appear in *The Unity of Torah*.

24 The actual Hebrew phrase is *Bein col Dibur v'Dibur* [between each Commandment and a Commandment]. Were the intent of this phrase only that the Ten Commandments generate the explanations and details in the rest of the Torah, a simpler and more direct phrase could have been used instead, such as *Mitokh HaDibrot* [from within the Commandments].

25 The Lutheran listing differs from the common Protestant listing and is closer to the Catholic listing.

26 The Jewish conception of the day beginning with the evening derives from the phrase "and it was evening and it was morning…" used repeatedly in the Creation story in Chapter 1 of Genesis. The ending of nightfall Saturday (as opposed to sundown) is explained by the *Mekhilta* on Exodus 20:10.

27 The connection between forbidden Sabbath activity and the Tabernacle

comes from the placement of God's directive: "However, My Sabbaths you will keep..." in Exodus 31:14, as Rashi explains on that verse. Because this instruction follows the instructions for building the Tabernacle, it is understood that those activities are prohibited on the Sabbath. See *Shabbat* 49b on the count of thirty-nine activities.

28 An example of a technical distinction occurs in the commandment not to take God's name in vain, where there are differences over whether certain oaths can justify using God's name.

29 There is also a briefly stated opinion in the *Mekhilta* that each tablet had all Ten Commandments, but that opinion does not actually oppose the Shared Principles. A slightly later work (*Midrash Tanchuma*, T'rumah 10) makes plain that the format of five and five is the accepted opinion.

30 This distinction was pointed out by the Spanish commentator Rabbenu Bachya (d. 1340).

31 The rendering of the Shared Principles in Display 2.3 reflects their elaboration in the commentary *Akedat Yitzchak* (fifteenth century) on Exodus 20. That elaboration accords with the Talmud's reinforcement of each of the Shared Principles. For example, *Sanhedrin* 37a reinforces Shared Principle A = respecting Creation, which connects belief in God with the prohibition of murder. There the Talmud states that mankind was created through a single man (Adam) to teach that taking a human life is like destroying an entire world.

32 This is the interpretation articulated in the *Or HaChayim* (eighteenth century) on Exodus 20:7. However, it is likely that even according to those who do not explicitly include this behavior under what is prohibited by Commandment 3, that commandment would still present the underlying principle in forbidding it.

33 Deuteronomy 4:45 speaks of three categories of laws: *edot* [testimonial ritual observances], *chukim* [non-testimonial ritual observances], and *mishpatim* [civil laws]. In the version of the Ten Commandments that appears in Exodus 20, the Fourth Commandment begins with the imperative *Zakhor et yom haShabbat*...[Remember the Sabbath day...], which is understood to mean remembrance through testimony. The association with testimony comes from a longstanding interpretation of *Shabbat* 119b, which refers to potential transgression [*avon*] being removed from someone who recites Genesis 2:1–3. This interpretation connects the reference to *avon* with Leviticus 5:1, which speaks of someone who fails to testify (despite the knowledge to do

so) as carrying *avon*. Thus someone who does not recite Genesis 2:1–3 on Friday evening would carry the transgression of failing to testify.

34 It is through this idea that Nachmanides (thirteenth century), in his comment on Exodus 20:12, explains placing Commandment 5 on the tablet that guides the relationship between Man and God (rather than on the other tablet between Man and Man).

35 I added this explanation to Rabbi Honigwachs' observation about *edah* and *edut* two sentences later.

36 In a private communication, Rabbi Honigwachs expressed the view that the later waging of war in Numbers indicates that Shared Principle D was partly attained by the end of that book.

37 The focus on differences in the two versions is my idea, but Nachmanides' introduction to Deuteronomy guided my thinking.

38 This is the idea that group transgressions (even those against God) always include an element of trespass against one's fellow. Such inclusion recognizes each person's role in the group in reinforcing the improper behavior of other members. An indication of one party's responsibility for having promoted improper behavior in others comes in the Torah law for a high court whose incorrect ruling leads to transgression by the public (see Leviticus 4:13–21).

39 The Fourth Commandment, as it appears in Exodus 20, begins with imperative *Zakhor* [Remember], while the version in Deuteronomy 5 begins *Shamor* [Guard]. According to the *Mekhilta*, *Yitro*, Chapter 7, both imperatives were present in each version of the Commandments. The first imperative requires the positive act of remembering the Sabbath through its sanctification (which includes the recitation of Gen. 2:1–3 as testimony), while the second imperative requires refraining from prohibited activity identified as *m'lakhah*, which is commonly (and poorly) translated as "work."

40 The annotated English translation of the Ramban's commentary by C. Chavel, *Ramban: Commentary on the Torah* (New York: Shilo Publishing House, Inc., 1973), Volume Two, draws the inference in footnote 8 on page 4 and cites the Talmudic and Midrashic evidence for the Ramban's explanation in footnote 12 on pages 4–5.

41 For a Pentateuch with clear delineation of paragraphs, a good choice is *The Stone Edition Chumash* (Brooklyn: Mesorah Publications, 1993), which features Hebrew with facing English translation.

42 The Talmud in *Shabbat* 115b–116a speaks of Numbers being divided at this point.

STAGE II

Sizing Up the Pattern

Checking It in Genesis and Developing a Strategy

Section 5

Analyzing the Pattern

here, we provide a preliminary analysis using the two expectations from Section 4. These are the expectations by which a proposed pattern must be judged:

- The pattern should help resolve logical problems in the order of Biblical topics, especially the adjoining of topics lacking a clear connection. (Recall that the lack of clear connection between consecutive topics can occur where both are narrative, where one is narrative and one legal, or where both are legal.)
- The pattern should show itself in a convincing and unforced way, which would establish its validity.

This analysis will set the stage for Section 6, where the pattern will actually be checked in Genesis. As an aid in following the both the analysis and the verification, a framed summary of the Shared Principles appears at the foot of every other page in the present stage.

i. Capacity to Help Resolve Order Challenges

To judge the pattern's capacity to resolve order challenges in the Bible, let us return to the five difficult transitions from one topic to another in Display 1.1 of Section 1. Recall that these five cases (numbered 1 to 5 below) each occur at a *p'tuchah* [space open to left edge of column] as the shift point, and cover every situation where difficulty can arise: narrative after narrative, law after law, law after narrative, or

---

A = respecting Creation; B = loyalty to primary relationship; C = limited access to sanctity/resources; D = duties of testimony/community; E = accepting one's place/status (with ties to land/future)

vice-versa. With this coverage, these five cases will serve as a proxy for all order challenges in our initial analysis. As will be seen, a systematic explanation for each transition emerges from the progression of the pattern within the Book and the Part where the transition falls. Please note that these particular progressions were illustrated in the subdivision of Parts in Section 4.

Case 1: Sale of Joseph in Genesis followed by affair of Judah and Tamar (shift after 37:36)

The sale of Joseph actually began as attempted murder (Principle A) and thus is included in Subpart A of Part E (35:23–37:36), while the affair of Judah and Tamar is placed in Subpart B (38:1–39:23) and reflects loyalty (Principle B). The shift point coincides with the pattern's progression. Note that the attempted seduction of Joseph by Potiphar's wife follows Judah's affair with Tamar, which also occurs in Subpart B. This explains why the text turns to this attempted seduction in reverting to Joseph's life. Subparts A and B of Part E are restated below from Display 4.7.

A (Creation)   35:23–37:36

   Descendants of murderous Esau/ planned murder of Joseph, the dreamer, who is sold as slave.

B (Loyalty)   38:1–39:23

   Judah's affair with daughter-in-law Tamar/ Potiphar's wife's designs on Joseph.

Recall Rashi's explanation of this transition: that through Tamar's deception over her identity, Judah was punished for making his father think Joseph had been killed. Thus Rashi's explanation for the affair of Judah and Tamar following Joseph's sale is more specific — but still fully consistent — with the partition we have described.

> **Case 2: Laws of altars in Exodus followed by civil laws (shift after 20:23)**

The laws of altars and the statement of civil law each relate to Principle C (Limits). However, the treatment of altars in the text involves both idolatry and illicit sexual unions, each themes for Principle B (Loyalty). For civil law, however, the association ties fully with Principle C through concern with damages. Thus, the shift point reflects the transition from Subpart B to Subpart C of Part C and aligns with the Shared Principles. Subparts B and C of Part C are restated below from Display 4.8.

> B (Loyalty)   20:15–20:23
> Banned images and altars revealing nakedness — like illicit union.
>
> C (Limits)   21:1–22:12
> Laws involving damages to persons and to property.

Rashi's explanation about the location of the high court next to the altar of the Temple is, of course, more specific to the two adjoining topics.

> **Case 3: Aaron's sons' deaths in Leviticus followed by rules for priestly service (shift after 10:7)**

Both of the topics here fall in Part A through the overlay of *korbanot* [offerings]. According to the pattern, the sequence of deaths followed by conditions on priestly service marks the transition from a theme of special relationship (Principle B) to one of limited access (Principle C). The shift point from the narrative subtext to the legal subtext is a *p'tuchah* exactly between Subparts B and C of Part A, thus aligning with progression through the Shared Principles. Subparts B and C are restated from Display 4.9.

> A = respecting Creation; B = loyalty to primary relationship; C = limited access to sanctity/resources; D = duties of testimony/community; E = accepting one's place/status (with ties to land/future)

> B (Loyalty)   8:1–10:7
>
> Consecration of Priests, marking special relationship with them/ Aaron's sons die in bringing "strange fire" (violating relationship).
>
> C (Limits)   10:8–12:8
>
> Conditions on priestly service/ dietary laws.

Recall Rashi's explanation from Display 1.1: that Aaron's sons were intoxicated (which is expressly prohibited in the conditions on priestly service), thus leading them to bring the strange fire. Though more specific, this explanation accords with the partition according to the pattern.

> **Case 4: Laws of suspected adulteress in Numbers followed by laws of Nazirite (shift after 5:31)**

Part A includes both of these legal topics through a common involvement with *korbanot*. In fact, the suspected adulteress (for whom God's name is erased from written curses — see 5:21–23) and the Nazirite (who uses God's name in a vow) both reflect Principle C (limited access to sanctity/resources). Thus, both topics fall within Subpart C (5:1–7:89), a difference from the first three cases whose respective topics fell in successive Subparts. This means that the transition from the suspected adulteress to the Nazirite cannot be explained by a succession of Subparts (as in the prior cases).

However, what does explain the transition is a further subdivision of Subpart C into the next deeper level of components, which you may recall are called Segments. As shown below in Display 5.1, the suspected adulteress falls in Segment B because of the concern with Principle B (Loyalty). Meanwhile, the Nazirite falls into Segment C in taking on certain limitations, including abstinence from wine in return for higher spiritual status. Thus, the shift point between the suspected adulteress and the Nazirite is the *p'tuchah* between Segments B and C of Subpart C.

DISPLAY 5.1: Subpart C of Part A Subdivided According to the Shared Principles	
Segment A 5:1–5:4	People with certain conditions (including those touching a corpse) must leave the camp temporarily because God dwells in the camp.
Segment B 5:5–5:31	Prohibited use of items dedicated to Tabernacle (as violation of relationship with God)/ laws of suspected adulteress.
Segment C 6:1–7:17	Laws of Nazirite/ use of God's Name in blessing Jewish people.
Segment D 7:18–7:83	Communal dedicatory offerings brought by leaders of Tribes.
Segment E 7:84–7:89	Moses' exclusive role in communicating with God in Tabernacle.

We find once more that Rashi's traditional explanation on 6:2 — that seeing the disgrace of the suspected adulteress may bring someone to swear off wine, which loosens inhibitions — is more specific but consistent with the partition above.

Case 5: Inheritance laws in Numbers followed by Moses' barred entry to land (shift after 27:11)

Both the law and the narrative account fall into Part E of Numbers by reflecting the future in Canaan and thus Principle E (Acceptance). In subdividing this Part, the laws of inheritance go in Subpart B (27:6–27:11) since these laws are guided by family relationships tied to Principle B (Loyalty). The bar on Moses' entry fits in Subpart C (27:12–30:17), with denied entry signaling Principle C (Limits). The shift point from the legal topic to the narrative topic is a *p'tuchah* between Subparts B and C of Part E, once again following the pattern.

A = respecting Creation; B = loyalty to primary relationship; C = limited access to sanctity/resources; D = duties of testimony/community; E = accepting one's place/status (with ties to land/future)

> B (Loyalty)   27:6–27:11
>
> Laws of inheritance based on familial relationship.
>
> C (Limits)   27:12–30:17
>
> Moses denied entry to Canaan/ laws of additional holiday offerings/ nullification of vows (using God's Name).

Once again, traditional explanation linking the law and the narrative (as presented in Rashi on 27:12) is more specific, but still consistent, with textual placement according to the Shared Principles. According to that explanation, the inheritance laws were stated with the intensive wording *naton titen* [you shall surely give (the inheritance)]. Consequently, says Rashi, Moses might have thought he was being specifically directed to apportion the inheritance of the tribes, which would have meant his entering the land after all — despite the earlier decree (in Numbers 20:12) against his entry.

Summary

As shown in the five cases above, the pattern of Shared Principles fits each of the selected difficult transitions and helps rationalize them. More specifically, in four of the five (Cases 1, 2, 3, and 5), the change from one topic to another parallels the progression through successive Shared Principles at the level of Subparts. With Case 4, the transition from one set of law to another aligns with the further subdivision into Segments according to the pattern.

Thus, the Shared Principles applied to transitions in these five cases seem to provide an overall structure that unifies the text. However, one might still contend that while these five cases nicely exhibit the pattern of Shared Principles, other cases may not as easily fit or be rationalized by the pattern. For this reason, the discussion in subsequent units will give continued attention to the capacity of the Shared Principles to resolve all such challenges.

ii. Validity of the Pattern

While the preceding analysis showed the pattern's capability to explain representative shifts from one topic to another, its validity still seemed, to me, highly suspect. In other words, the division of Books into Parts and then Parts into Sections would probably not occur in a convincing and unforced way. In this subunit, we will refer back further to the discussion and displays in Section 4, as we explore four major reasons for doubt over validity:

DISPLAY 5.2: **Four Reasons to Doubt the Validity of the Pattern**

a. Likelihood of forced organization in division of Biblical books and alignment of Parts;
b. Likelihood of forced organization in division of Parts and in alignment of Sections;
c. Poor prospects for matching my division points with those of Rabbi Honigwachs;
d. Lack of precedent for parallel sequences of subtexts in established study of Biblical structure.

(We will explain the concept of "parallel sequence" in our discussion.)

Note that, at this point, we intend only to understand potential doubts, not to bring resolution.

a. Likelihood of forced organization in division of Books and alignment of Parts.

The Parts Claim stood out as the most immediate place for forced organization. If the claim were true, there would be a natural division of each Book into five Parts. Yes, one can see that Genesis presented a natural fivefold division: (1) universal history (from Creation), (2) the life of Abraham, (3) the life of Isaac, (4) the life of Jacob, and (5) the lives of

---

A = respecting Creation; B = loyalty to primary relationship; C = limited access to sanctity/resources; D = duties of testimony/community; E = accepting one's place/status (with ties to land/future)

Joseph and his brothers. Also, one can see an immediate link between four of these five periods and their corresponding Shared Principles:

- The period of universal history (1), including the incidence of violence clearly aligns with Principle A (respecting Creation).
- The central event of the period of Isaac (3) is his binding on an altar, which fits directly with Principle C (limited access to sanctity/resources).
- For the period of Jacob (4), deceit stands out as the dominant theme, thus corresponding to Principle D (duties of testimony/community). Because of the conflict over Joseph's role, as well as the stress on dreams and on the blessings given to the Tribes, the period of Joseph and his brothers (5) fits Principle E (accepting one's place/status — with ties to land and future).

The challenge of Abraham

However, one particular period does not immediately seem to correspond to its Principle: how does the period of Abraham correspond to Principle B (loyalty to a primary relationship)? As noted in Section 4 (see the discussion about Display 4.3), the link between the life of Abraham and Principle B seems to come, at least on its face, from a notion outside the text: that of Abraham as the father of monotheism.[1] Would this link with Shared Principle B be actually borne out by the text itself for the period of Abraham? We will see in Section 6.

Exodus

The prospects for confirming the Parts Claim beyond Genesis would be yet more remote since no other Book seems, on its face, to split naturally into five portions — much less to fit the order of the Shared Principles. Just for starters, why must we split Exodus into five portions? Why not the following seven topics (given in the order they appear in Exodus), which cannot align with the fivefold progression of the Shared Principles? These seven seem just as fitting:

1. enslavement of Jewish people;
2. revelation of God to Moses at Burning Bush;

3. liberation through Plagues and Splitting of Sea;
4. laws given at Mount Sinai;
5. directions for building Tabernacle;
6. incident of Golden Calf;
7. actual building of Tabernacle.

Compare the above arrangement and with Display 4.4 of the division of Exodus into five Parts, which we saw in Section 4. That display is reproduced below.

DISPLAY 4.4: Exodus Divided According to the Shared Principles		
Part	Verses	Features Related to Shared Principle
A (Creation)	1:1–6:30*	Egyptian oppression of Jewish people with infanticide/ midwives' belief in God/ revelation to Moses.
B (Loyalty)	7:1*– 18:27	God's unique power shown in Plagues and Splitting of Sea/ Jews' sacrifice Pascal Lamb to break from Egyptian idolatry.
C (Limits)	19:1– 23:33*	Giving of Ten Commandments/ more detailed laws largely involving property obligations.
D (Community)	24:1*– 33:23*	Declaration to do and understand/ communal instructions for building/funding the Tabernacle with repeated mention of Sabbath and Tent of Meeting/ Sin of Golden Calf.
E (Acceptance)	34:1*– 40:38	Revelation to Moses fulfilled/ Tabernacle built by chosen artisans/ Priesthood given special duties while others must accept lesser roles.

* Rabbi Honigwachs ends Part A after 17:16, Part C after 24:18, and Part D after 35:3.

Labeling the initial topic

this comparison raises an immediate question in the initial disparity. As you can see, the first Part in Display 4.4 is linked to Principle

A = respecting Creation; B = loyalty to primary relationship; C = limited access to sanctity/resources; D = duties of testimony/community; E = accepting one's place/status (with ties to land/future)

A (Creation) through murder and belief, while the first topic in the alternative listing is linked to Principle B (Loyalty) through enslavement of the Jewish people to Egyptian masters. Since all those themes are present, should we not choose the latter as the most general? By picking just on murder and belief initially, Display 4.4 appears to force ordered alignment with the Shared Principles. We grapple with this point in Section 8.

The Golden Calf
Another problem exposed in the comparison involves the Golden Calf, which is included in Part D (Community) in Display 4.4. Isn't this incident vital to the Biblical account and deserving of its own portion, as in the alternative sequence of topics? If so, then would it not be associated with Principle B (Loyalty) on account of idolatry or something very close to idolatry? Yet Part D in Display 4.4 takes the Golden Calf as a communal matter. This seeming forced classification of topics will also be addressed in Section 8.

Other books
Furthermore, forced partition/alignment apparently occurs beyond Exodus. For example, according to Display 4.6, Part B of Numbers includes both the Incident of the Spies and the Rebellion of Korach, which were linked in Section 3 to Principles D (Community) and E (Acceptance), respectively. Instead, that display links both events to disloyalty, rationalizing the connection with Principle B. Does the pattern require then that we associate the same events with different Principles just to make the pattern fit or that we ignore the events that don't fit? As with all the issues that will be raised here, keep this one in mind for its full treatment (and resolution) later. The point of mentioning all these prospective issues now is to explain why I did not believe the pattern would hold up under thorough scrutiny.

b. Likelihood of forced organization in division of Parts and in aligning Subparts with pattern.

Some of the same concerns over forced partition/alignment that emerged with Parts also occur with Subparts (into which Parts are subdivided). However, there is a difference because Parts generally contain more *parshiyot* than Subparts. The larger number of *parshiyot* in Parts gives rise, as we saw in Item a above, to questions about the selective ignoring of topics within a given Part (e.g., the Golden Calf in Part D of Exodus and both the Spies and Korach's Rebellion in Part B of Numbers). In contrast, the problem in aligning a Subpart with a Shared Principle seems less in ignoring topics than in forcing a Shared Principle on a single *parshah* whose underlying theme may be uncertain.

Eliezer and Rebecca in Genesis

Let us take an example: how shall we classify the single *parshah* (23:1–24:67) that deals with the mission of Abraham's servant Eliezer to find a wife for Isaac? In that *parshah*, the overall purpose of finding a wife involves a primary relationship, as does Eliezer's duty to his master. These factors suggest a link with Principle B (Loyalty). However, the significant attention to Eliezer's oaths (both using God's Name) in the *parshah*, as well as the concern with obtaining Rebecca's consent (so as not to kidnap) suggests instead Principle C (Limits).

In fact, there is also the very long passage within the *parshah* with Eliezer's testimony to Rebecca and her family, which could fit Principle D (Community). True, the combination of the Parts Claim and the Subparts Claim could take into account different themes with different Principles (e.g., Subpart C of Part B would encompass both Principles B and C). Then the Shared Principle associated with the Book might even add a third. Still, how are we to disentangle these layers in a reasonably objective way? Several particular aspects of this problem are addressed in later units, but the conceptual problem also needs to be dealt with.

A = respecting Creation; B = loyalty to primary relationship; C = limited access to sanctity/resources; D = duties of testimony/community; E = accepting one's place/status (with ties to land/future)

Ambiguous classification

This problem of ambiguity in classification takes on an additional twist in the legal character of many passages outside Genesis. While in some legal passages the laws do range over different themes (thus making it difficult to choose one), a more acute problem is that individual laws themselves can be ambiguous.

Take the prohibition on placing a stumbling block before the blind (Leviticus 19:14). Like many other laws in the Pentateuch, its meaning depends on the level of interpretation:

- At the most literal level, we might classify this law under personal injury and associate it with Principle A (respecting Creation).
- Less literally, we could take the word "blind" to mean ignorant, so that the injunction targets harmful advice, which would be more akin to false testimony and Principle D.
- A third possibility is to treat "blind" as morally weak, which frames our law as a prohibition against assisting someone in his personal transgression and ties it to Principle C (limited access to sanctity/resources).

As we saw in Display 4.10, Chapter 19 of Leviticus (which includes this prohibition) was linked with Principle C (Limits), but not by choosing among the different interpretations of laws. Rather, the link was made through the repeated punctuation of the laws in Chapter 19 with "I am God" or "I am the Lord, your God," thus suggesting limits related to sanctity.

Our ability to explain (or "finesse") this particular case does not remove the general worry in classifying a legal subtext whose laws have multiple interpretations.

c. Poor prospects for matching my points of division with those of Rabbi Honigwachs.

Beyond the doubts already stated, there is the problem of matching my own division points between Parts with those of Rabbi Honigwachs. (You will recall that these points of division occur at *p'tuchot* [blank spaces open to the left margin in columns of text], and that the locations of all *p'tuchot* are listed in Appendix a.) To confirm that a declared pattern is truly present in a certain environment, different informed viewers — in this case, Rabbi Honigwachs and I — should recognize the pattern in at least roughly the same way. If, instead, substantial discrepancies recur between different viewers' perceptions of the pattern, we may infer that the pattern is so poorly defined or so fungible as to lose validity.

This consideration leads us to ask how likely it would be to randomly achieve matches between Rabbi Honigwachs' points of division and mine. The issues involved in calculating such probabilities would slow our progress excessively were we to deal with them at length here. Instead, the interested reader will find these matters addressed in some detail in Section 17. For our purposes now, it is enough to indicate some of the odds of getting a substantial match (enough to confirm some sense of validity).

The odds of matching division points between Parts in a given Book of the Bible depend on the number of *p'tuchot* in that Book. This is because the number of *p'tuchot* determine how many possible choices there are for division points; the more choices, the poorer the odds of random matches. Not counting the enlarged spacing at the end of each Book, Genesis has 43 *p'tuchot*; Exodus 69; Leviticus 52; and Numbers 92. We are not concerned with Deuteronomy, as we have accepted the fact that it ranges over different Shared Principles and thus would not be expected to divide with the same regularity into Parts.

On this basis alone, the odds of matching Rabbi Honigwachs' four points with my independent selection in Genesis would run higher than in the other Books. However, another factor in Genesis greatly favors random matches: its natural fivefold partition into (1) universal history, (2) the life of Abraham, (3) the life of Isaac, (4) the life of Jacob, and (5) the lives of Joseph and his brothers. As a result of the natural partition,

---

A = respecting Creation; B = loyalty to primary relationship; C = limited access to sanctity/resources; D = duties of testimony/community; E = accepting one's place/status (with ties to land/future)

any Part that focuses on an individual life can begin no earlier than birth and can begin no later than the first material action of the individual. This limitation drastically reduces the choices for beginning Parts.

For example, Part C (focusing on the life of Isaac) could begin only as early as Isaac's birth (in the *parshah* beginning 18:1) and only as late as his marriage to Rebecca (in the *parshah* beginning 23:1). There are exactly five *p'tuchot* that begin just before birth and end just before marriage, so the odds of randomly getting a match for the beginning of Part C are one in five, or 20%. Using the same approach for the beginning of Parts B, D, and E (we don't have to do A, because we know it starts at 1:1),[2] we find the odds of all four of my points matching those of Rabbi Honigwachs less than 1.25%. Should we be satisfied with matching any three of the four division points for Parts in Genesis, the odds rise to 16.25% — challenging but not overwhelming.

Outside Genesis, however, the odds become prohibitive without a natural fivefold partition that limits where Parts can begin. In Exodus, for example, with its 69 *p'tuchot*, the odds are 4 in 69 of randomly choosing one of Rabbi Honigwachs' points of division for Parts. Assuming success on the first choice, there would be three more points among 68 *p'tuchot* for odds of 3 in 68. Continuing in this way, we would find the odds for randomly choosing all four points as < .00012%. Even dropping expectations to three or more matches raises the odds to only .03%. (Details of these calculations for Genesis and Exodus can be found in Section 17.) In any event, extensive agreement seems a poor bet.

Two other considerations arise in comparing my division points for Parts to those of Rabbi Honigwachs. One involves setting a threshold for how close points of division must be to constitute an acceptable match. In other words, must they match exactly, or can the respective points of division be, say, up to one *p'tuchah* away from each other? A second consideration involves the proportion of pairs of points that we would require to match acceptably. We will address these considerations in Section 7, with more details in Section 17.

d. Lack of precedent for parallel sequences in established study of Biblical structure.

For yet a fourth reason, the pattern of Shared Principles presented further cause for doubt, especially outside Genesis. Within Genesis, and particularly for the lives of the Patriarchs Abraham, Isaac, and Jacob, the ordered recurrence of certain themes has been traditionally recognized.[3] The account of each Patriarch begins with Divine Revelation, which fits Principle A (Creation). Then each account includes some obstacle to the marriage of the Patriarch, with Sarah's abduction (in Abraham's life), Rebecca's abduction (in Isaac's life), and the switching of Leah for Rachel (in Jacob's life). These obstacles would fit with Principle B (Loyalty). While a link with Shared Principles C and D needs confirmation, the text principally linked to each Patriarch concludes with an account of lineage that could accord with Principle E (Acceptance). In other words, we see that at least much of the pattern recurs in the same order for the Patriarchs. This type of recurrence in the same order is known as parallelism, and the lives of the Patriarchs would be said to follow a **parallel** sequence of ordered themes.

Both within Genesis and within the next three Books, the pattern of Shared Principles calls for such parallel sequences involving the Parts and Subparts:

Part A	Part B	Part C
Subparts A-B-C-D-E	Subparts A-B-C-D-E	Subparts A-B-C-D-E
Part D	Part E	
Subparts A-B-C-D-E	Subparts A-B-C-D-E	

Yet, in exploring patterns for large portions of text outside Genesis, current structural scholarship has stressed a type of sequence different from parallel sequences of ordered themes. To appreciate this lack of

---

A = respecting Creation; B = loyalty to primary relationship; C = limited access to sanctity/resources; D = duties of testimony/community; E = accepting one's place/status (with ties to land/future)

attention to parallel sequences, we must first understand how such scholarship communicates about patterns. While parallel sequences of passages are occasionally recognized (especially within the context of smaller portions of text), these sequences are typically represented with a notation employing apostrophes as shown below:

A-B-C-D-E-A'-B'-C'-D'-E'…where passages A and A' have a common theme, passages B and B' have a common theme, and so on.[4]

In the context of the Shared Principles, the sequence A-B-C-D-E represents Subparts A-B-C-D-E of Part A, and the sequence A'-B'-C'-D'-E' represents Subparts A-B-C-D-E of Part B.[5]

Current scholars of Biblical structure have more often found repeated themes in Torah sequences to be **symmetric** (also known as "chiastic") rather than parallel.[6] By a symmetric pattern on five themes, we mean a sequence of subtexts of one of two forms (with bolding inserted for clearer visual recognition):

A-B-C-D-E-D'-C'-B'-A' with passages A and A' of like theme, B and B' of like theme, etc.

or

A-B-C-D-E-E'-D'-C'-B'-A' with passages A and A' of like theme, B and B' of like theme, etc.

Note that the symmetry in these sequences is relative to their midpoints: passage E for the first form and the shift point between passages E and E' for the second.

Please note that where Biblical scholars have found parallel sequences, the scope of the sequences has generally been too small to constitute a pattern for a whole Book, much less for the whole Torah. I weighed this condition against the possibility that current structural scholarship could reflect a secular mindset promoting structural similarity of the Torah and other ancient works, such as the Epic of Gilgamesh,[7] with clear symmetric patterns. All things considered, it still seemed unlikely that the purported pattern of Shared Principles would depart so markedly from what had been analyzed thus far.

Summary

In summary, the following factors suggest that the pattern would not be independently validated:

- Although Genesis naturally splits into five portions, it is not clear that one of these portions aligns with the respective Shared Principles. Outside Genesis, there is no obvious division of a Book into five portions, much less a division that would align in order with the Shared Principles as Parts.
- In subdividing Parts into Subparts, the identification of some portions of text with a particular Shared Principle may be difficult because the respective portion ranges over or can be identified with different themes; legal subtexts that can be interpreted with different levels of literalism add a further difficulty.
- Even within Genesis (but especially outside Genesis), the number of *p'tuchot* makes it unlikely that the division points in an independent partition would sufficiently match those of Rabbi Honigwachs to give any sense of validation.
- Outside Genesis, recurrent patterns within books have been found predominantly in symmetric sequences, rather than in parallel sequences that would reflect Subparts in the Shared Principles.

With an eye to these concerns, Section 6 checks how well the pattern works in Genesis.

A = respecting Creation; B = loyalty to primary relationship; C = limited access to sanctity/resources; D = duties of testimony/community; E = accepting one's place/status (with ties to land/future)

Section 6

Checking Genesis

Our first order of business is checking whether the pattern actually holds up in Genesis. The choice of Genesis for initial scrutiny makes sense for three reasons:

1. Genesis comes first among the Books;
2. Also, on the basis of the initial analysis in the previous unit, it is the Book most likely to fit the pattern of Shared Principles. Recall that this pattern is defined by two claims:
   - the Parts Claim that each of the first four Books can be divided into five Parts that align in order with the Shared Principles;
   - the Subparts Claim that each Part containing at least five paragraphs can be subdivided into five Subparts that align in order with the Shared Principles.

   If the Parts and Subparts Claims do not work in this Book (where there is at least some known supporting framework in the text), there is no point looking elsewhere.
3. Furthermore, the Source Critics' most basic argument for multiple authors of the Torah occurs in Genesis. This argument involves the two successive accounts of Creation, the first in Genesis 1:1–2:3 (the seven days of Creation) and second in 2:4–3:21 (scene in the Garden of Eden). These two accounts have many differences, most acute the different names of God used therein. Thus, they constitute a "consistency challenge" and are cited by Bible critics as evidence of different source documents. On a Torah scroll, a *p'tuchah* divides the two accounts, so their succession also constitutes an "order challenge" as a difficult transition. If the Shared Principles survive

our checking of the Parts Claim and Sections Claim in Genesis, the resulting Parts and Subparts should then have something to say about this order challenge.

In light of these considerations, our approach in this unit will proceed in four steps:

1. Checking the Parts Claim.
2. Checking the Subparts Claim.
3. Examining the two accounts of Creation in light of the resulting Parts and Subparts.
4. Summarizing the findings on the Shared Principles in Genesis.

i. Checking the Parts Claim

As we have said, Genesis naturally divides into five portions (universal history, the life of Abraham, the life of Isaac, the life of Jacob, and the lives of Joseph and his brothers). Consequently, we will be using this partition and will not need to test, as in the other Books, for the existence of a natural fivefold partition. This means that, in Genesis, we must only check

a. whether our points of division match those dividing the Parts of Rabbi Honigwachs, and
b. whether the Parts actually align in order with the Shared Principles.

After checking these issues, we will move to the Subparts Claim.

(a) Do our points of division match those dividing the Parts of Rabbi Honigwachs?

To refer to the five natural components of Genesis without presuming this match, let us just number them:

(1) universal history, (2) the life of Abraham, (3) the life of Isaac, (4) the life of Jacob, and (5) the lives of Joseph and his brothers.

A = respecting Creation; B = loyalty to primary relationship; C = limited access to sanctity/resources; D = duties of testimony/community; E = accepting one's place/status (with ties to land/future)

We will need to locate the four points of division between succeeding portions, i.e., between (1) and (2), between (2) and (3), between (3) and (4), and between (4) and (5).

Since the end of (5) is also the end of Genesis (which, like the end of all books, is marked by three full blank lines), no point of division is needed there. (Now would be a good time to slip a bookmark into Appendix a and to make sure your English Bible is handy.)

Here is how to locate our points of division in line with the Shared Principles. Recall that according to the Subparts Claim, every Part with enough *parshiyot* will subdivide into five Sections aligned with the Five Shared Principles. This means that the division point for successive Parts, say A and B, also divides Subpart E of Part A from Subpart A of Part B, as shown below:

DISPLAY 6.1: Point of Division between Parts A and B, with Sections Shown

Part A   =>   Part B

Subparts A-B-C-D-**E**   Subparts **A**-B-C-D-E

As shown by the arrow above, the point of division between Parts A and B marks not only a shift from Principle A (Creation) to B (Loyalty), but also a shift from Principle E (Acceptance) to A (Creation) in going from Subpart E of Part A to Subpart A of Part B. Since Part A and its last Subpart, Subpart E, end together, that end will coincide with completion of a theme or themes linked to Principle E (Acceptance). And since Part B and its first Subpart, Subpart A, kick in at the same place, a new theme or themes linked to Principle A (Creation) will begin immediately thereafter. This idea also holds true for

- the end of Part B and its Subpart E in relation to Part C and its Subpart A;
- the end of Part C and its Subpart E in relation to Part D and its

Subpart A;
- the end of Part D and its Subpart E in relation to Part E and its Subpart A.

Each division of Parts occurs at the completion of a theme or themes linked to Principle E, which is then followed immediately by a new theme or themes linked to Principle A.

We can now use the completion of a theme or themes linked to Principle E (Acceptance) to locate the four points of division between the five natural components of Genesis, beginning with the point of division between (1) universal history and (2) the life of Abraham.

The division between (1) universal history and (2) the life of Abraham

Within universal history, we encounter a series of accounts beginning with Creation and extending through the story of Noah and then the Tower of Babel. The story of Noah concludes with the *parshah* (9:18–9:29) that tells of the exposure of Noah's nakedness by his son Ham whom he subsequently cursed. That *parshah* thus displays two themes (disrespect for one's parent and a curse for the future) associated with Principle E. This association continues in the next *parshah* (10:1–11:9) with the Tower of Babel, which was built to magnify the name of Man (see 11:4). Flowing from this account is a genealogical *parshah* (10:1–11:32), followed in 12:1 with God's initial contact with Abraham (then with the name Abram). Because that contact constitutes revelation, it goes with Principle A. Thus the *p'tuchah* after 11:32 (following the genealogical *parshah*) marks the end of universal history.

> We have just shown that, in line with the Shared Principles, the division point between (1) universal history and (2) the life of Abraham is the *p'tuchah* after 11:32. This point divides Part A and Part B. In addition to identifying this point of division between Parts, we have also identified Subpart E of Part A as the text covering Noah, the Tower of Babel, and the succeeding genealogy. This text consists of the verses 9:18–11:32.

> A = respecting Creation; B = loyalty to primary relationship; C = limited access to sanctity/resources; D = duties of testimony/community; E = accepting one's place/status (with ties to land/future)

The division between (2) the life of Abraham and (3) the life of Isaac

The same approach of looking for a distinctive association with Principle E works well in choosing the division point between the lives of Abraham and Isaac in Genesis. Here also the division point will divide Subpart E of the life of Abraham and Subpart A of the life of Isaac. Thus we are seeking the completion of a theme or themes in Abraham's life tied to Principle E (Acceptance) followed immediately by a new theme or themes related to Isaac.

With that idea in mind, there is an obvious incident to try with Subpart A of Isaac's life: God's directive to Abraham to sacrifice his son Isaac (a directive countermanded when Abraham demonstrated his commitment to follow God's word — see 22:12). The *parshah* with this incident (22:1–19) thus includes themes of revelation and murder, both reflecting Principle A (Creation). Recognizing these Principle A themes prompts us to look at the *parshah* just before (21:22–21:34), which recounts Abraham's treaty with the Philistines. Because that treaty involved the land and the future, it reflects Principle E, which ties to both of those elements. Thus, the point of division between the lives of Abraham and Isaac is the *p'tuchah* following 21:34.

> We have just shown that, in line with the Shared Principles, the division point between (2) the life of Abraham and (3) the life of Isaac is the *p'tuchah* after 21:34. This point divides Part B and Part C. Beyond identifying the division point between these Parts, we have identified Subpart E of Part B as the single *parshah* 21:22–21:34 on Abraham's treaty with the Philistines.

The division between (3) the life of Isaac and (4) the life of Jacob

We use the same method seeking a theme associated with Principle E (Acceptance) that occurs after the past point of division, i.e., beginning with 22:1. Such a theme first presents itself in the *parshah* 25:12–18, which at first appears to simply recount the death of Ishmael and to list his offspring and their destinations (which would not relate to any particular Shared Principle). However, the final verse contains the phrase *al p'nei echav* [in the face of his brothers] to describe those destinations. This phrase occurs only one other time in the Torah, in the prophecy given to Ishmael's mother Hagar in regard to his future (see 16:12). That correspondence casts the *parshah* 25:12–18 as the fulfillment of Ishmael's destiny and aligns it with Principle E.

The next *parshah* (beginning with 25:19) involves prayers to God over the failure of Isaac's wife Rebecca to yet bear children. This content, along with God's revelation to Rebecca about the cause of her difficult pregnancy, shows a shift to Principle A (Creation). Thus the point of division comes just after 25:18.

> We have shown that, in line with the Shared Principles, the division point between (3) the life of Isaac and (4) the life of Jacob is the *p'tuchah* after 25:18. This point divides Part C from Part D. Beyond identifying the division point between these Parts, we have also identified Subpart E of Part C as the single *parshah* 25:12–18 on fulfillment of Ishmael's destiny.

Before we move to the last division point between portions, let me address an important question: If Part B focuses on Abraham's life, why end Part B before he dies (which does not happen until the end of Part C focusing on Isaac's life)? After all, Abraham still actively participates in some events that occur in Part C, such as the binding of Isaac (22:1–22:24) and sending the servant Eliezer to find a wife for Isaac (24:1–24:9). The resolution is simple: our categorization of portions depends not on who remains active, but on whose life is the focus.

The division between (4) the life of Jacob and (5) the lives of Joseph and his brothers

Unlike the three previous intersections of portions in Genesis, this last intersection presents some uncertainty. The *parshah* that begins with 35:9 describes Reuben dishonoring his father by interfering in his father's relationship with Rachel's maidservant. The theme thus fits

> A = respecting Creation; B = loyalty to primary relationship; C = limited access to sanctity/resources; D = duties of testimony/community; E = accepting one's place/status (with ties to land/future)

Principle E. Now, the next *parshah* that clearly deals with a theme for Principle A is the one coinciding with Chapter 37, which concerns the planned murder of Joseph. Until Chapter 37, there are three intervening *parshiyot*, the first reporting the death of Isaac and his burial by Esau and Jacob, and the second and third giving an account of Esau's progeny and warlords. These *parshiyot* could be allocated between portions (4) and (5) in several ways, though each resulting division point (between (4) and (5)) fell within a limited area of the text.

However, a more careful look at the *parshiyot* dealing with Esau's progeny and warlords made it clear that those *parshiyot* should be linked with Chapter 37 and the life of Joseph and his brothers. That choice drew on shared use of the distinctive term *toldot* [progeny] in 36:1 and 37:2, a point noted by Rashi. In other words, by common use of this term, the text sets the stage for Joseph and his brothers as the main actors by comparing them to Esau's progeny.

Yet, removing the two paragraphs about Esau's progeny and warlords still leaves two options to divide (4) the life of Jacob from (5) the lives of Joseph and his brothers. The division point could fall either in the middle of 35:22 or after 35:29 (which are only seven verses apart). The choice of the former came from a technical consideration as a *baal korei* [one who reads the Torah for the public].[8] This consideration is explained in an endnote because the difference in the two choices is too small to effect the overall matching.

> We have shown that, in line with the Shared Principles, the division point between (4) the life of Jacob and (5) the lives of Joseph and his brothers is the *p'tuchah* in the middle of 35:22. This point divides Part D from Part E. Beyond identifying the point of division between these Parts, we have also identified Subpart E of Part D 35:9–middle of 22 on Isaac's burial.

Summary on matching points of division

We can now compare all four independently chosen points of division with those of Rabbi Honigwachs. They agree in each case, but regarding the fourth point, I would not be surprised and could not object if the other choice were made. Yet because this one case of alternate choices involved a very limited range of text, we can conclude that our points of division match those of Rabbi Honigwachs well enough in Genesis. That brings us to the ultimate question in checking the Parts Claim.

(b) Do the Parts align in order with the Shared Principles?

To answer this question, let us refer to the Parts of Genesis in a single display, as they were rendered in Section 4. For each Part, this display lists themes aligned with the respective Shared Principle. For example, themes listed for the focus on Jacob correspond to Principle D.

DISPLAY 6.2: = DISPLAY 4.3: Parts of Genesis According to the Five Shared Principles

Part	Verses	Features Related to Shared Principle
A (Creation)	1:1–11:32	Universal History — Creation/ violence before Flood.
B (Loyalty)	12:1–21:34	Focus on Abraham — monotheism introduced/ threats of Sarah's violation/ special relationship with Abraham's offspring via the Covenant between the Parts.
C (Limits)	22:1–25:18	Focus on Isaac — the Binding (how to approach God)/ Eliezer's mission (mention of God in his oath and need for Rebecca's agreement so as not to kidnap).
D (Community)	25:19–35:22	Focus on Jacob — birthright testimony and Laban's false promises.
E (Acceptance)	35:22–50:26	Focus on Tribes — Joseph's dreams of ruling/ his brothers' early rejection of that primary role/ Jacob foretells sons' future roles.

While the events or topics listed above for each Part fit the respective

---

A = respecting Creation; B = loyalty to primary relationship; C = limited access to sanctity/resources; D = duties of testimony/community; E = accepting one's place/status (with ties to land/future)

Shared Principle, their presence does not establish the alignment. Perhaps other events or topics in the same Part fit a different Shared Principle. The question is: do the events or topics that fit the respective Shared Principle form a dominant theme in that Part of the Biblical text? (This question did not arise in aligning whole Books because the dominant theme of a whole Book comes from the opening context.) If not, linking a Part to a given Shared Principle would mean choosing only events and topics that fit the linkage and ignoring the rest. And that is exactly the recipe for forced (and therefore unjustified) organization. Let us review:

- In Part A, it was easy to see that Principle A (related to Creation and violence) is dominant in that Part over any other Shared Principle.
- And, similarly, in Parts C, D, and E, the topics and events for the respective Shared Principle were the ones that overwhelmingly occupied the most verses and occurred most frequently.
- In particular, the binding of Isaac (i.e., his planned sacrifice by his father Abraham), constitutes the central event in Isaac's life. Since sacrifice is a means of approaching God (and gaining access to sanctity), the life of Isaac is clearly associated with Principle C (Limits).
- Likewise, the life of Jacob is dominated by testimony in keeping with Principle D (Community); and
- The dreams and blessings in the lives of Joseph and his brothers suggest Principle E (Acceptance).

In each of Parts A, C, D, and E, the dominant theme came directly from the text. Thus we turn now to the remaining Part, which is Part B and the life of Abraham.

The challenge of Abraham

However, the link between the life of Abraham and Shared Principle B (Loyalty) seemed, at first blush, to depend on Abraham's being the father of monotheism, an accepted notion but one that takes more than a plain reading of the text itself.[9] (Monotheism does clearly reflect loyalty — to one and only one God.) If the Shared Principles truly reflect themes in the text, such a notion would not be incontrovertible evidence. We must find events in the text itself linked with Shared Principle B. There are five I can see that involve threats to marriage or that involve forbidden sexual relations, potential or actual:

- two abductions of Sarah (by Pharaoh and then by Abimelekh);
- the attempt by the residents of Sodom to sexually molest Lot's visitors;
- the cohabitation of Lot with his daughters following the destruction of Sodom;
- the strain to Abraham's marriage brought by his concubine Hagar.

Yet, if these events are unique enough to Abraham's life to count as "defining characteristics" in matching "his" text to Shared Principles, we encounter a problem: in the three subsequent Parts of Genesis, there are also such incidents. To wit:

- Isaac also experienced the abduction of his wife Rebecca;
- Jacob's first marital relations were with Leah, who had been switched for Rachel (whom Jacob actually married);
- Jacob's daughter Dinah was raped;
- Judah's affair with Tamar, as well as
- the attempted seduction of Joseph by the wife of Potiphar.

One might argue that such themes are more pervasive in Abraham's life than in the subsequent Parts, but is this a sufficient basis to link Principle B to Abraham in particular, as opposed to Isaac, Jacob, or Joseph and his brothers?

Moreover, there were other major events or circumstances in Abraham's life more closely associated with other Shared Principles. For example:

A = respecting Creation; B = loyalty to primary relationship; C = limited access to sanctity/resources; D = duties of testimony/community; E = accepting one's place/status (with ties to land/future)

- Principle C (Limits) comes to mind with the kidnapping of Lot and Abraham's rejection of booty after rescuing him, habitual thievery as a trait of Ishmael, and the change of names for Abraham (from Abram) and for Sarah (from Sarai).
- Principle D (Community) reminds us of Abraham's acts of kindness to visitors (as communal relations) and Abraham's pleas on behalf of Sodom.

In light of these other events, something else is necessary to justify associating Principle B with the life of Abraham.

On further reflection, a particular set of promises also emerges in the text: God's blessing to Abraham in 12:1–3, the Covenant between the Parts in 15:1–22, and the Covenant of Circumcision in 17:1–14. While each of these promises speaks of the future and could possibly relate to Principle E (Acceptance), there is more fundamentally a special relationship between God and Abraham's descendants intrinsic to each promise. That special relationship links to Principle B. For the Covenant of Circumcision, the sign of that covenant is made on the reproductive organ, further suggesting this link. In light of these additional textual indications in the life of Abraham, it becomes clearer to associate that Part of Genesis with Principle B and to move on to checking the Subparts Claim.

ii. Checking the Subparts Claim

In finding the division points between the Parts in Genesis above, we actually began the work of checking the Subparts Claim by identifying Subpart E in each of Parts A, B, C, and D. We repeat them here for ease of reference:

Subpart E of Part A is Genesis 9:18–11:32; of Part B 21:22–34; of Part C 25:12–18; and of Part D 35:9–middle of 22.

Let us now attempt to finalize the subdivision of the Parts and thereby identify all of the Subparts within Genesis. We will proceed through five items (a) through (e), with (a) describing the full subdivision of Part A; (b) describing the full subdivision of Part B; and so on. Then we will see how well these Subparts match up with those of Rabbi Honigwachs.

But first, consider a key difference in making these subdivisions, as we verify progression through the pattern.

Because many Subparts lack enough *parshiyot* (at least five) to be further subdivided using the Shared Principles, we cannot employ the technique used in finding points of division between Parts. That technique allowed us to find a theme linked to Principle E (Acceptance), which would then mark the last Subpart (Subpart E) in a Part. However, when it comes to finding division points between Subparts, as opposed to division points between Parts, we often cannot identify the last Segment of a Subpart (since that particular Subpart does not always subdivide).

The Special Challenge of Subdividing Parts

Thus we are left with a less definitive approach in identifying a change in themes (not particularly involving Principle E) to mark the transition from one Subpart to the next. In other words, we must start reading at the beginning of a given Part, say Part A, which should coincide with Subpart A and should link to Shared Principle A. When we get to a shift in themes to Shared Principle B, that shift should mark the end of Subpart A and the beginning of Subpart B. Similarly, we read on and come to a shift to themes associated with Shared Principle C, marking the end of Subpart B and the beginning of Subpart C, and so on. While we can describe this process easily enough, it can present a substantial challenge because successive Subparts of the same Part share much in common, making it difficult to detect a shift.[10]

Genesis: Subdivision of Part A (1:1–11:32)

As noted earlier, we have already identified the last Subpart E of Part A as 9:18–11:32, which covers Ham's disrespect for his father Noah, Noah's curse of Ham, the Tower of Babel, and a consequent genealogy. This means we are seeking to identify the remaining four Subparts of Part A: Subpart A, Subpart B, Subpart C, and Subpart D. To help

---

A = respecting Creation; B = loyalty to primary relationship; C = limited access to sanctity/resources; D = duties of testimony/community; E = accepting one's place/status (with ties to land/future)

navigate these four pieces as we check the progression through the Shared Principles, each identification appears in a box followed by a description/rationale.

> *Subpart A (1:1–2:3) corresponds to the seven days of Creation.*

The first seven *parshiyot* (1:1–2:3) in Genesis correspond to the seven days of Creation, with the seventh *parshah* stating (in 2:2) that God completed the work of Creation. From these words, it appears that "pure Creation" (Principle A within Part A) ends. Keep in mind that these seven *parshiyot* also form what Source Critics view as the account of Creation coming from the first source document.

> *Subpart B (Genesis 2:4–3:21) recounts the scene in the Garden of Eden.*

The next *parshah* (2:4–3:21) includes God's first direct relationship with Man, as well as the concept of Woman as *ezer k'negdo* [a helpmate to balance him (Man)] in 2:20. This marks a shift to Principle B (Loyalty) and confirms this *parshah* as beginning a new Subpart. According to Source Criticism, the first part of this *parshah* forms the account of Creation that comes from a second and different source document.

While the *parshah* 2:4–3:21 seems most tied to Principle B, other themes occur in this *parshah* as well. Before the concept of Woman as a helpmate comes the creation of plants and trees and then of Man, all of which suggest Principle A (Creation). Then, after Woman as a helpmate, we find God forbids in 2:17 eating from the Tree of Knowledge, a limit on access that Woman and Man break, thus reflecting Principle C (Limits). This episode leads to Man's testimony (Principle D) in 3:12 blaming Woman, with God's curse for the future (Principle E) following in 3:14–19. Thus, this *parshah* touches on the Shared Principles in order, but with the relationship of Man and Woman a constant factor, which defines it as (primarily) Principle B.

> Subpart C (Genesis 3:22–6:4) recounts the expulsion from Eden of Adam and Eve, the story of Cain and Abel, and a genealogy culminating in the degradation of mankind.

The *parshah* (3:22–6:4) begins with the expulsion of Adam and Eve from Eden and the bar on their reentry in 3:24. From this limit on access, the *parshah* turns to the birth of the first couple's sons, Cain and Abel, who were the first people to approach God with offerings. In 3:4–5, we learn that Abel's offering was accepted but not Cain's, a further indication of a shift to Principle C (Limits) in this *parshah*, thus confirming the end of the previous Subpart.

Continuing on in this *parshah*, Cain murders Abel out of jealousy, which accords with Principle A, not C. However, keep in mind that we are still in Part A, so the pattern would predict themes associated with Principle A throughout this Part. Cain is then cursed in 4:14 to wander the rest of his life, a punishment limiting settlement (Principle C). The text proceeds with a lengthy account mainly of lineage. However, bloodshed, reflecting Principle A (Creation) occurs again early in that account in 4:23, while three verses later the text speaks of people calling out in God's name (access to sanctity and Principle C). The focus on lineage, which projects no particular Shared Principle, continues almost to the end of the *parshah*. The last verses of the *parshah* tell of women being taken (implicitly against their will) by men of power, thus violating Principle B (Loyalty). All told, the full *parshah* 3:22–6:4 seems most related to Principle C (Limits), though the linkage does not come through as plainly as the linkage to Principle B in the previous *parshah*.

We move on to the next *parshah*, which consists of the four verses 6:5–8. We are told that the world had gone bad, that God regretted Creation, but that Noah found favor with God. This *parshah* seems to combine Principle A (because of the reference to Creation) and Principle

---

A = respecting Creation; B = loyalty to primary relationship; C = limited access to sanctity/resources; D = duties of testimony/community; E = accepting one's place/status (with ties to land/future)

C (because of Noah's spiritual access). It does not look like a shift away from Principle C.

> Subpart D (Genesis 6:9-9:17) recounts Noah's Ark, the Flood, and Rainbow.

At the outset of this single *parshah*, the story of the Ark and the Flood represents rescue of a group, a communally directed effort aligned with Principle D (Community). As such, it marks a shift from Principle C (Limits) and signals the beginning of a new Subpart. Later in this *parshah*, the rainbow appears in 9:12 as a sign of God's promise not to flood the world again. In other words, the rainbow testifies to this promise and also aligns with Principle D.

Summary of Subdivision of Part A of Genesis

With Subpart D now identified, we have left in Part A of Genesis only 9:18–11:32, which we already know as being Subpart E. This means all five Subparts of Part A have been found and smoothly fit the pattern of the Shared Principles. They are summarized below.

DISPLAY 6.3: Part A of Genesis Subdivided According to the Shared Principles

Subpart A 1:1–2:3	The seven days of Creation.
Subpart B 2:4–3:21	Garden of Eden/ Man's relation to Woman/ mankind's relation to God.
Subpart C 3:22–6:8	Expulsion from Eden/ story of Cain and Abel/ genealogy culminating in mankind's degradation.
Subpart D 6:9–9:17	Noah's Ark/ the Flood/ the rainbow afterwards.
Subpart E 9:18–11:32	Noah disgraced by Ham/ Noah's curse of Ham/ the Tower of Babel/ consequent genealogy.

Summary of Subdivision of Other Parts of Genesis

For each of the other Parts of Genesis (Parts B, C, D, and E), the identification and analysis of the respective Subparts appear in Section

15 and follows the same approach as for Part A. To summarize that Section, three of these four remaining Parts in Genesis (all but Part C) clearly and cleanly subdivide into five Subparts that align in order with the Shared Principles. In Part C, three of its five *parshiyot* align very plainly with the corresponding Shared Principles, and a fourth *parshah* aligns fairly well after applying some judgment. However, the association of the second *parshah* with Principle B (as Subpart B of Part C) is less obvious than the others.

This leaves the matter of matching our division points between Subparts in Genesis with those of Rabbi Honigwachs. These division points all correspond except in Part A, which still shows a progression through the Shared Principles when broken into Subparts. As a result, we find that overall there is strong, though not perfect, confirmation of the Subparts Claim: that each Part in Genesis subdivides according to the Shared Principles.

iii. God's Names and the Two Accounts of Creation

While the first account of Creation corresponds to the seven days, identical with Subpart A as shown above, the second account matches Subpart B. Following the Shared Principles, the first account reflects "pure Creation" and so reflects Principle A (Creation). The second account, through its focus on primary relationships, reflects Principle B (Loyalty). In noting this link between the two accounts, we now examine the most fundamental argument advanced by Source Critics in support of multiple authorship: the variation in God's names between these subtexts. First, though, we must identify the specific variation and know its place in Source Criticism.

E and J

To begin with, let us understand that there are two prevalent Hebrew names for God in the Pentateuch. (In deference to the sanctity

---

A = respecting Creation; B = loyalty to primary relationship; C = limited access to sanctity/resources; D = duties of testimony/community; E = accepting one's place/status (with ties to land/future)

of these names, I will describe them rather than writing them directly in transliteration.) The first name is the only one that appears in the first account of Creation. It is a five-letter Hebrew word whose English transliteration begins with *E*. I will refer to this name as the **E-Name**. It is generally translated as "God." This word also appears in secular legal contexts where it is transliterated without capitalization as *elohim* [judge]. Bible scholars use the adjective "elohist" to refer to subtexts, like the first account of Creation, where the E-Name occurs predominantly.

The second name is a four-letter word that begins with the Hebrew letter *yud* and appears only as a Divine name. It is known in scholarly circles by its Greek label, the Tetragrammaton. However, in order to avoid scholarly mouthfuls, we will use an alternative label. This alternative uses the standard convention for rendering into English those Hebrew names that begin with the letter *yud* (and whose transliteration should logically begin with the sound of "y"). According to that convention, the "Y" in transliteration is replaced by "J," as in Jacob for the Hebrew name Yaakov, Judah for Yehudah, Joseph for Yosef, and Jerusalem for Yerushalayim. Thus we label this second name for God as the **J-Name**. The J-Name, typically translated as "the Lord," may be seen in corrupted transliteration as "Yahweh" or "Jehovah," with the associated adjective of "yahwist" or "jahwist."

Throughout the Torah, God is nearly always referred to either by the E-Name alone or by the J-Name alone. In twenty-one places, both names appear together with the J-Name first, and other names are used (e.g., Genesis 17:1) only a few times. In the second account of Creation, God is predominantly referred to by the J-Name followed by the E-Name. In particular, all eighteen narrative references to God in that account use the J-E combination, but when God is mentioned four times in dialogue in Genesis 3:1–5 in the third person, the E-Name is used by itself. (In many places later in the text, we also see various possessive forms of the E-Name, often directly following the J-Name, which itself never takes a possessive form. Thus, we find, for example, in Genesis 27:20 the expression "the Lord your God.")

Bible Critics argue that a single author would not use the E-Name for God in one account of Creation and the J-E Combination in a second.

Moreover, apparent discrepancies between the accounts, especially in creating Woman, seem to preclude a single author. In particular, the first account has men and women created at the same time, perhaps as part of the same being:

> *And God created Man in His image…male and female He created them (1:27).*

In contrast, the second account has the first man being created and placed (alone) in the Garden: "And God formed the man of dust from the earth, and He blew into his nostrils a living soul…And God planted a garden in Eden…and placed there the man…" (2:7–8).

Then, only when God sensed that the first man needed a helper and could not find one from among all the animals and birds (see 2:20), was the first woman created: "And God cast a deep sleep on the man…and He took one of his sides and enclosed it in flesh…And God fashioned the side…into a woman, and He brought her to the man" (2:21–22).

Thus the two accounts of Creation form what Source Critics call a **doublet**, two separate and seemingly discrepant stories about the same thing that Critics find in various places in the Five Books. (Some of the purported doublets, though "found" by the Critics, are not separate accounts at all; we will explore this issue and others involving perceived inconsistency in Section 12.) Within our language on textual challenges, doublets would be regarded as consistency challenges because of their perceived inconsistency, thus implying multiple authorship. Yet, in the case of the two consecutive accounts of Creation (which are separated by a *p'tuchah*), we also have the order challenge of why the text would reiterate what had just been reported.

Since the two accounts of Creation constitute the very first (and the most obvious) doublet, they are fundamental to Source Criticism as an outgrowth of Wellhausen. According to the most recent renderings of this approach, the first account belongs to the "P" source, which primarily includes subtexts involving law and priestly rituals (thus "P"), while

---

A = respecting Creation; B = loyalty to primary relationship; C = limited access to sanctity/resources; D = duties of testimony/community; E = accepting one's place/status (with ties to land/future)

the second account belongs to the "E" source, which mainly includes narratives involving people in which the E-Name predominates. The Wellhausen Hypothesis also asserts the presence of two further source documents: "J" for narratives where the J-Name predominates and "D" for Deuteronomy. Though the first account of Creation is associated with the "P" source, Wellhausen and his intellectual disciples assert that nearly all of Genesis was cobbled together from just "E" and "J." Indeed, the classification of most subtexts in Genesis is remarkably simple in Source Criticism: just decide on the basis of which name of God is used predominantly.

In fact, Wellhausen's classification of subtexts in Genesis doesn't always work (and we will see why in Section 12). However, our purpose here is not to rebut Source Critics fully on the matter of doublets. Rather it is to examine, in light of the Shared Principles, only this most basic case involving the two accounts of Creation. From this examination, we will come to better understand the Torah's view of God, which is critical to an accurate reading of the text.

Powerful God/His relation to man

The seven days of Creation recounted in Genesis 1:1–2:3, which use only the E-Name, report no interaction between God and anything that has been created. The only points in this account (comprising Subpart A of Part A) that connect God and mankind are the following:

1. The creation of mankind in God's image (1:27), and
2. God commanding mankind to populate the earth and to subdue it, and Him giving herbage and trees to mankind as food (1:28–29).

As noted earlier, the E-Name also has a meaning apart from a name of God — *elohim* [decision-maker or judge]. This connotation of authority implies God created the world without consulting mankind. Mankind's only choice about Creation is whether to believe in God.

As for mankind's choices once the world has been created, things are different in the second account, and so is God's name (the J-E Combination). In particular, mankind has, as part of the relationship with God (simultaneous with the addition of the J-Name), the capacity to fulfill or ignore His wishes, as indicated by the story of the Tree of Knowledge in 3:1–6, which is contained in Subpart B of Part A of Genesis. Also, carrying the mantle of the J-E Combination, God intercedes in the second account in the lives of people, making them subject to certain relationships (not just to a predetermined physical environment) as a consequence of their behavior. One need not take the text literally to grasp these features.

Thus in line with the Shared Principles, the two accounts describe two aspects of God in Creation: the first dealing with His independent decision to create the world with various characteristics, and the second with His special relationship with mankind. We see now the perfect sense that God would be known by different names in these differing contexts of the two Creation accounts.

Cassuto's Approach

Rabbi Dr. Umberto Cassuto, who died before the pattern of Shared Principles was proposed, nonetheless offered a remarkably apt and supportive illustration, which goes something like this:

> *The two accounts were like those of a child whose father was king of his country. In the first account, the child wrote about the king's actions in relation to the country as a whole, but in the second the child wrote about the king in matters involving the father-son relationship. Thus, the child referred to his father in the first account as "King," but referred to him in the second as "Father."*[11]

This illustration of Cassuto, who held a professorship in Hebrew language and literature at the University of Florence, was also built on an important characteristic of languages of the ancient Near East. Specifically, as he noted, such languages generally included one name of God as a general term for the God of the world and another name for the distinct God of the particular people, i.e., their national God

---

A = respecting Creation; B = loyalty to primary relationship; C = limited access to sanctity/resources; D = duties of testimony/community; E = accepting one's place/status (with ties to land/future)

that interacts with them. And so it is that the E-Name fits the more general term, and the J-Name fits the God of Israel. Isn't it striking that the second account of Creation contains eighteen of the twenty-one J-E Combinations in the Torah and also constitutes Subpart B of Part A of Genesis, which combines respecting Creation with loyalty to a primary relationship?

Midrash Rabbah

A slightly different but equally concordant idea comes from the *Midrash Rabbah* on Genesis. (This source was quoted earlier, but in regard to its comment on the Song of Songs that concerned the Ten Commandments as the basis for the rest of the Torah.) This source tells us the use of the E-Name in Genesis 1:1 means the world was created with the Divine attribute of *Din* [Judgment]. Rashi, on the same verse, explains that the Divine attribute of *Chesed* [Kindness] is associated with the other predominant name of God in the Torah, the J-Name. In other words, God creates the world in Judgment but relates to it in Kindness. Authentic Jewish sources consistently understand this distinction in Divine names, and while Source Critics naturally deny any credence to such sources, open-minded readers can appreciate why the use of different names does not imply different authors.

We have yet to deal with the discrepancy in the description of the creation of Man and Woman between the two accounts. Actually, Rashi has already taken care of this "problem" in his comments on 1:27 (where the text does not identify an order of creation with Man first and Woman second). Citing a passage from *Midrash Rabbah* on Genesis, Rashi tells us that this verse is, in effect, an executive summary of what is described at greater length in the second account. In fact, if we compare the first account with the second, we see that there are other respects in which the first appears to be an executive summary (e.g., in the creation of plant life). In fact, viewing the second account through the Shared Principles resolves any supposed discrepancy with the first account. Differences in order of events merely reflect the change in focus to God's closer relationship to Man than that of the rest of Creation.

iv. Summarizing the Five Shared Principles in Genesis

Drawing on the results from the first three subunits here, we can report our findings for Genesis regarding the Shared Principles as follows:

- The Parts Claim checks out quite well. Genesis naturally divides into Five Parts (universal history, the life of Abraham, the life of Isaac, the life of Jacob, and the lives of Joseph and his brothers), which align in order with the Shared Principles. Our four points of division match those of Rabbi Honigwachs, even though in one case the placement could vary within a very small range of the text.
- The Subparts Claim checks out in almost all respects. Each Part subdivides into five Subparts, and, except for Subpart B of Part C, they clearly align in order with the Shared Principles. There are grounds to align that Subpart with Principle B, but they are materially weaker than the grounds for alignment of the fourteen other Subparts with their respective Shared Principles. The points of division between successive Subparts within each Part agree with the divisions of Rabbi Honigwachs, except in Part A.
- Major questions concerning the two accounts of Creation are resolved by the application of the Shared Principles in Subparts A and B of Part A of Genesis. This application reinforces traditional responses given to Bible Critics by Cassuto and others.

A = respecting Creation; B = loyalty to primary relationship; C = limited access to sanctity/resources; D = duties of testimony/community; E = accepting one's place/status (with ties to land/future)

Section 7
Strategy for Testing the Pattern

Let's briefly take stock. We just saw in Section 6 that for the Book of Genesis, the pattern aligns for its Parts and Subparts, and that our points between Parts match those of Rabbi Honigwachs exactly. However, the preliminary analysis in Section 5 noted four grounds to expect (especially in Exodus, Leviticus, and Numbers) the pattern's failure to align or the division points' failure to match. (Recall that Deuteronomy was already excluded from review because of the Jewish people's arrested progress in Numbers in meeting the Shared Principles. That arrested progress led to Deuteronomy not having a dominant theme like the other Books.) The four grounds to expect failure are now restated in Display 7.1 (opp.) in the order making most sense for systematic consideration.

Only three of the four grounds (i, ii, and iii) suggest practical factors in failure. Thus a strategy that firmly tests the Shared Principles should invite these three factors into play. This idea leads to a three-pronged strategy with a test corresponding to each of the factors, as described below. While the last of the four grounds will not have a specific test associated with it, it still casts doubt on whether the pattern will work.

i. Test of Alternate Partition

The Parts Claim asserts that each Book adheres to a fivefold partition following the five Principles in order: A-B-C-D-E. In Exodus, Leviticus, and Numbers, we could test this assertion by proposing an alternate partition of a natural sequence of topics. These topics would be chosen so that their respective Principles differ from the pattern A-B-C-D-E. If such a partition can be found and verified, its sequence of topics would contradict the pattern. That contradiction would establish the forced character of the pattern by showing the Shared Principles align in dividing the Book only with the "right" partition. This would invalidate the Parts Claim.

DISPLAY 7.1: Grounds to Expect the Pattern's Failure to Align or to Match

i. Outside Genesis, no book is commonly divided into five subtexts, much less into a partition that would (as the Parts Claim asserts) align with the Shared Principles.
ii. Especially outside Genesis, the number of *p'tuchot* makes it unlikely that independently chosen division points between Parts would match those identified by Rabbi Honigwachs well enough for validation.
iii. In subdividing Parts into Subparts, assigning a single Shared Principle to a subtext may be difficult because the subtext ranges over different themes; legal subtexts that can be interpreted with different levels of literalism add a further test of the Sections Claim. In other words, one text has different themes.
iv. Outside Genesis, recurrent patterns within books have been found most often in symmetric sequences, not in parallel sequences that would fit with Subparts in the Shared Principles.

To illustrate the idea of an alternate partition, we revisit the one in Exodus mentioned earlier in Section 5. As shown below in Display 7.2, this partition presents a sequence of seven natural topics. Within the Display, a parenthetical indication of a Shared Principle follows each topic; this is the Principle we would expect initially to be associated with that topic. (Readers seeking the general scope and rationale for each topic can check the endnote.[12])

A = respecting Creation; B = loyalty to primary relationship; C = limited access to sanctity/resources; D = duties of testimony/community; E = accepting one's place/status (with ties to land/future)

> **DISPLAY 7.2**: Alternate Partition of Exodus into a Sequence of Topics
>
> 1. Enslavement of Jewish people (B);
> 2. Revelation of God to Moses (A);
> 3. Liberation through Plagues, Splitting of Sea (B);
> 4. Ten Commandments and civil law (C);
> 5. Directions for making Tabernacle (D);
> 6. Incident of Golden Calf (B);
> 7. Actual making of Tabernacle (D or E).

In viewing this Display, one might be tempted to focus only on there being seven topics without checking the assignment of Shared Principles. From that focus, one might immediately conclude that the alternate partition cannot possibly align with five Shared Principles. But suppose the sequence of seven associated Shared Principles turned out as A-A-B-C-D-D-E. This sequence would align after combining the first two topics and combining the fifth and sixth.

However, in Display 7.2, the topics initially generate the following sequence of Shared Principles: B-A-B-C-D-B-(D or E), which seemingly allows for no combination. Thus, should this partition hold up under textual scrutiny, it would contradict the pattern. In this way, the Test of Alternate Partition could undermine the Shared Principles in Exodus.

A few observations about this alternate partition are in order. First, we are not precluded from testing the pattern in Exodus with other partitions. However, the partition here does provide a reasonable sequence of topics in Exodus that clearly seem to depart from the pattern. And the departure involves much more than a simple excess over the five portions for the five Shared Principles. For starters, the first topic in our alternate partition for Exodus is not linked to Principle A (which would be necessary to align with the pattern).

To make our partition stand up, the text must be checked more carefully to confirm the Shared Principles are properly assigned to its topics. Regarding the first topic, we must confirm that Principle B

(Loyalty) and not Principle A (Creation) should be assigned to it. For suppose instead that upon further scrutiny the first topic presents clear substantial signs of Principle A. This would lead to combining the first topic (Enslavement) with the second topic (Revelation), which was already linked to Principle A, thus forming a new first topic linked to Principle A: Enslavement and Revelation.

This combination would reduce the first five topics in Display 7.2 to four as follows:

- Enslavement and revelation (Shared Principle A);
- Liberation from slavery (Shared Principle B);
- Ten Commandments and civil law (Shared Principle C);
- Directions for making Tabernacle (Shared Principle D).

That partial sequence would thus align with the first four Shared Principles, leaving only the last two topics (the incident of the Golden Calf, and the actual making of the Tabernacle). If the latter of the two were linked to Shared Principle E (already seen as a possibility) and if the former were somehow aligned with Principle D or E, then our partition would be transformed into full alignment with the Shared Principles. The prospect of such a transformation seemed extremely remote, but the text had to be examined against that possibility so as to rule out the Parts Claim in Exodus. This examination of the text is shown in Section 8.

In Leviticus and Numbers, we use the same Test of Alternate Partition as in Exodus to challenge the Parts Claim. In each case, we begin with a natural sequence of topics that, on its face, does not align with the Shared Principles. Then we attempt to confirm that non-alignment by closely examining the text: in Section 9 for Leviticus and in Section 10 for Numbers. Only if this examination leads to a repartition aligned with the pattern do we even get to the other tests.

A = respecting Creation; B = loyalty to primary relationship; C = limited access to sanctity/resources; D = duties of testimony/community; E = accepting one's place/status (with ties to land/future)

ii. Test of Point Disparity

This test compares our division points between Parts with those of Rabbi Honigwachs to see whether they match well enough. You will recall the need for a sufficient match: that unless different informed observers perceive the pattern in roughly the same way, the pattern can be doubted as ill-defined or fungible. Thus the respective division points must match well enough. Please keep in mind that the Test of Point Disparity would be applied only if the pattern first survived the Test of Alternate Partition. In other words, even if a book is shown to divide into Parts according to the Shared Principles, is there too much disparity between our division points for those Parts and those of Rabbi Honigwachs to portray a meaningful pattern?

Before we can determine whether there is too much disparity between our points and those of Rabbi Honigwachs, we need to decide two things:

1. the variance allowed between two corresponding division points (one of ours and the other of Rabbi Honigwachs) to still be considered a successful match; and
2. the total number of failed matches allowed before the pattern is invalidated.

We will outline our approach below to these decisions, with elaboration of the details in Section 17.

Variance allowed between corresponding division points

To be clear, we are talking about, for example, our division point between our Part A and our Part B in a certain book versus Rabbi Honigwachs' division point between his Part A and his Part B. (Keep in mind that surviving the Test of Alternate Partition does not demand that our Parts be identical to those of Rabbi Honigwachs.) While our comfort with the pattern would be highest when the two points in question are identical, visual pattern recognition surely does not require an exact fit.

In fact, statisticians typically draw inferences from data without absolute certainty. Most often, such inferences come with what is known as "95% confidence" with a particular range of uncertainty, i.e., plus or minus a particular number. This type of statistical inference appears frequently in pre-election polls. While our task of comparing division points does not actually involve random sampling as it does in such polls, it is still natural to allow for some discrepancy.

In this vein, say we allow an inexactness of up to 5% in the agreement of two respective division points. This statement still requires setting the basis for determining 5% — in other words, 5% of what quantity. A natural possibility would be 5% of the number of verses. Since Leviticus has the fewest verses among the first four books (at 859), we could take 5% of 859, which is 43, as the maximum distance between respective division points for a match.

However, a better choice is 5% of the number of *p'tuchot* [blank spaces open to the left margin in Torah text], which takes into account the relative density of *p'tuchot* within each book. Since Genesis has the fewest *p'tuchot* (forty-three) of the first four books, a stringent allowance for such inexactness would use forty-three as the basis, with 5% of forty-three equaling a tiny fraction over two. That means the total distance between two respective points can be no more than two *p'tuchot* for a successful match anywhere in the first four books.

In other words, for the two respective points to be considered a successful match, they can differ by no more than two *p'tuchot* in the Torah. (Recall that all *p'tuchot* in the Torah are listed in Appendix a.)

Total failed matches allowed

With the above standard of closeness of respective points in hand, we can count the applications of the standard in the first four Books. Because there are four Books, this count would be four times the number of pairs of respective points in each Book. Recall that these division points between Parts in a Book occur at four places: between Parts A and B, between Parts B and C, between Parts C and D, and between Parts D and E. (We need no division point between Part E of one Book

---

A = respecting Creation; B = loyalty to primary relationship; C = limited access to sanctity/resources; D = duties of testimony/community; E = accepting one's place/status (with ties to land/future)

and Part A of the next Book because several rows of *p'tuchot* mark the end of each Book.) Thus there are four points of division in one Book, and 4x4=16 in the first four Books. This means sixteen applications of the standard of closeness.

In this light, how many of the sixteen applications could fail before tossing out the pattern for having insufficient matching of division points? This decision requires some subjectivity, no matter the lengths taken to avoid it. One thing is clear: the decision should be keyed to our closeness standard for division points. As explained in Section 17, a detailed consideration of probabilities can inform our choice.

In the end, this consideration led to setting the allowable number of failures to match closely enough at two out of sixteen.

iii. Test of Ambiguous Subdivision

Let's assume that the pattern has survived the first two tests: the first involving alternate partition and the second involving disparity of division points. Both of these tests focused on the division of a Book into Parts aligning with the Shared Principles. The idea now is to test the Subparts Claim: that Parts (those with at least five *parshiyot*) themselves subdivide into five Subparts aligning in order with the Shared Principles. In a sense, this third test involving Subparts mirrors the first test involving Parts. However, in the third test, we offer no alternative subdivision (that would have emulated the first test) because Parts are much smaller than Books, with less leeway for an alternate sequence of topics. (Largely for the same reason, we do not test for the disparity of subdivision points between Subparts.)[13]

While there is less leeway for topics conflicting with Subparts, the subdivision of a Part into Subparts brings greater ambiguity in two respects than does the division of a Book into Parts. Hence, this third test is identified with "ambiguous subdivision." The first respect is in introducing a third layer of themes (over those for Books and Parts) within which shifts must be found. The second respect is the loss of a technique we can generally use to find shifts from one Part to the next within a Book. Let us understand that loss by first recalling the process of dividing a Book.

To tell where one Part ends and another begins in Genesis, we used a specific technique: finding (if possible) the end of themes in the first Part tied to Principle E (Acceptance). That end would coincide with the end of Subpart E of the first Part. Then we would check that a theme or themes reflecting Principle A (Creation) immediately follows, thus marking Subpart A of the next Part. As you can see, this approach relies on the subdivision of Parts into Subparts.

Subparts lacking a further subdivision

While each Part of Genesis subdivides into five Subparts, most of the Subparts do not subdivide further — simply because they have fewer than five *parshiyot*. (Those Subparts that do subdivide further are said to subdivide into "Segments."). Besides further subdivision, however, we cannot look within a given Subpart for the end of themes tied to Principle E, which would close Segment E of that Subpart. This inability complicates the task of finding the progression of the Shared Principles through the Subparts of a given Part. In Genesis with its relatively few *p'tuchot*, the task is more manageable, but in the next three Books, the ambiguity in finding the shifts from one Subpart to another greatly increases. And if we cannot find these shifts, the pattern will fail the Test of Ambiguous Subdivision.

A further complication involving legal texts

Within legal texts, *parshiyot* commonly open with the following verse: "And God spoke to Moses, saying."[14]

We will refer to this language as the **standard opening**. Rabbi Honigwachs uses the Standard Opening to find the progression of the pattern, especially through Subparts of a given Part. In particular, when a string of *parshiyot* each begins with the standard opening, he posits that a division point must come before the first of these *parshiyot*.[15] In other words, he could use this device to place division points without actually identifying a shift in Shared Principles.

A = respecting Creation; B = loyalty to primary relationship; C = limited access to sanctity/resources; D = duties of testimony/community; E = accepting one's place/status (with ties to land/future)

While there is a persuasive rationale for this device,[16] the pattern should pass the Test of Ambiguous Subdivision only with clean progressions on its own. For us, that means forgoing use of a first standard opening in finding shifts to mark progression through the pattern. In other words, if we are in Subpart D of a given Part and are trying to find a shift to Subpart E, we must find an actual new theme or themes associated with Principle E (Acceptance). For example, Rabbi Honigwachs sets the beginning of Subpart E of Part A in Leviticus as 12:1, in accord with the standard opening, but we see no shift to Principle E there.

Personal Reflection and Summary

Before moving on to summarize this Section, it is worth stressing my state of knowledge of Rabbi Honigwachs' work before I began to test the pattern. I had set *The Unity of Torah* aside for more than two years, and what recollection of it I had was almost entirely limited to Genesis, on which the book focused. In particular, I recalled only Rabbi Honigwachs' explanation of his later use of the standard opening, but without any particular application. I did not observe his specific use again until after I had gone through my own exercise of trying to identify successive Subparts in alignment with the Shared Principles, and I did not modify my own work after seeing his transitions. Thus my read of *The Unity of Torah* should not have influenced any decisions regarding how I saw the pattern in Exodus, Leviticus, and Numbers. In particular, it should not have influenced me in finding the points between Parts and between Subparts.

In line with this reflection, my strategy to challenge the pattern in Exodus, Leviticus, and Numbers would involve the three tests summarized below.

- The Test of Alternate Partition, a test proposing partitions of each Book that depart from the pattern and that, if upheld, would signal a forced character.
- The Test of Point Disparity, a test of the pattern's replication, limiting respective division points to a distance of two or fewer *p'tuchot*, with failures limited to two.

- The Test of Ambiguous Subdivision, a test of tracking the pattern's progression in Subparts that ignores the standard opening of *parshiyot* in finding shifts.

I was confident that the pattern would not survive this three-pronged strategy.

A = respecting Creation; B = loyalty to primary relationship; C = limited access to sanctity/resources; D = duties of testimony/community; E = accepting one's place/status (with ties to land/future)

A Review with Murals and Stairways

Here we stand after completing the first two phases of our journey. Let us review our progress to this point.

In Stage I:

- We saw how the debate over authorship of the Five Books hinges on whether or not there is an overall pattern in the text.
- We saw further that any such pattern must resolve order challenges in the text, and especially those involving the adjoining of apparently unconnected topics.
- We also came to understand an overall pattern proposed by Rabbi Yehoshua Honigwachs based on five Shared Principles in the Ten Commandments.
- Finally, Stage I exposed us to both major features and possible problems in the proposed pattern. This exposure came through partitioning each of the first four Books into five Parts and through examples of subdividing Parts into five Sections.

In Stage II:
Our initial analysis of the proposed pattern suggested it could resolve some better known order challenges with consecutive topics that do not seem connected.

- However, the analysis also suggested the pattern probably requires forced organization, especially outside Genesis. While we noted the pattern does hold up in Genesis, we witnessed in Stage II the development of a strategy likely to invalidate the pattern in the middle three books. The strategy tests whether each of these Books reliably divides into five Parts aligned with the pattern and whether the division points between the Parts would match closely enough with an independent partition. The strategy also tests whether those Parts with enough *parshiyot* reliably subdivide into five Subparts aligned with the pattern.

We are now about to enter Stage III of the journey where we apply the strategy. This application will involve a close examination with details of the text and how well they fit the proposed pattern. To avoid getting mired in these details and losing sight of the objective of our investigation, we pause briefly for a concrete illustration to place our completed travel and the path ahead in proper perspective.

Imagine the discovery many centuries ago of five mysterious covered stairways built into the side of five concentric hills in a remote part of the world, each hill rising from the one below. Each stairway features a mural with a single distinct motif on its entrance and another much longer mural running continuously along its ceiling with many different scenes. The longer murals sometimes depict a series of actions involving people and sometimes depict favorable or unfavorable symbols of a single action; adjoining scenes often appear disjointed or unconnected. The number of steps differs among the stairways, and within each stairway the horizontal distance from one step to another may vary greatly.

The five stairways represent the Five Books, with each entrance mural marking the opening theme of the particular Book and with each longer mural reflecting the text of the Book. A series of human actions is identified with narrative, and favorable and unfavorable symbols with positive law and negative law (prohibition) respectively. Each step corresponds to a *p'tuchah*, and the horizontal distance from one step to the next represents the length of a *parshah*. Just as anthropologists would try to make sense of the overall structure, so too do readers of the Five Books attempt to understand the organization of the text.

Respect for the murals' history and values, which are still embraced by many people today, depends on artistic integrity and authenticity. However, the dominant anthropologists (the Source Critics) attribute the fragmentation within the murals to multiple artists with different agendas, thus promoting cynicism towards the murals' values. But a new anthropologist (Rabbi Honigwachs) sees recurring motifs based

---

A = respecting Creation; B = loyalty to primary relationship; C = limited access to sanctity/resources; D = duties of testimony/community; E = accepting one's place/status (with ties to land/future)

on five symbols at one point within the second mural (the Shared Principles in the Ten Commandments).

We are a body of independent investigators brought in to evaluate the claims of the new anthropologist. So far, we have confirmed his assertion regarding the sequence of entrance murals for the five stairways, i.e., the context of the Five Books aligns with the Shared Principles. Regarding the presence of five motif areas of the ceiling mural inside the first stairway (Genesis), we have confirmed (the Parts Claim) that they exist and parallel the five entrance motifs. In fact, we independently identify the same four steps in the first stairway where the new anthropologist claims the mural changes in the ceiling above from one motif to another. We have even found that, within each of the five motif areas on the first stairway ceiling, there is a sub-progression that follows the same order (the Subparts Claim).

However, we are highly skeptical of the validity of the pattern beyond the first stairway, which is the only stairway to show human action (narrative) on its ceiling mural without any presence of symbols (law). Furthermore, the mural inside the first stairway features a series of four main figures (Abraham, Isaac, Jacob, and Joseph) who appear and become dominant in order. This series of figures makes it easier to find the steps between motifs in the first stairway, but there are no such cues in the ceilings of the other stairways.

Now we are about to enter the second stairway (Exodus). We see no obvious breakdown on the ceiling into five motif areas as we did in the first stairway. Thus we will test the new anthropologist's first claim by trying to divide the mural into motif areas that do not follow the proposed pattern (Test of Alternate Partition). Even if, upon analysis, our alternative division ends up reducing to five motif areas (Parts) consistent with the pattern, we will check how closely the points of division match those of the new anthropologist (Test of Point Disparity). After examining a specific scene in the ceiling mural with special importance, we return to test the new anthropologist's claim (Test of Ambiguous Subdivision) regarding the sub-progressions within the five motif areas in the second stairway.

In the third stairway (Leviticus) and again in the fourth (Numbers), we follow this same approach of two tests followed by a special examination and then a third test. We will report our findings for the three tests in each stairway separately and then provide a concluding analysis that combines the first four stairways. The fifth stairway, which is almost entirely symbolic (legal), does not go through progressions like the first four, so we decide to treat it separately.

In the event (as unlikely as it may seem) that new anthropologist's claims are confirmed by our findings, we will have no recourse but to say the murals came from a single hand. And with that conclusion, the grounds for much of the cynicism towards the murals' values should vanish.

A = respecting Creation; B = loyalty to primary relationship; C = limited access to sanctity/resources; D = duties of testimony/community; E = accepting one's place/status (with ties to land/future)

Notes

1. One might argue that the reference in Genesis 12:5 to "the souls they (Abraham and Sarah) made in Haran" means conversions to monotheism. However, the inference that the conversions were to monotheism, as opposed to some other form of faith, still requires going outside the text.
2. For the lives of each of Abraham, Jacob, and Joseph, possible choices for the beginning the respective Subparts are as follows:

    Subpart B focusing on Abraham: 11:1–32 (birth), 12:1–9 (first independent action);

    Subpart D focusing on Jacob: 25:19–34 (birth and first independent action);

    Subpart E focusing on Joseph: 26:1–32:3 (birth), 32:4–34:31, 35:1–8, 35:9–22, 35:22–29, 36:1–30, 36:31–43, 37:1–36 (first independent action).

    Note that there is a *p'tuchah* in the middle of the verse 35:22.
3. This idea can be found in Ramban's comment on Genesis 12:6, which comes from Chapter 9 of *Midrash Tanchuma, Lekh L'kha*.
4. Cf. Professor D. Dorsey in *The Literary Structure of the Old Testament* (Grand Rapids, MI: Baker Academic, 1999).
5. There is a subtle distinction, however. In the parallel sequences of conventional Biblical scholarship, corresponding passages share a theme (which may be a closer link than a common association with a Shared Principle). For example, two Subparts C — one in one Part and one in another — may each have different themes that are nonetheless both linked to Principle C (Limits). This could occur if Subpart C of Part A involves a limitation on sanctity, while Subpart C of Part B involves theft of possessions.
6. Ibid.
7. An ancient poem from Mesopotamia written in cuneiform on clay tablets and predominantly thought to predate the Torah.
8. The problem was how to view the *parshah* in between (dealing with Isaac's burial by his sons):

    On one hand, the burial could demonstrate honoring one's parents reflecting Principle E (Acceptance), which would place this *parshah* at the end of Jacob's life and Part D;

    At the same time, the burial could also be linked to murder and Principle

A (Creation) with Esau yearning for his father's demise (see 27:41) and his plan to exact revenge on Jacob. That association would place the *parshah* with portion (5).

While each view of Isaac's burial had something to aid it, I was finally influenced by the highly unusual circumstance surrounding the previous *parshah* treating Reuben's transgression: it ends in the middle of a verse. This abrupt ending of a *parshah* evoked the following interpretation: times have changed with Isaac's death. Accordingly, the shift from portion (4) to (5) occurs in the middle of 35:22.

9   See Endnote 1 above. The interpretation of "the souls they made" in Genesis 12:5 as conversions to monotheism reflects Rashi's comments that are, of course, authoritative. Yet for the Shared Principles to be a verifiable textual pattern, evidence of the pattern should be found more directly in the text itself.

10 Successive Subparts of the same Part already share an association with the Shared Principle of the Biblical book, as well as association with the Shared Principle of the Part. Making distinctions with this degree of similarity is hard enough in Genesis, but it becomes harder in subsequent books, which contain more paragraphs (and therefore more choices for division points). For example, Subparts B and C of Part C of Exodus both reflect Shared Principle B by being in Exodus, as well as Principle C by being in Part C. Can the point dividing Subparts B and C be identified to verify progression through the pattern, when the two Subparts have so much in common? In particular, let's say we are in Subpart B trying to look for the shift into Subpart C, and we encounter a theme associated with Principle C (Limits). Can we tell whether that theme is substantially different enough to signal moving from Subpart B to Subpart C? Perhaps this Principle C theme reflects Part C of Exodus and not Subpart C of Part C.

11 This explanation paraphrases Cassuto's ideas in *The Documentary Hypothesis and the Composition of the Pentateuch*, tr. by I. Abrahams, (Jerusalem: Shalem, 2006). The original version was published in Hebrew in 1941 after Cassuto joined the faculty of Hebrew University. It was first translated into English in 1961, ten years after Cassuto's death, and has served as a major resource in rebutting Source Criticism.

12 Here are the approximate scopes and rationales for assigning Shared Principle in Display 7.2.

In assigning Principle B (Loyalty) to enslavement of the Jewish people in Chapters 1–2, enslavement is seen as imposing a master other than God, showing disloyalty to a primary relationship.

Because Divine revelation is naturally associated with belief in God, Shared Principle A (Creation) is tentatively assigned to the revelation at the Burning Bush (roughly Chapters 3–4).

Liberation from slavery again signals loyalty to a primary relationship and thus Shared Principle B for the Plagues and the Exodus (~Chapters 5–17). Note the notation "~" signifies "roughly."

Law inherently sets limits and limits access, so T4 (~Chapters 18-24) fits Shared Principle C.

The directions for making the Tabernacle (~Chapters 25–31) involve communal responsibility, which accords with the tentative assignment to Principle D (Community).

Idolatry or something close to it is the theme of the Golden Calf (~Chapters 32–33), thus reflecting Principle B (Loyalty).

The actual making of the Tabernacle (~Chapters 34–40) could suggest Principle D (Community) as a communal task, or it could suggest Principle E (Acceptance) through the limiting of certain work to those with particular talents.

13 Besides there being less leeway for different placement of subdivision points (between Subparts), several other factors complicate comparisons of our subdivision points with those of Rabbi Honigwachs:

Not all of the subdivisions of Parts into Subparts are presented in *The Unity of Torah*. Thus, it is impossible to get a full comparison.

Two Parts in Leviticus (Parts B and E) and one Part in Numbers (Part C) do not have enough *parshiyot* for subdivision. Shall we simply ignore these cases (reducing the comparison pool), or shall we give credit to the pattern by default?

Suppose my point of division between specific Parts does not match its counterpart from Rabbi Honigwachs. Then what allowance (if any) in the matching of Subparts from those Parts should be given? This question arises where, for example, I identify a certain point as dividing Part A from Part B, but Rabbi Honigwachs identifies it as dividing Subpart A and Subpart B in Part A.

For all these reasons, the most straightforward approach is to compare only division points between Parts and to set aside subdivision points between Subparts. Where there are known differences in such points, we will still deal with them, but not in the context of the overall fit.

14 This language does not occur in Genesis (where Moses does not appear) or in Deuteronomy (where Moses speaks in the first person), but it is found pervasively in the other three Books.

15 Rabbi Honigwachs does not always use the first standard opening in a string to signal a shift from one Subpart to another. Indeed, sometimes he has it signaling a shift from one Segment to another within a Subpart. For example, in the string of two consecutive *parshiyot* in Leviticus with standard openings in 7:28 and 8:1, verse 7:28 is viewed as beginning Segment E in Subpart A, just after the end of Segment D.

16 A string of English paragraphs with the same distinctive opening (for example, "whereas") might also mark a transition from the preceding subtext.

STAGE III

Applying the Strategy and Analyzing the Results

Section 8
Testing the Pattern in Exodus

Here in Section 8 for Exodus (as well as in Section 9 for Leviticus and in Section 10 for Numbers), we will use the strategy developed in Section 7. That strategy includes three tests:

- the Test of Alternate Partition, which proposes a sequence of topics that conflicts with the pattern in regards to Parts;
- the Test of Point Disparity, which compares our division points for Parts with those of Rabbi Honigwachs; and
- the Test of Ambiguous Subdivision, which challenges the pattern to progress through Subparts with more layers of themes and without the technique to divide Parts.

We will apply these tests in order, but before the third test, we will discuss a special case of the Shared Principles that comes about when dividing Parts and deserves our attention. Thus, our approach in Exodus, Leviticus, and Numbers will proceed as:

(i) Alternate Partition, (ii) Point Disparity, (iii) Special Case, (iv) Ambiguous Subdivision.

After Ambiguous Subdivision, a summary follows covering all three tests and the special case. Like Stage II, Stage III provides a framed footer fully identifying the Shared Principles.

i. Test of Alternate Partition

In Section 7 we cited a possible alternate partition for Exodus that seems to conflict with the pattern, based on the idea that Exodus could be divided into seven topics just as naturally as five. That partition with tentatively assigned Shared Principles appeared earlier as Display 7.2, but now we add each topic's text range. This partition challenges the pattern over alignment with the five Shared Principles. In listing text ranges below, the symbol "~" means **approximately**; we need only approximate text ranges for this test to identify the topics. The Shared Principles for most topics will be explained in the course of our discussion, but short reasons for each are listed in an endnote.[1]

DISPLAY 8: Alternate Partition of Exodus into a Sequence of Topics

1. Enslavement of Jewish people	~Chapters 1–2	B (Loyalty)
2. Revelations of God to Moses and Aaron	~Chapters 3–5	A (Creation)
3. Liberation through Plagues, Splitting of Sea	~Chapters 6–17	B (Loyalty)
4. Ten Commandments and civil law	~Chapters 18–24	C (Limits)
5. Directions for making Tabernacle	~Chapters 25–31	D (Community)
6. Incident of Golden Calf	~Chapters 32–33	B (Loyalty)
7. Actual making of Tabernacle	~ Chapters 34–40	D (Community) or E (Acceptance)

We see three topics (the first, sixth, and seventh) whose alignment with the pattern of Shared Principles seems faulty or uncertain. We will address these cases in order.

a. *The Seeming Misalignment of Enslavement of the Jewish People*

Keep in mind that according to the pattern, the first topic in this sequence should be linked to Principle A (Creation). Instead, enslavement apparently involves imposing a master other than God and so reflects Principle B (Loyalty). To make this violation of the pattern stick, we must just confirm that the enslavement text does not link to Principle A. It turns out, however, that strong signs of this Principle do appear in the text of this topic, as we now show.

The enslavement text consists of the first three *parshiyot* in Exodus, ending with 2:22. That border becomes plain through the fourth *parshah*'s focus on the revelation at the Burning Bush, which belongs to the second topic, i.e., revelations. The first *parshah* of the three (1:1–7) describes lineage rather than enslavement and links to neither Principle A nor B in any obvious way.[2] The second *parshah* (1:8–23), while dealing with enslavement, cites Pharaoh's planned infanticide and the midwives' refusal to carry it out because of their belief in God. Murder and belief in God suggest Principle A (Creation). The third *parshah* (2:1–22) also involves enslavement, but stresses the incident where Moses kills an Egyptian and Pharaoh's attempt to kill Moses, again reflecting Principle A. Thus while enslavement provides a backdrop for the second and third *parshiyot*, those *parshiyot* fit Principle A better than B (Loyalty). (See if you don't agree!)

The consecutive topics of enslavement and revelations now both align with Principle A (Creation). Thus we merge them into a single topic, which we will call "oppression of the Jewish people and revelations to Moses and Aaron," or "oppression and revelations," for short. Note the substitution of the word "enslavement" by "oppression," which reflects the repeated use of the word *b'farekh* [with oppression] in 1:13–14. The root of this Hebrew word connotes "breaking" or "crushing," thus implying bodily injury. Of course, infanticide actually took place in the most severe period of enslavement. Also note that the overlay of enslavement still fits the Book of Exodus, which, as an entire Book, aligns with Principle B (Loyalty). We can now restructure the seven topics in the original alternative into six as shown below.

DISPLAY 8.1: First Revised Partition (with Assignment of Shared Principles)

1. Oppression and Revelations	~Chapters 1–5	A (Creation)
2. Liberation through Plagues, Splitting of Sea	~Chapters 6–17	B (Loyalty)
3. Ten Commandments and civil law	~Chapters 18–24	C (Limits)
4. Directions for making Tabernacle	~Chapters 25–31	D (Community)
5. Incident of Golden Calf	~Chapters 32–33	B (Loyalty)
6. Actual making of Tabernacle	~Chapters 34–40	D (Community) or E (Acceptance)

b. The Seeming Misalignment of the Incident of the Golden Calf

In the revised partition above, the first four topics do align in order with the first four Principles, A, B, C, and D. However, the fifth topic, the Incident of the Golden Calf, again presents a topic seemingly out of alignment, since the theme of idolatry in this topic goes with Principle B (Loyalty), not with D or E (which would fit the pattern). To check the misalignment, we must examine carefully the coverage of the Golden Calf within the text. To do so in every detail (as completed later in Section 16) would unduly impede our progress. Thus, in what now follows, we will provide key elements of the analysis.

The account of the incident spans fifty-two verses: 31:18–33:16, made up of five components:

- When Moses does not return from the mountain by the time expected, Aaron is bullied into making a replacement; the resulting Golden Calf is worshipped (Subparagraph 31:18–32:6);
- There is a dialogue between God and Moses on Mount Sinai in the immediate aftermath, in which God intends to destroy the people and replace them with a new nation of Moses' descendants, but relents in the face of Moses' argument (*Parshah* 32:7–14);

- Moses returns to the camp. He breaks the tablets and grinds the Calf to dust to be force-fed to the people. He elicits the testimony of Aaron and proclaims a civil war, which, together with a plague, claims many lives. Through Moses' action and further appeal, God forgives the people but will no longer lead the way (Subparagraph 32:15–35);
- God gives directions on new relationship: an angel will lead the way in God's stead, and Moses must leave the camp to communicate with God (Subparagraph 33:1–11);
- Moses' additional appeal: Moses pleads that God stay in the midst of the people, to which God later agrees (*Parshah* 33:12–16).

Signs of Principle D (Community) in the Incident of the Golden Calf

In scanning these components of the Golden Calf, we do see signs of Principle D. Take the first component 31:18–32:6, which directly mentions worship of the Calf in 31:5: "They arose early the next day and brought up elevation and peace offerings (to the Calf)…"

This clearly reflects Principle B (Loyalty). However, this component forms the second subparagraph of *parshah* 31:12–32:6, whose first subparagraph deals solely and at equal length with the Sabbath. Because the Sabbath is "remembered" in the Fourth Commandment with testimony, it is plainly linked to Principle D (Community).

Even in the first component itself, the instigators of the Calf give false testimony, by saying: "This is your god, Israel, that brought you up from the land of Egypt (31:4)." And before this testimony, mob behavior is indicated in the approach to Aaron to make the idol: "…and the people congregated on Aaron…"(31:1)

In the second component, God clearly mentions the sin of worshipping the Calf (most directly related to Principle B) in 32:8, but we also find a strong focus in the remainder of this component on whether the Jewish people will remain God's people. In particular, we find: "…and I (God) shall destroy them and…make you (Moses' family) a great nation." (32:10); the focus of this verse could either link (via the theme of primary relationship) to Principle B or (via communal identity) to Principle D.

Then the third component shifts to the aftermath of the Golden Calf and treats several themes aligned with the Principle D (Community), such as Aaron's testimony, which includes: "they said, '…make us a god that will go before us, for…we know not his (Moses') fate' " (32:23).

We also have the civil war in 32:26–29, which, in its communal context, reflects Principle D. Mention of the Golden Calf in this component is less direct and does not include actual worship.

Further removed from the sin, the fourth and fifth components refer to the Golden Calf only obliquely and tend toward testimonial and communal themes. These include stripping the people of their testimonial ornaments, whose Hebrew root *adi* is a variant of *ed* [witness], and Moses' speaking with God outside the camp. These clearly suggest Principle D (Community).

Categorizing the Components

In checking the relative weight of Principle B (Loyalty) and Principle D (Community) in each component, Principle B seems stronger in the first two components and Principle D in the last three. Even balancing the first component against its preceding subparagraph (on the Sabbath), there still seems enough of a failure in the Parts Claim of ordered alignment with the Shared Principles to reject it — unless something else impels us to link the Incident to Principle D. Otherwise, adhering to the Parts Claim would involve forcing Principle D on the text where themes of testimony/community do not dominate. And should one rationalize placement of this sin as a brief (and perhaps allowable) interruption of the pattern, that approach would lead us to view much of Numbers (with so many sins committed in the Wilderness) as an interruption.

Now, a defender of the pattern might bring the great codifier Maimonides to support the Parts Claim here. In his *Guide for the Perplexed*, Maimonides wrote that the Tabernacle and its rituals (notably sacrifices) were meant to wean the people from idolatry by replacing pagan icons with physical expressions of God.[3] This "replacement" approach could link the Golden Calf (as idolatry) to the Tabernacle (as a communal institution) and Shared Principle D. Yet, with little in the text itself to promote this explanation, it seems arbitrary to view the most obvious case of Principle B as a different Shared Principle. Furthermore, in spite of Maimonides' unequaled standing, his view of the Tabernacle replacing idolatry has not won clear acceptance.[4] Thus I remained unwilling to combine the Golden Calf with Principle D.

Conclusive Evidence for Principle D

To change my mind would take an explicit feature intrinsic to the Golden Calf text with a communal or testimonial character. Rashi, in fact, led me to such a feature in his comment on 32:4 highlighting (beyond the single verse cited earlier) the behavior of a mob. His comment seems partly inspired by the use of the word *am* [people] to refer to participants in the Incident. This word (as opposed to the more common ancestral term *b'nei Yisrael* [the children of Israel]) carries a communal connotation, and therefore a connection with Principle D.

In the fifty-two verses comprising the Incident, the word *am* or its variants occur twenty-eight times, more than once every two verses, while the term *b'nei Yisrael* appears only three times — and never in the first two components (this usage contrasts with the other 1,157 verses of Exodus where *b'nei Yisrael* occurs 139 times and *am* 78). Moreover, the subtext of the Incident contains the only places in Exodus where the word *am* serves as the subject for a verb of independent action. In other places, action is done to the *am*, or the *am* reacts to something.

In marking the relative absence of *b'nei Yisrael* in the Incident, this analysis lends credence to a different reading of the Jewish people's sin with the Golden Calf. Relying on the *Midrash Pesikta Rabati* — *Eichah*, the nineteenth century work *Bet HaLevi* does not see the main sin as worshipping an idol (which can be seen by the relatively few resulting deaths, suggesting that many didn't actually worship it). Rather, when the Jewish people (commonly known as *b'nei Yisrael*) heard the *am* (i.e., the instigators) declare that the Calf brought the people out of Egypt, they failed to protest, i.e., they didn't testify in opposition, which more closely reflects Principle D (Community).

With the Incident of the Golden Calf now associated with Principle D, we can revise Display 8.1 by merging this topic with the fourth topic, the directions for making the Tabernacle, which is already tied to Principle D. We will call this combination: "Tabernacle Directions and the Golden Calf."

DISPLAY 8.2: Second Revised Partition (with Assignment of Shared Principles)		
1. Oppression and Revelation	~Chapters 1–5	A (Creation)
2. Liberation through Plagues, Splitting of Sea	~Chapters 6–17	B (Loyalty)
3. Ten Commandments and civil law	~Chapters 18–24	C (Limits)
4. Tabernacle Directions and Golden Calf	~Chapters 25–33	D (Community)
5. Actual making of Tabernacle	~Chapters 34–40	D (Community) or E (Acceptance)

c. The Uncertain Alignment of the Actual Making of the Tabernacle

As indicated above, the actual making of the Tabernacle could be aligned naturally with either Principle D (Community) or E (Acceptance). An alignment with Principle D would continue to stress the communal nature of the task of construction — as is the case with the fourth topic above, Tabernacle Directions and the Golden Calf. In contrast, alignment with Shared Principle E would stress special talents used in the task: e.g., "the work of a weaver" (38:18) and "wreathen work (of a silversmith)" (39:15). This stress fits Principle E because one's talents determine whether he could play a role in making the Tabernacle and its contents. A person accepts his own talents as part of accepting his place thus reflecting Principle E.

Before addressing the proper alignment itself, let us note how closely this issue touches one of the most vexing problems with the text. Why do Chapters 35–40 of Exodus (the actual making of the Tabernacle) repeat the details that had already been given in Chapters 25–30 in the directions for the Tabernacle? Put another way, the text could have naturally dispensed with nearly all of the last six chapters in Exodus and said merely, "And Moses and the people did as God commanded." (Of course, to Source Critics, such apparently needless repetition presents no problem at all. It merely confirms multiple authorship, since the two similar accounts may come from two different sources that were later stitched together. Such an explanation would thus mirror Source Critics' view of other pairs of subtexts they call "doublets" — recall the discussion of this term in Section 6.)

Yet, if the actual making of the Tabernacle were linked to Principle E (Acceptance), this alignment would rationalize the degree to which Chapters 25–30 are repeated by Chapters 35–40. In particular, we could say the details given in the instructions for the Tabernacle appeared again in its actual construction to call attention to the talents employed. And this progression from the instructions to the actual task would follow the pattern's order from Principle D (Community) to Principle E. While linking this topic to Shared Principle E would neatly explain the otherwise needless repetition of details of the Tabernacle, that linkage would need to be checked in the text.

In particular, we demand full confidence in linking the actual making of the Tabernacle to special talents (and thus to Principle E). For that confidence, such skills should occur first in the building itself — not before. Yet, the two key artisans for the Tabernacle, Bezalel and Oholiab, are introduced along with their skills in 31:1–6, which falls in the fourth topic of Tabernacle Directions and the Golden Calf. Thus, while the actual making of the Tabernacle mentions skills much more extensively than does the fourth topic, we may regard the latter citations as continued from the Tabernacle directions, and thus tied to Principle D (Community). If so, that would argue for aligning the actual making of the Tabernacle with Principle D. That alignment would mean failure of the Parts Claim, since no topic would then align with Principle E (Acceptance).

A True Failure or Not?

Though a convenient support for the pattern in Exodus had just been struck down, I had not fully established the pattern's failure in meeting the Parts Claim. Before claiming victory, I would need to verify that no significant theme besides special talents links the making of the Tabernacle with Principle E (Acceptance). As it turns out, another such theme (and a very powerful one) does present itself at the end of Exodus — fulfillment of a promise by God, thus reflecting the future orientation of Principle E.

The promise in question is found in *parshah* 33:17–23. That *parshah* begins with God's acceptance of Moses' request in the previous *parshah* to stay in the midst of the people and Moses' further request that he (Moses) be allowed to see *c'vodekha* [Your (God's) **glory**]. God responds in 33:20 that no person can see God and live. However, Moses is told in 33:23 he will be allowed to see *achorai*, simply translated as "My [God's] back."[5] Thus God's promise means two things: Him staying in the midst of the people and giving Moses a special revelation.

Just past 33:23, we encounter God's command to Moses to make the second tablets. After Moses carves out the tablets from stone (but before he engraves the Commandments), God descends in a **cloud** (now also hold this image) and passes before him, i.e., with Moses at God's back. Clearly, this is the revelation alluded to by the term *achorai* in the past *parshah*, whereby God fulfills His commitment in how Moses may see Him. But what about God's commitment to dwell in the midst of the people? Where is that commitment fulfilled? The answer lies with the words "glory" and "cloud" as highlighted above.

At the end of Exodus in 40:34, after the Tabernacle is finished, the **cloud** appears again and settles upon the structure reflecting God's **glory**. In other words, when the Jewish people complete their task of construction, God's presence once again resides with them in the visible form of a cloud. Why a cloud? As we saw earlier in text, no person can see God and live, so His glory must be obscured from the people in a mist. Yet the cloud reassures them that He is there. Through the fulfillment of both aspects of God's promise (with its future orientation), the last topic in the partition, the actual making of the Tabernacle, aligns with Principle E.

In light of this conclusion about the last topic and Principle E, we can now restate the topical sequence in Exodus in its final form of five Parts below. Note: we have tweaked the name of the last topic to stress the key role of the cloud of glory. Remarkably, the Parts Claim has been upheld in Exodus, with each of the topics aligning in order with the Shared Principles. These five topics are Parts A, B, C, D, and E, respectively.

DISPLAY 8.3: Third Revised Partition (with Assignment of Shared Principles)		
1. Oppression and Revelations	~Chapters 1–5	A (Creation)
2. Liberation through Plagues, Splitting of Sea	~Chapters 6–17	B (Loyalty)
3. Ten Commandments and civil law	~Chapters 18–24	C (Limits)
4. Tabernacle Directions and Golden Calf	~Chapters 32–33	D (Community)
5. Tabernacle Completion with Cloud of Glory	~Chapters 34–40	E (Acceptance)

ii. Test of Point Disparity

This test proceeds in two steps. First, we find the endpoint of each Part, i.e., where it shifts to the next Part. Note that these division points (between successive Parts) may vary slightly from the approximate Chapter ranges given above in Display 8.3. Such variation can occur because those ranges were intended only to help identify the topics, not to pinpoint them. Second, we compare these points with those of Rabbi Honigwachs in *The Unity of Torah* (pages 78–79) to evaluate the fit.

a. Identifying Division Points between Successive Parts

Because the end of Part E corresponds to the end of the Book, we need only identify four division points: between A and B, between B and

C, between C and D, and between D and E.

> **Division Point in Exodus between Part A and Part B**
>
> Part A = oppression of the Jewish people and the revelation of God to Moses;
>
> Part B = liberation through the Plagues and the Splitting of the Sea.

As explained in Section 7, we seek a *p'tuchah* between the topics where a shift occurs from Principle E (Acceptance) to Principle A (Creation). This will mark the end of Subpart E of Part A and the beginning of Subpart A of Part B, and thus the division point between Part A and Part B. Such a shift does occur after Exodus 6:30.

Before that point, in the *parshah* 6:10–30, Moses fails in his initial request to release the people from Pharaoh's rule to worship God in the Wilderness, and Moses tells God his failure was inevitable because of his "unrefined lips" [*aral s'fataiyim*]. This reference clearly reflects Principle E (Acceptance) since Moses is saying he does not have the tools to lead, even though God had told him in 4:14–16 that Aaron would be his spokesman. Just after 6:30, in *parshah* 7:1–7, God responds that He will bring many signs and wonders and that Egypt will know God (7:5). This passage signals belief in God (reflecting Principle A) and reads like a prelude to the Plagues. Thus, we divide Parts A and B after 6:30.

> **Division Point in Exodus between Part B and Part C**
>
> Part B = liberation through the Plagues and the Splitting of the Sea;
>
> Part C = Ten Commandments and civil law.

As with the division point between Parts A and B, we seek a theme linked to Principle E (Acceptance) at the end of the first Part. After the Plagues and Splitting of the Sea, such a theme clearly occurs in the *parshah* 18:1–27. There, Jethro (Yitro in Hebrew) advises Moses to reduce his heavy involvement in judging the people. Jethro suggests a court system with judges at different tiers of authority and for different jurisdictions. People must accept their place within that system. From that theme, we move to the Revelation at Sinai and the Ten Commandments, thus reflecting Principle A. This makes the end of 18:27 our division point for Parts B and C.

> **Division Point in Exodus between Part C and Part D**
>
> Part C = Ten Commandments and Civil Law;
>
> Part D = directions for making the Tabernacle and the Incident of the Golden Calf.

Once again, we seek a theme linked to Principle E (Acceptance), this time at the end of Part C. After the civil law portions, but before the directions for the Tabernacle, we find in *parshah* 23:20–33 God's promises to the Jewish people if they remain faithful in conquering Canaan. These promises include annihilation of the inhabitants (23:23), blessing of bread and water and removal of illness (23:25), and healthy births and fertility (23:26). These promises relate to the future and the land, and are thus linked to Principle E. The next *parshah* 24:1–18 contains the people's declaration of "we will do and we will understand" (24:7), expressing faith (Principle A) and immediate obedience to God (with understanding coming only afterwards).[6] In addition, there is a special revelation of God to Moses, Aaron, Nadab, Abihu, and the seventy elders (24:9–11), further suggesting Principle A. Thus, Parts C and D are divided after 23:33.

> **Division Point in Exodus between Part D and Part E**
>
> Part D = Directions for Making the Tabernacle and the Incident of the Golden Calf;
>
> Part E = Actual Making of the Tabernacle.

As we noted above in the test of the Parts Claim, *parshah* 33:17–23 (which follows the last component of the Incident of the Golden Calf) includes the following vital elements: God's promise to stay with the people, Moses' request to see God's glory, God's response that no one can see the Divine Presence and live but promising to show Moses *achorai* [My back]. Each of these elements relates to a promise for the future or to accepting one's place. Thus, this *parshah* clearly aligns with Principle E. Then the next *parshah* recounts the revelation (Principle A) to Moses in which God passes before him. This makes 33:23 the point of division between Parts D and E. Now all four points dividing the Parts of Exodus can be inserted below in keeping with Display 8.3.

DISPLAY 8.4: Parts of Exodus and their Endpoints		
Part	Verses	General Description
A (Creation)	1:1–6:30	Oppression and Revelations
B (Loyalty)	7:1–18:27	Plagues and Splitting of Sea
C (Limits)	19:1–23:33	Ten Commandments and Civil Law
D (Community)	24:1–33:23	Tabernacle Directions and Golden Calf
E (Acceptance)	34:1–40:38	Tabernacle Completion with Cloud of Glory

b. *Comparing Division Points with Those of Rabbi Honigwachs*

In comparing respective division points for Parts, recall from Section 7 that we consider such points matching if, and only if, they are no more than two *p'tuchot* apart. (Note that the distance in *p'tuchot* between respective points can be counted from Appendix a.) We see from Display 8.5 below that the respective points of division are positioned more than two *p'tuchot* apart in the first case (in the division of Parts A and B). However, in the last three cases, the respective points lie within two *p'tuchot* of each other. This means we have one failure in Exodus in the Test of Point Disparity.

A = respecting Creation; B = loyalty to primary relationship; C = limited access to sanctity/resources; D = duties of testimony/community; E = accepting one's place/status (with ties to land/future)

DISPLAY 8.5: Comparison of Respective Points of Division in Exodus

Successive Parts to be divided	Last verse before division Mine	Last verse before division Rabbi Honigwachs'	Distance in *p'tuchot*
Parts A and B	6:30	17:16	24
Parts B and C	18:27	18:27	0
Parts C and D	23:33	25:1	1
Parts D and E	33:23	35:4	2

As we developed the Test of Point Disparity in Section 7, whether the pattern ultimately survives rests on the total number of failures (no more than two) to match in the first four Books. Because this outcome cannot be known without the results for Leviticus and Numbers, judgment must be withheld for now. We know only one failure so far for Genesis and Exodus combined.

While not knowing the ultimate outcome of the Test of Point Disparity, we can still tell why the respective division points in Exodus between Parts A and B did not match. We noted earlier in Section 5 that the pattern's three levels (Part, Subpart, and Segment) make it difficult to know the level at which a shift in Principles is taking place. Owing to that difficulty, Rabbi Honigwachs takes Part A of Exodus to cover the oppression of the Jewish people, the revelations to Moses and Aaron, the Plagues, and the Splitting of the Sea,[7] while my Part A covers only the first two topics. In this particular case, we each saw a shift in themes at the beginning of Chapter 7 of Exodus, as the plagues were about to start. I see this shift as dividing Parts A and B, while he sees it as dividing Subparts A and B of Part A. My concern here lies not with whose divisions are correct, but rather with being able to replicate the pattern adequately overall.

iii. A Striking Suggestion of the Pattern in the Terms of Redemption

In our discussion above, we divided each Part of Exodus from its successor. For the division of Parts A and B, we proceeded through Part

A until we found a substantial theme of Shared Principle E with which to end that Part. That approach led us to *parshah* 6:10–30, where Moses does not accept his place as leader because of a physiological limitation (*aral s'fataiyim* [unrefined lips]). On these grounds, Moses asserts twice (in 6:12 and 6:30) his inability to deal with Pharaoh. Between these two assertions, God promises liberation in language reflected in the Jewish observance of Passover. This language, it turns out, also carries a striking suggestion of the Shared Principles that connects with this observance.

Passover begins with the Seder, the ritual meal during which the story of the Exodus is recounted. In line with one of seven primary rabbinic enactments, participants drink four cups of wine at prescribed points in the Seder. Most commonly, this enactment is viewed as symbolizing the four verbs (known as the "four terms of redemption") found in Exodus 6:6–7, by which God promises liberation.[8] These four verbs are bolded within the passage below:

"[1]...***v'hotzeiti*** etkhem mitachat sivlot Mitzraiyim;	and I will take you out from under the sufferings of Egypt;
[2] ***v'hitzalti*** etkhem me'avodatam;	and I will save you from their bondage;
[3] ***v'gaalti*** etkhem bizroa n'tuyah ubish'fatim g'dolim	and I will redeem you with an outstretched arm and with great judgments;
[4] ***v'lakachti*** etkhem li l'am	and I will take you as a people for Me..."

There is also a fifth verb that appears close afterwards in Exodus 6:8:

[5] ***v'heiveiti*** etkhem el haaretz	and I will bring you to the land...

A = respecting Creation; B = loyalty to primary relationship; C = limited access to sanctity/resources; D = duties of testimony/community; E = accepting one's place/status (with ties to land/future)

This fifth verb corresponds to a fifth cup that is poured at the Seder but over which no blessing is made, thereby marking the resolution to a controversy over the Talmudic text in *Pesachim* 18a. The version of the text we have today attributes to Rabbi Tarfon a reference to making a blessing over "the fourth cup" (which accords with the "four terms of redemption"). However, a number of respected authorities (going back 900 years!) report the reference in their text as being to "the fifth cup." The fifth cup is referred to as Elijah's Cup, because, according to Jewish tradition, the prophet Elijah will one day return to settle the controversy.[9]

As we shall now see, the five phrases align in order with the Shared Principles, thus suggesting the pattern in the terms of liberation.

1. In this first phrase above, the word *sivlot* [sufferings] suggests physical oppression, which reflects Principle A (Creation).
2. Principle B (Loyalty) comes with the word *me'avodatam* [from their bondage] in the second phrase signaling service [*avodah*] to a master other than God.
3. The word *sh'fatim* [judgments] in the third phrase calls to mind decisions by a court, notably monetary judgments, which involve resources and thus Principle C (Limits).
4. God taking an *am* [people] carries a communal theme in the fourth phrase consistent with Principle D (Community).
5. In the fifth phrase, the promise of being brought to the land coincides with Principle E (Acceptance) because living on the land is mentioned in the Fifth Commandment.

Such a correspondence actually builds on one made by several great commentators between the "four terms of redemption" and the liberation from three levels of oppression followed by the giving of the Torah.[10] The three levels of oppression were foretold by God to Abraham in the Covenant between the Parts in Genesis 15:13:

- First was the level of estrangement [*geirut*], with the Jewish

people labeled a disloyal population undeserving of resources available to others.
- Second came forced labor [*avdut*].
- Personal suffering [*inui*], as reflected in murdering male children, completed the three levels.

The liberation came in reverse:

- from *inui* first,
- from *avdut* second,
- and from *geirut* third.

This corresponds to the first three terms of redemption. The giving of the Torah ties to the fourth term, in which the Jewish people become God's *am*. Alignment of all five terms of redemption with the Shared Principles may hint at the history and future of the Jewish people.

iv. Test of Ambiguous Subdivision

In this test of the Subparts Claim, we check whether each Part in Exodus subdivides into Subparts aligned in order with the five Shared Principles. As noted with the Parts Claim earlier, a total examination requires so many details that will impede reasonable progress. We thus present here full details only for the subdivision of Part A, some details for Part B, and summaries for the rest; Section 16 gives further details. The underlined headings that list the Part to be subdivided come from Display 8.4 above.

Subdivision in Exodus of Part A 1:1–6:30: Oppression and Revelations

As shown in Display 8.5A, Part A of Exodus subdivides into five Subparts aligned in order with the Shared Principles. As noted following the display, the seven *parshiyot* in Part A progress smoothly according to the pattern, though the fifth one is not quite as clean a fit as the others. However, there is no substantial difficulty.

A = respecting Creation; B = loyalty to primary relationship; C = limited access to sanctity/resources; D = duties of testimony/community; E = accepting one's place/status (with ties to land/future)

DISPLAY 8.5A: Part A of Exodus Subdivided According to Shared Principles		
Subpart	Verses	Features Related to Shared Principle
A (Creation)	1:1–1:22	Oppression of Jewish people culminating in infanticide/ midwives' belief in God;
B (Loyalty)	2:1–2:22	Moses' father takes wife/ Moses born, brought to Pharaoh's court/ Moses kills Egyptian beating Jew, flees to Midian where he weds;
C (Limits)	2:23–4:17	Burning Bush revelation where Moses must remove shoes and where he asks for God's name;
D (Community)	4:18–6:9	Moses' return to Egypt as communal leader/ first approach to Pharaoh fails, with people's added task to gather straw for bricks;
E (Acceptance)	6:10–30	Moses attributes initial failure to his own unrefined lips.

Subpart A: In the Test of Alternate Partition above, we examined the opening *parshiyot* in Exodus. We found that the first *parshah* (1:1–7) provides context for the descent into Egypt and is not linked to any particular Shared Principle. However, the second (1:8–22) has the plot to kill male children at birth and the midwives' refusal to cooperate out of a fear of God, thus involving murder and belief in God, both tied to Principle A (Creation). These themes suggest assigning the first two *parshiyot* (together comprising verses 1:1–22) to Subpart A of Part A of Exodus.

Subpart B: the third *parshah* (2:1–22) of Exodus still involves themes of Principle A (Creation), e.g., Moses killing an Egyptian and Pharaoh's attempt to kill Moses. Because the *parshah* begins with the union of Moses' parents and ends with him marrying Zipporah, it also reflects Principle B (Loyalty). The shift to a new Subpart is also marked by the transition from the general situation in Subpart A to the situation of a single family, with its context of primary relationship. Thus the third *parshah* of Part A is identified with Subpart B consisting of verses 2:1–22.

Subpart C: Of greater length, the fourth *parshah* (2:23–4:17) of Exodus treats God's revelation to Moses at the Burning Bush. In recounting revelation, this *parshah* remains linked to Principle A (Creation). However, several obvious themes of Principle C (Limits) also appear. In particular, Moses must remove his shoes to retain access to revelation (3:5); there is a very strong concern with God's name (3:13–15); and Moses is given access to signs to gain the people's faith (4:1–9). This combination of Principles A and C identifies Subpart C of Part A as verses 2:23–4:17.

Subpart D: As the fifth *parshah* (4:18–26) of Exodus opens, we read of Moses' return to Egypt and communal duty (4:18). This purpose clearly suggests Principle D (Community) and signals a shift from the prior Subpart. The *parshah* next presents more Godly guidance for Moses' words to Pharaoh, which does not link as well to Principle D. Then comes Zipporah's saving Moses from God's wrath by circumcising their son (which Moses had failed to do). This event partly reflects Principle D (Community) through Zipporah's associated testimony. While Principle D is not found as robustly in this *parshah*, there is nonetheless a shift from Subpart C of Part A.

The sixth *parshah* (4:27–6:9) of Exodus follows with God's instructions to Aaron to meet his brother's return and to gather the people's elders. It then describes the first effort to have Pharaoh let the people leave for a three-day holiday to worship God. This effort is not only rejected, but also met by a decree that the straw required for making bricks will no longer be supplied. Further, the Jewish foremen are beaten when brick quotas are not met. While the decree could tie to access and hence Shared Principle C (Limits), the themes in this *parshah* relate mainly to communal activity in line with Principle D (Community). Thus Subpart D of Part A is viewed as verses 4:18–6:9 (including this *parshah* and the prior one).

Subpart E: In our earlier discussion of the points dividing Parts in Exodus, we identified *parshah* 6:10–30 as tied to Principle E (Acceptance)

A = respecting Creation; B = loyalty to primary relationship; C = limited access to sanctity/resources; D = duties of testimony/community; E = accepting one's place/status (with ties to land/future)

on account of Moses reflecting on his own lack of qualification for leadership. With this link, we have thus identified that *parshah* as Subpart E.

Subdivision in Exodus of Part B 7:1–18:27: Plagues and Splitting of Sea

As shown in Display 8.5B, Part B of Exodus subdivides into five Subparts aligned in order with the Shared Principles. As explained below, the only seeming issue is the clear presence of Principle C (Limits) within Subpart D of Part B, which might have weakened that alignment. However, Section 16 will show that Subpart D further subdivides into Segments aligned with the pattern, with the presence of Principle C reflecting Segment C of Subpart D. Thus the pattern passes the Test of Ambiguous Subdivision for Part B, just as it did for Part A.

DISPLAY 8.5B: Part B of Exodus Subdivided According to the Shared Principles		
Subpart	Verses	Features Related to Shared Principle
A (Creation)	7:1–7	Moses told that goal of plagues is making Egypt recognize God;
B (Loyalty)	7:8–10:29	First nine plagues asserting Jews' freedom from human masters;
C (Limits)	11:1–14:10	Laws of Passover with Tenth Plague in between/ firstborn sanctified;
D (Community)	14:11–17:16	Communal Exodus/ Splitting of Sea/ communal complaint/ war with Amalek;
E (Acceptance)	18:1–27	Judicial hierarchy set as proposed by Moses' father-in-law, Jethro.

Subpart A: As we also saw earlier in dividing Parts A and B, the first *parshah* in Part B (7:1–7) serves to introduce the plagues with the purpose of making "Egypt know that I am God" (7:5). Belief in God resides in the First Commandment and thus relates to Principle A (Creation). This *parshah* (Exodus 7:1–7) constitutes Subpart A of Part B of Exodus.

Subpart B: We come next in Exodus to the plagues themselves, with repeated demands by Moses of Pharaoh to "let my people go." Moses' clearly declares that God must be served instead of Pharaoh, thus reflecting Principle B (Loyalty). This means we have entered Subpart B of Part B. The plague narrative goes on through the Ninth Plague (Darkness) for a total of seven *parshiyot*. Subpart B of Part B of Exodus consists of Verses 7:8–10:29, comprising these seven *parshiyot*.

Subpart C: With Subpart A and Subpart B accounting together for eight *parshiyot*, we now begin the ninth *parshah* in Part B (11:1–12:20). That *parshah* records God's plan to bring one more plague (Slaying the Firstborn), with the Jewish people told to borrow the Egyptians' possessions (11:2). This access to resources reflects Principle C (Limits). The rest of the *parshah* focuses on God's instructions for Passover, the first in how to worship God (i.e., gain spiritual access), another sign of Principle C. With this thematic shift, we enter Subpart C of Part B of Exodus.

Next, the tenth *parshah* (12:21–36) of Part B opens with Moses' instructions for Passover to the elders, with the ban in 12:22 on leaving one's home that night (involving access). This link to Principle C is followed by the slaying of the firstborn and by final release of the Jewish people to serve God (again access), with further mention of taking Egyptian property (12:35–6). In giving more laws of Passover, the next three *parshiyot* also involve access, continuing in the fourteenth *parshah* (13:11–22) with redemption of the firstborn and denial of a direct route to Canaan.

It should be noted that throughout the six *parshiyot* since we entered Subpart C, Principle B (Loyalty) also plays a strong role through (1) freedom from human masters and (2) rejection of the Egyptian idolatry of sheep. Therefore, verses 11:1–13:22, which make up the ninth through fourteenth *parshiyot* of Part B in Exodus, are identified with Subpart C.

Subpart D: The fifteenth *parshah* of Part B (14:1–14) then shifts from themes related to Principle C to the impending war with Egypt, a

---

A = respecting Creation; B = loyalty to primary relationship; C = limited access to sanctity/resources; D = duties of testimony/community; E = accepting one's place/status (with ties to land/future)

communal theme related to Principle D, making it clear we have moved into Subpart D of Part B of Exodus. The theme of war, with the backdrop of liberation from slavery, continues in the next three *parshiyot*, the sixteenth through to the eighteenth in Part B, with the Splitting of the Sea, the drowning of the Egyptians, and the Song of the Sea.

This brings us to the nineteenth *parshah* (15:20–16:10) of Part B, which begins in the same vein as the Song of the Sea but shifts to communal travel from the site of battle. The text then reports a string of complaints from the people over water and food. The term "the entire assembly of the Children of Israel" occurs three times in this *parshah*, thus reinforcing Principle D (Community). (Principle C [Limits] is also suggested in the complaints over deprivation of access.) This link to Principle D through communal complaint shows up in next two *parshiyot* with other reinforcing themes (e.g., the Sabbath in 16:22–30). The twenty-second (17:8–13) and -third (17:14–16) *parshiyot* concern the battle with Amalek and God's instruction to write a remembrance (i.e., testimony) of the battle, which continue to reflect Principle D. Thus, Subpart D of Part B of Exodus spans the fifteenth through to the twenty-third *parshiyot*, comprising verses 14:1–17:16.

Subpart E: We saw earlier in dividing the Parts of Exodus that Subpart E of Part B is the *parshah* 18:1–27), which includes the judicial hierarchy.

Connection of Law to Surrounding Narrative

Part B in Exodus is the first Part in the Torah to combine narrative (regarding the plagues) with a substantial body of law (for Passover), which, as seen above, constitutes Subpart C of Part B. Recall that our first discussion of perceived textual disorder in the Torah (in Section 1) stressed the order challenge presented by seemingly abrupt joining of law to narrative. Thus Part B offers the first venue to confront this type of challenge with the Shared Principles.

How Subpart C fits within the Shared Principles is a vital point to stress. There are, of course, more legal subtexts to come, and how they fit with the pattern must also be tested. For now, though, consider how Source Critics view ritual (versus civil) law — as written by priests long after the narrative text to enhance their own power (see Section 13 for details).[11] Thus, the subtexts of ritual law, including those in Subpart C of Part B, would not be expected to fit any particular pattern with surrounding narrative.

Yet the ritual law in Subpart C of Part B *does* fit the surrounding narrative! We see that key elements of that narrative share with the Passover ritual a clear link to Principles B (Loyalty) and C (Limits). While rituals typically involve spiritual access (and Principle C), the Passover ritual specifically calls for abandoning idolatry (Principle B) in the focus on the sacrifice of sheep, a key Egyptian god. For its part, the surrounding narrative ties into Principle B in the Tenth Plague in freeing the Jewish people from enslavement, while touching on Principle C both in despoiling the Egyptians (who took their property) and in denial of direct access into Canaan.

Results of Test of Ambiguous Subdivision for Parts C, D, and E of Exodus

The remaining Parts of Exodus (Parts C, D, and E) are subdivided into Subparts in Section 16. In looking over those additional subdivisions, we find that the one for Part C works very smoothly. There are only six *parshiyot* in Part C, i.e., just one more than the minimum to subdivide into Subparts, and it is easy to see the alignment with the pattern and division points.

As for Parts D and E, alignment of each Subpart with its Shared Principle goes smoothly overall, but with less clarity in Subpart C of Part E (as explored more fully in Section 16). Also note that the respective Subparts B of Parts D and E describe the specifications and actual making of the priestly garments. Thus, to tie these Subparts to Principle B (Loyalty), we must view God and the priests as having a primary relationship in Tabernacle service. This view has a basis in the text, even if the primacy of that relationship is not as obvious as others we have seen (notably, between God and Man, between spouses, and between God and the Jewish people).

A = respecting Creation; B = loyalty to primary relationship; C = limited access to sanctity/resources; D = duties of testimony/community; E = accepting one's place/status (with ties to land/future)

Summary

With our overview of the results of the test of the Sections Claim, we may now summarize our findings concerning the Shared Principles in Exodus:

- The pattern withstood the Test of Alternate Partition in Exodus. A natural sequence of topics that seemingly did not align in order with the five Shared Principles was offered. Under careful scrutiny, this alternative partition resolved into a fivefold partition in such alignment, thereby representing the five Parts. The Parts Claim was thus upheld.
- The Test of Point Disparity compared our four division points between Parts with those of Rabbi Honigwachs. One pair of points was not close enough to match, while the other three pairs matched. The final outcome will require results from Leviticus and Numbers.
- The five terms of redemption in Exodus 6:6–8, and thus the four cups at the Passover Seder, plus the fifth cup for Elijah, align with the Shared Principles. This correspondence may hint at the history and future of the Jewish people.
- The pattern withstood the Test of Ambiguous Subdivision. For each of the five Parts, all had Subparts that divided in ordered alignment with the Shared Principles. Within individual Parts, nearly all *parshiyot* directly fit the appropriate Subpart for progression through the pattern, with the only possible problem in Subpart C of Part E. Thus, the Subparts Claim was upheld.

SECTION 9
Testing the Pattern in Leviticus

As in Exodus, we will test the pattern in Leviticus using the three-pronged strategy described in Section 7, with discussion of a special case before the third test. Our overall approach will thus follow the following steps:

1. the Test of Alternate Partition, which proposes a sequence of topics that conflicts with the pattern in regards to Parts;
2. the Test of Point Disparity, which compares our division points for Parts with those of Rabbi Honigwachs;
3. the case of a passage that seems to support Source Criticism; and
4. the Test of Ambiguous Subdivision, which challenges the pattern to progress through Subparts with more layers of themes and without the technique to divide Parts.

i. Test of Alternate Partition

Before choosing a sequence of topics (that seems not to align with the Shared Principles), let us weigh a vital factor that guides that choice. Clearly, Leviticus opens with the subject of *korbanot* [offerings] — also referred to as "sacrifices." Because the singular form *korban* means literally "coming close (to God)," the beginning of Leviticus clearly links with Principle A (Creation). In fact, we find *korbanot* mentioned throughout the first fourteen chapters of Leviticus.

We find immediately thereafter, in Chapters 15–18, laws dealing with sexual matters and atonement (which means restoring a primary

---

A = respecting Creation; B = loyalty to primary relationship; C = limited access to sanctity/resources;
D = duties of testimony/community; E = accepting one's place/status (with ties to land/future)

relationship), which are both themes relating to Shared Principle B (Loyalty). Thus, if we take our first two topics as the first fourteen chapters followed by the next four, we would already build in the alignment of Principles A and B.

Then, since Chapters 19–22 can be connected to spiritual access (through the repeated imprimatur of God's Name), those chapters would then link to Principle C (Limits). After that, as we shall soon see, the remainder of the book can be partitioned into subtexts corresponding to Principles D (Community) and E (Acceptance), respectively. Conveniently for the pattern, this approach would yield the Shared Principles in order — but it would also be fundamentally flawed.

The flaw in the approach lies in associating the first fourteen chapters with Principle A purely through the presence of *korbanot* in those chapters. As a matter of fact, Chapters 15–17 (though not 18) continue to mention offerings, even though they feature themes of Principle B. Thus, to end the first topic just before Chapter 15 creates an arbitrary alignment with the pattern. Furthermore, while the early portions of the first fourteen chapters do focus on sacrifices, the latter portions of those chapters also feature other substantial topics (notably, the dietary laws in Chapter 11 and the laws of biblical leprosy in Chapters 13–14).

In seeking to check the validity of the pattern rigorously (and not let it off without a challenge), I was led to view sacrifice as the key theme only in the first seven chapters, where other topics were not so apparent. Yes, that would still put Principle A (Creation) at the beginning (aligning there with the pattern). However, for Chapters 8–12, with their topics of sacrificial ritual, the strange fire brought by Aaron's sons, and the dietary laws, I could link those chapters to Principle C (Limits) rather than A. That link would conflict with the pattern, since Principle B (Loyalty) goes second in the Shared Principles, and not Principle C. Also, Chapters 13–14 can link to Principle D (Community) through the leper's separation from the camp.

This approach led to the alternate partition below showing tentative assignment of Shared Principles, with Principles A, C, and D assigned respectively to the first three topics in Leviticus. Again, chapter ranges for the topics are identified using the symbol "~" to mean approximately.

DISPLAY 9: Alternative Partition of Leviticus into Sequence of Topics		
1. Description of sacrifices	~Chapters 1–7	A (Creation)
2. Consecration, strange fire, dietary law, childbirth	~Chapters 8–12	C (Limits)
3. Biblical leprosy — separation from camp	~Chapters 13–14	D (Community)
4. Sexual matters and atonement	~Chapters 15–18	B (Loyalty)
5. Laws associated with holiness	~Chapters 19–22	C (Limits)
6. Sabbath, holidays, release years	~Chapters 23–25	D (Community)
7. Blessings and curses for future	~Chapters 26–27	E (Acceptance)

Let us briefly review the tentative assignments of Shared Principles for each topic above.

1. Assigning the first topic to Principle A (Creation) makes sense because the Hebrew word *korban* is rooted in "coming close" (to God).
2. The themes within the second topic (e.g., strange fire brought by Aaron's sons, conditions on woman after giving birth) involve limited access and link to Principle C (Limits).
3. Lepers in the third topic must leave the camp, signaling Principle D (Community).
4. Principle B (Loyalty) clearly goes with sexual matters and atonement in the fourth topic.
5. The fifth topic ranges over diverse laws, many punctuated with the declaration "I am God." This association with holiness (access to sanctity) calls for Principle C (Limits).
6. In the sixth topic, the Sabbath (as focus of the Fourth Commandment) and holidays (as times of assembly) signal Principle D (Community). The Sabbatical and Jubilee years also testify to God providing enough produce in prior years when planting and harvesting are allowed.
7. The blessings and curses in the seventh topic state results of future

A = respecting Creation; B = loyalty to primary relationship; C = limited access to sanctity/resources; D = duties of testimony/community; E = accepting one's place/status (with ties to land/future)

actions by the Jewish people, thus setting, in line with Principle E (Acceptance), the conditions to be accepted.

Focus on the First Three Topics

Note that the last four topics of the alternate partition (the fourth through the seventh) are assigned the sequence of Principles B-C-D-E, so those topics would align with the pattern. Thus, we need to focus on the first fourteen chapters of Leviticus that make up the first three topics if this partition is to undermine the Shared Principles. To begin, let us restate those three topics:

1. Description of sacrifices	~Chapters 1–7	A (Creation)
2. Consecration, strange fire, dietary law, childbirth	~Chapters 8–12	C (Limits)
3. Leprosy — separation from camp	~Chapters 13–14	D (Community)

Because the fourth topic (sexual matters and atonement) links to Principle B (Loyalty), the sequence of Principles for the first four topics would seem to be A - C - D - B, which violates the pattern. And if this sequence holds up under further scrutiny, we will have found an expected failure in the order of the Shared Principles. Remember that the unified structure we are discussing in the Bible is largely based on the order of the recurring themes, not just their existence.

In fact, since the fourth topic is so clearly linked to Principle B, the pattern could be restored only should we find an actual sequence of A - B - C - D - E, where we now have A - C - D. Finding that fivefold sequence would mean identifying both

- another topic linked to Principle B (Loyalty) "between" the first two topics (i.e., in a subtext at the end of first topic and/or at the start of the second topic); and
- another topic linked to Principle E (Acceptance) at the end of the third topic.

Only in that event, which seemed highly unlikely, would we convert the three topics now aligned with A - C - D into a proper sequence of all five topics in order, so that together they could comprise five Subparts of Part A. That conversion would make Part A the first fourteen chapters of Leviticus.

This conversion of the first three topics into a sequence of topics aligned in order with the pattern would amount to a validation of the Subparts Claim for those first fourteen chapters. In other words, those chapters would be identified as Part A and withstand the Test of Ambiguous Subdivision, showing a subdivision into five Subparts. Thus, to see whether those chapters somehow comprise Part A, we temporarily skip ahead to the Test of Ambiguous Subdivision for Part A.

Are There Five Subparts in the First Fourteen Chapters?

Leviticus opens with various sacrifices and how they are offered. This is why Principle A (Creation) is assigned to Chapters 1–7. Our initial sense of the shift afterwards to Principle C (Limits) focused on the key event of a "strange fire" brought in consecrating the Tabernacle. Yet, the fire comes in the last seven verses of a single *parshah* (8:1–10:7) whose first sixty verses describe the consecration, which begins by dedicating the priests in Chapter 8. This priestly dedication and references to "atonement" in their offerings in Chapter 9 reflect a special relationship with God and thus Principle B (Loyalty). Even though "strange fire" signals improper access and Principle C (Limits), the word *zarah* [strange] in 10:1 also signals violation of the sons' priestly relationship.[12] Thus this *parshah* presents clear themes linked to Principle B (Loyalty).

The next *parshah* (10:8–11) bars priests from serving under certain conditions, even after the consecration, thus marking a shift to Principle C (Limits). The rest of Chapter 10 mostly concerns priestly access to offerings after losing a relative, with implicit reference to the deaths of Aaron's two sons in bringing the fire. Chapters 11 and 12 relate

---

A = respecting Creation; B = loyalty to primary relationship; C = limited access to sanctity/resources; D = duties of testimony/community; E = accepting one's place/status (with ties to land/future)

respectively to the Principle C themes of dietary law and restrictions on women after childbirth, with no mention of priests or consecration to suggest Principle B (Loyalty).

This brings us to Chapters 13–14 and the topic of Biblical leprosy requiring separation from the camp, with its link to Principle D (Community). We should note that the Talmud (in *Arachin* 15b) states that one afflicted with Biblical leprosy has spoken about others, with such speech suggesting testimony. This Talmudic explanation reinforces the link to Principle D. Thus the first fourteen chapters of Leviticus have generated a sequence so far of four topics:

(a) Description of sacrifices	Principle A (Creation)
(b) Consecration, strange fire of Aaron's sons	Principle B (Loyalty)
(c) Eligibility of priests, dietary laws, restrictions after childbirth	Principle C (Limits)
(d) Biblical leprosy	Principle D (Community)

But this sequence aligns in order with the first four Shared Principles only.

I thought I had caught a flaw in the pattern here with the absence of anything closing the topic of leprosy (which extends through the end of Chapter 14) tied to Principle E (Acceptance). Clearly, the beginning of next chapter does not suggest Principle E because Chapter 15 launches at once into nocturnal (sexual) emissions, tied only to Principle B (Loyalty). The absence of a Principle E theme would contradict full subdivision of the alleged Part A made up of the first fourteen chapters of Leviticus. This contradiction would then cause Leviticus to fail the Test of Alternate Partition, since our alternate partition would not resolve into five Parts aligning with the pattern.

Yet, upon more careful examination of Chapter 14, I realized that it ends with a *parshah* (14:33–57) dealing with a form of leprosy unrelated to Principle D (Community). It actually deals with what might be called leprous houses, i.e., houses whose walls become discolored on their own, a condition not causing separation from the camp. Because this subject is introduced in 14:34 with the phrase "when you come into the land...", the themes of future and land are invoked. These themes connect closely with Principle E (Acceptance).

With the first fourteen chapters of Leviticus now subdivided into five Subparts, these chapters form Part A. That means that the first three original topics in the alternate partition — description of sacrifices, consecration with strange fire, priestly eligibility, dietary law, childbirth; and Biblical leprosy — will have been combined into Part A. Recall that the rest of Leviticus (Chapters 15–27) was already seen in the alternate partition to align in order with the last four Shared Principles as B-C-D-E. Thus the alternate partition has resolved fully into five parts following the pattern. This resolution is shown below.

DISPLAY 9.1: Revised Partition of Leviticus (with Assignment of Shared Principles)		
1. Types of sacrifices, consecration and strange fire/ restrictions on service by priests, diet, and childbearing women/ Biblical leprosy	~Chapters 1–14	A (Creation)
2. Sexual matters and atonement	~Chapters 15–18	B (Loyalty)
3. Laws associated with holiness	~Chapters 19–22	C (Limits)
4. Sabbath, holidays, and years of release (Jubilee)	~Chapters 23–25	D (Community)
5. Blessings and curses for future	~Chapters 26–27	E (Acceptance)

Though I now had to accept the Parts Claim, I remained troubled that the first fourteen chapters could not be uniquely associated with sacrifices, since the next three chapters also deal with sacrifices. This

---

A = respecting Creation; B = loyalty to primary relationship; C = limited access to sanctity/resources; D = duties of testimony/community; E = accepting one's place/status (with ties to land/future)

situation led to a discursive description of the first topic above in re-stating the revised partition in Display 9.1.

ii. Test of Point Disparity

As in Exodus, this test proceeds in two steps. First, we must identify the endpoints of each Part, after which the text shifts to the next Part. (Again note that these division points [between successive Parts] may vary slightly from the approximate chapter ranges given above in Display 9.1.) In the second step, we compare these division points with those named by Rabbi Honigwachs in *The Unity of Torah* (pages 78–79) to evaluate the fit.

a. Identifying Division Points Between Successive Parts

Because the end of Part E corresponds to the end of the Book, we need only identify four division points: between Parts A and B, between Parts B and C, between Parts C and D, and between Parts D and E. Note that the descriptions of the Parts below come from Display 9.1.

Division Point in Leviticus between Part A and Part B

Part A = types of sacrifices, consecration with strange fire; restrictions on service by priests, diet, and childbearing women; leprosy;

Part B = sexual matters and atonement.

As explained in Section 7, we seek a *p'tuchah* between the topics where a shift occurs from Principle E (Acceptance) to Principle A (Creation). This will mark the end of Subpart E of Part A and the beginning of Subpart A of Part B, and thus the division point between Part A and Part B. Such a shift does occur after Leviticus 14:57 in line with the leprosy of houses in *parshah* 14:33–57, which we saw touches Principle E in its reference to the land.

> **Division Point in Leviticus between Part B and Part C**
>
> Part B = sexual matters and atonement;
>
> Part C = laws associated with holiness.

Clearly, we have already left Part B by the beginning of Chapter 17, which deals with improper slaughtering (reflecting bloodshed) and the need to cover the blood of a slaughtered animal. These laws fit Principle A (Creation), but Principle C (Limits) also emerges in barring consumption of blood.

From 15:1 (the beginning of Part B) until the beginning of Chapter 17, there are exactly three *p'tuchot*: after 15:18, 15:33, and 16:34 respectively. This tells us that Part B consists of just three *parshiyot*, which makes it impossible to subdivide Part B into five Sections. Thus we cannot expect a theme of Principle E (Acceptance) to end Part B. Fortunately, the *parshah* that concludes Chapter 16 concerns atonement, so 17:1 must be the beginning of Part C, making 16:34 the end of Part B.

> **Division Point between Part C and Part D**
>
> Part C = laws associated with holiness;
>
> Part D = Sabbath, holidays, release years (Sabbatical and Jubilee).

Unlike the situation with Part B (which contains only three *parshiyot*), there seem to be enough *parshiyot* in Part C to seek its end in a theme connected with Principle E (Acceptance). Indeed, we do find such a theme in *parshah* 21:1–24, which discusses the special status of priests relative to the burial of relatives and to fitness for service in the Tabernacle. And because the next *parshah* (which begins with 22:1) involves contact with the dead in disqualifying a sacrifice, we have found a theme suggesting Principle A (Creation). Thus, Part C ends after 21:24.

> A = respecting Creation; B = loyalty to primary relationship; C = limited access to sanctity/resources; D = duties of testimony/community; E = accepting one's place/status (with ties to land/future)

> **Division Point between Part D and Part E**
>
> Part D = Sabbath, holidays, release years (Sabbatical and Jubilee);
>
> Part E = blessings and curses for future.

Just as we looked for a theme of Principle E (Acceptance) to close Part C, so too we look for such a theme to close Part D. In *parshah* 25:1–26:2, we find several such themes. We have the years of release, the Sabbatical and the Jubilee, every seventh and every fiftieth year respectively. These years directly involve the land of Canaan in barring agricultural activity at those times. In addition, we find the valuation of slaves, which also relates to Principle E (Acceptance) in the sense of accepting one's place.

However, as we seek a theme of Principle A (Acceptance) to mark the end of Part D, we realize that the remainder of the Book, i.e., 26:3–27:34 consists of only three *parshiyot* — not enough to be subdivided into Sections. That means we cannot expect to find a Subpart corresponding to Shared Principle A that would normally begin Part E. Because the remainder of the Book deals with blessings and curses for the future, the Shared Principle suggested by this remainder is E. Thus we could say that this remainder is not Part E, but rather a continuation of Subpart E of Part D.

If we do link blessings and curses for the future to the preceding sub-text on release years and valuation of slaves, we would create a Subpart E (25:1–27:34) within Part D. That would mean there is no Part E in Leviticus, which would fundamentally undermine the pattern! Still, I had to admit to having already offered blessings and curses for the future as the last major topic in Leviticus, and thus kept the identification of blessings and curses with Part E.

For this reason, I could not declare real defeat of the Parts Claim. The pattern had, in fact, passed the Test of Alternate Partition in Leviticus. At the same time, I could describe the pattern as less than perfectly confirmed here, a fact worth noting in the concluding evaluation in Section 11. Moreover, by placing the division point between Parts D and E after 26:2 (as shown below), it was still possible that this division point would not match that of Rabbi Honigwachs.

DISPLAY 9.2: Parts of Leviticus and their Endpoints		
Part	Verses	General Description
A (Creation)	1:1–14:57	Types of sacrifices, consecration and strange fire/ restrictions on service by priests, diet, childbearing women/ Biblical leprosy;
B (Loyalty)	15:1–16:34	Sexual matters and atonement;
C (Limits)	17:1–21:24	Laws associated with holiness;
D (Community)	22:1–26:2	Sabbath, holidays, release years (Sabbatical, Jubilee);
E (Acceptance)	26:3–27:34	Blessings and curses for future.

b. *Comparing Points of Division for Parts with those of Rabbi Honigwachs*

In comparing respective points of division for Parts, recall from Section 7 that we will consider such points matching if and only if they are no more than two *p'tuchot* apart. (Note that the distance in *p'tuchot* between respective points can be counted from Appendix a.)

DISPLAY 9.3: Comparison of Respective Points of Division in Leviticus			
Successive Parts to be divided	Last verse before division Mine	Last verse before division Rabbi Honigwachs'	Distance in *p'tuchot*
Parts A and B	14:57	15:33	1

A = respecting Creation; B = loyalty to primary relationship; C = limited access to sanctity/resources; D = duties of testimony/community; E = accepting one's place/status (with ties to land/future)

Parts B and C	16:34	16:34	0
Parts C and D	21:24	21:24	0
Parts D and E	26:2	26:46	2

As Display 9.3 makes plain, each of our division points between Parts differs from the respective point of Rabbi Honigwachs by no more than two *p'tuchot*. Because this distance is within the tolerance for points to match, the pattern withstands the test of overall fit in Leviticus. The division between Parts D and E bears special explanation for the difference in our respective points. Rabbi Honigwachs placed his point of division just before the standard opening ("And the Lord spoke to Moses saying") where he begins Part E. His placement follows his convention to set division points at the first of a sequence of standard openings. In contrast, I began Part E at the beginning of the blessings and curses, where a standard opening does not occur.

iii. A Passage Seeming — At First — to Support Source Criticism

Early on, we spoke of a particular assumption on which Source Criticism depends — that cultural structures become more complex with time. This assumption leads to Source Critics' claim that the text for simple forms of worship emerged before the text for more complex forms.[13] In Section 1, we clearly saw the falsity of this assumption shown in the field of language, where for example contemporary English is less complex than its predecessor Anglo-Saxon. Nonetheless, Source Critics hold to their conclusion as it applied to time order of different ritual passages in the Torah. (See Section 12 for further analysis of that conclusion.)

Despite the problems with Source Criticism in this regard, there is a passage in Leviticus that, on its face, seems to give credence to a "time order" for ritual texts based on complexity. In fact, the verse in question (26:1) relates to dividing Parts D and E. The verse presents the prohibition of erecting a *matzeivah* [single stone pillar for worship] and refers to "on your land," thus serving as evidence of a Principle E (Acceptance) theme at the end of Part D.

This prohibition of a single stone pillar seems, at first, to confirm Source Critics' beliefs about religious practice increasing in complexity over time. After all, the single stone pillar was a simple form of spiritual testament, whose prior (accepted) use was recorded by the Torah itself. In particular, Jacob built a *matzeivah* in Genesis 28:18, while the Jewish people built twelve of them in Exodus 24:4. Yet, here in Leviticus 26:1, after the completion of the Tabernacle (in all its complexity), the simple *matzeivah* is no longer permitted! Does this mean the Jewish people were meant to have "graduated" to more complex worship?

But listen to what Ramban had to say about 26:1. In his times he did not have to contend with the Documentary Hypothesis and Source Critics, but he still found the reversal of past practice to demand an explanation. He began by citing the nearby preceding verses (see especially 25:47) that speak of a Jew who sells himself as a slave to an alien until the Jubilee year. In light of these verses, Ramban viewed the forbidden pillar of 26:1 being put together with the graven image and the prostration stone of the same verse as those of an alien living in Canaan. Ramban understood that a Jew purchased by an idolatrous household may be especially prone to emulate the mores of his master, which the Torah comes to prohibit at this point.

In other words, with the Ramban's approach, we still have the banning of the simpler *matzeivah*, but not because of its simplicity. Rather, the *matzeivah* is now banned (after the giving of the Torah) as having been embraced in Canaan's idolatry. Indeed, perhaps because the *matzeivah* was familiar to the Jewish people, it would prove alluring to the alien's Jewish slave.

Moreover, we can see a connection to the Shared Principles in 26:1 that fits well with Ramban's approach. Our verse appears at Part D's

---

A = respecting Creation; B = loyalty to primary relationship; C = limited access to sanctity/resources; D = duties of testimony/community; E = accepting one's place/status (with ties to land/future)

end, where we find Principle E (Acceptance). While idolatry suggests Principle B (Loyalty), the issue here is a Jewish slave who may not seek idolatry per se, but simply wants to be comfortable with his alien master. Such a slave may be drawn to the *matzeivah* if he does not accept his place as a Jew. This understanding explains why Leviticus 26:1 need not be viewed as supporting an assumption of Source Criticism.

iv. Test of Ambiguous Subdivision

Of the five Parts in Leviticus, two Parts lack enough *parshiyot* [paragraphs] to subdivide into Subparts; Part B has two *parshiyot*, and Part E three. Thus, we need only apply the Test of Ambiguous Subdivision to the other three Parts. In fact, we have actually applied this test for Part A in the course of the Test of Alternate Partition. For that reason, we only briefly revisit the Part A subdivision before moving on to the subdivisions for Parts C and D.

DISPLAY 9.4: Part A of Leviticus Subdivided According to the Shared Principles

Subpart	Verses	Features Related to Shared Principle
A (Creation)	1:1–7:38	Types of sacrifices
B (Loyalty)	8:1–10:7	Consecration and strange fire
C (Limits)	10:8–12:8	Restrictions on service by priests, diet, and childbearing women
D (Community)	13:1–14:32	Biblical leprosy, which requires separation from camp
E (Acceptance)	14:33–14:57	"Leprous" houses that will be found in Canaan

This subdivision of Part A aligns well with the Shared Principles, but one point regarding Subpart B bears repeating. If we look at that Subpart's second subject (two of Aaron's sons bringing a strange fire and dying) with no other information, we might assign it to Subpart C, as it is more related to Principle C as a violation of limited spiritual access than B (Loyalty). However, Subpart B consists of a single *parshah*, and we cannot separate the strange fire from the first and much lengthier topic (consecration), which clearly goes with Principle B. A single *parshah* must remain intact because the *Midrash Rabbah* on Song of Songs (5:14) speaks of what is between the Commandments ordering the *parshiyot* [paragraphs], and not subparagraphs. In addition, the adjective *zarah* [strange] used to describe the fire comes from the same root as *zar* [non-priest], thus implying the strange fire violated the priests' special relationship with God (Principle B).

Subdivision in Leviticus of Part C 17:1–21:24: Laws Associated with Holiness.

Part C contains six *parshiyot*, just enough to allow its subdivision into Subparts. Display 9.4 repeats the breakdown of Part C originally provided in Section 4, with more details provided following the display to explain the alignment with the Shared Principles.

DISPLAY 9.5: Part C of Leviticus Subdivided According to the Shared Principles

Subpart	Verses	Features Related to Shared Principle
A (Creation)	17:1– 17:16	Eating blood forbidden/ duty to cover blood of dead animal
B (Loyalty)	18:1– 18:30	Listing of illicit sexual relations that result in expulsion of inhabitants of Canaan
C (Limits)	19:1– 19:37	Diverse laws often followed by the phrase "I am God" or "I am the Lord, your God," ending in rule of fair weights and measures
D (Community)	20:1– 20:27	Punishments carried out by communal judicial system for idolatry and illicit sexual unions
E (Acceptance)	21:1– 21:24	Special rules for priests involving burial of relatives, marriage, and physical fitness for service in the Tabernacle.

A = respecting Creation; B = loyalty to primary relationship; C = limited access to sanctity/resources; D = duties of testimony/community; E = accepting one's place/status (with ties to land/future)

In analyzing this subdivision, several points should be mentioned in aligning the Subparts of Part C of Leviticus in order with the Shared Principles:

Subpart A: This Subpart consists of only one *parshah* (17:1–16), which, in its focus on blood, reflects a concern with the sanctity of life that is consistent with Principle A (Creation).

Subpart B: In treating forbidden sexual relations, the single *parshah* of Subpart B (Leviticus 18:1–30) clearly fits Principle B (Loyalty).

Subpart C: The two legal *parshiyot* that make up Subpart C (Leviticus 19:1–37) begin with the dictum "you shall be holy" (19:2). Because spiritual access requires holiness, this language signals, at least on its face, a shift to Principle C (Limits) with a new Subpart.[14] Moreover, the frequent refrain (sixteen times in thirty-seven verses of the two *parshiyot*) of "I am the Lord" and "I am the Lord, your God" connects the laws here with God's name. It is as if to say that violating these laws takes His name in vain, thereby signaling Principle C, as well.

Despite these strong indicators of Principle C, other factors emerge. First, the dictum "you shall be holy" may be interpreted as demanding sexual purity and Principle B (Loyalty).[15] If that interpretation were made, this dictum would signal no shift from Subpart B. Also, the frequent refrain may be read as not connecting with God's name, but rather with belief in God (as in the First Commandment). While these and other issues are explored more fully in Section 14, one rationale still allows comfort in the link to Principle C. This Subpart presents a wide range of law touching many Shared Principles. Taken broadly, law sets limits, and with such a wide range of law, the main thing the individual laws share is that very character. On balance, these two *parshiyot* fit Principle C (Limits), but the fit is not yet as clear as with other Subparts.

Subpart D: The previous Subpart focused on laws with scant regard for punishment. In contrast, the single *parshah* (20:1–27) of this Subpart focuses on punishment, specifically for idolatry and sexual impropriety, and the shift is obvious. The first punishment mentioned (see 20:2) is communal — stoning of someone who sacrifices his children in Molech worship. Then, if the people fail to carry out this punishment, God will cut the perpetrator and his family off from the people (see 20:5). This retribution is understood as an early death that ends the bloodline in the community. Indeed, the primary punishments throughout this *parshah* are (communal) execution and being cut off by God from the people, both reflecting Principle D (Community).

Still, both idolatry and sexual impropriety suggest Principle B (Loyalty), and one might question linking them in this *parshah* to Principle D. The text itself provides a link, especially in 20:23–24. According to those verses, the then-residents of Canaan practiced this forbidden behavior, which would lead to their expulsion and replacement by the Jewish people. Further, the Jewish people merit God separating them from other peoples by dint of refraining from this behavior. With that understanding, Subpart D aligns quite well with the pattern.

Subpart E: This Subpart, the single *parshah* (21:1–24), gives special requirements for priests in burial of relatives, in marriage, and in fitness for service. Clearly shifting from the prior Subpart focused on punishments. These requirements touch on respect for parents (in burial) and on certain priestly roles. Thus this *parshah* strongly suggests Principle E (Acceptance).

In sum, Part C can be subdivided into five Subparts. Each of the shifts is plain, and each Subpart fits its respective Shared Principle, though the fit for Subpart C requires further attention.

Subdivision in Leviticus of Part D 22:1–26:2: Sabbath, Holidays, Release Years

The subdivision for Part D, which consists of eleven *parshiyot*, is shown below.

A = respecting Creation; B = loyalty to primary relationship; C = limited access to sanctity/resources; D = duties of testimony/community; E = accepting one's place/status (with ties to land/future)

DISPLAY 9.6: Part D of Leviticus Subdivided According to the Shared Principles

Subpart	Verses	Features Related to Shared Principle
A (Creation)	22:1–22:16	Sacrifices disqualified by contact with death, other ritual impurity
B (Loyalty)	22:17–22:33	Other sacrifices disqualified as violating relationship with God
C (Limits)	23:1–24:12	Sabbath, holidays as calls to holiness/ God's name cursed
D (Community)	24:13–24:33	Blasphemer taken outside camp for communal stoning
E (Acceptance)	25:1–26:2	Effect of Sabbatical, Jubilee on land/ redeeming slaves/ valuation

Just as we analyzed the subdivisions of Parts A and C, let us now elaborate on the alignment of the Subparts of Part D in order with the Shared Principles:

Subpart A: This single *parshah* (22:1–16) suggests Principle A (Creation) through several references to death. Actually, the *parshah* bans impurity [*tuma*] from sanctified areas, with such impurity due to several causes — not just contact with the dead. Yet contact with the dead brings the strongest form of impurity, so the fit with Principle A seems reasonable.

Subpart B: The focus in this single *parshah* (22:17–33) shifts from Subpart A with people who cannot enter sanctified areas to sacrifices that cannot be offered (for reasons other than impurity). While the shift is plain, linking Subpart B to Principle B (Loyalty) takes some thought. That link treats the offering of unsuitable sacrifices as violating the relationship with God — like the "strange fire" brought by Aaron's sons in Subpart B of Part A. A further theme tied to Principle B comes in barring slaughter of animals within a week of birth and along with their mothers (22:22–28). Thus the mother-offspring relationship cannot be destroyed at will.

At the same time, we need to consider Principle C (Limits) for this Subpart, since forbidding sacrifices of blemished animals could be seen as limiting access. In fact, we raised this very issue regarding the strange fire of Aaron's sons. In that case, however, the link to Principle B was promoted by the earlier content of Subpart B of Part C in its single *parshah*. That initial content is the priestly element of consecration, clearly suggesting Principle B.

While we also have a single *parshah* here, no other subject in it so closely fits Principle B (Loyalty). Yet, the term *l'ratzon* [to find favor] found in 22:21 and in variant forms in 22:25 and 22:29 does seem more suited to Principle B than to Principle C (Limits). In other words, proper animals must be brought to find favor (and strengthen the relationship) with God. In the end, Principle B proves the most logical choice.

Subpart C: This Subpart (23:1–24:12) occupies seven *parshiyot*, the only Subpart in Part D with more than one. Its predominant subject matter of the Sabbath and holidays plainly suggests Principle C (Limits), in its repeated use (eight times) of the term *mikrah kodesh* [call to holiness] and its variants for such times of observance. The shift is also clear: this terminology occurs in each of the first five *parshiyot* of Subpart C applied collectively and individually to the Sabbath and each holiday.

The sixth and seventh *parshiyot* extend the link to Principle C. The sixth *parshah* (24:1–4) specifies the oil for the continual lamp, while the seventh (24:5–12) sets rules for the showbread and then reports a case of blasphemy. Note that these two topics in the last *parshah* (in two subparagraphs) would seem unconnected without the link to the same Shared Principle.

Subpart D: A single *parshah*, this Subpart (24:13–23) continues the account of the blasphemer but focuses on his punishment, stoning by *col ha-edah* [the entire assembly]. In its linguistic linkage to *edut* [testimony], the term *edah* strongly suggests Principle D (Community). This link is supported in 24:13 by having the witnesses place their hands on the perpetrator before execution. Further, the text takes pains to state that *edah* covers both the native and the convert (24:16 and 24:22).

A = respecting Creation; B = loyalty to primary relationship; C = limited access to sanctity/resources; D = duties of testimony/community; E = accepting one's place/status (with ties to land/future)

The only thing lacking full clarity is the shift from the prior Subpart (which ended with the actual act of blasphemy). However, the early use of *edah* (in 24:14) sends a strong signal, especially as a term used only infrequently before the Book of Numbers.

Subpart E: Another single *parshah* (25:1–26:2), this Subpart gives the laws of Sabbatical and Jubilee years and of monetary valuation of individuals. The Sabbatical year requires (1) abstinence from planting and harvesting and (2) the release of slaves. In addition, the Jubilee year adds the return of land to the family of the original owner. In the concern with land and the status of individuals (free vs. slave), these laws clearly shift from Subpart D and reflect Principle E (Acceptance). Monetary valuation of individuals extends this linkage.

Review of the Test of Ambiguous Subdivision

We can now review the results of this test in Leviticus for the three Parts capable of subdivision into Subparts:

- Part A subdivides cleanly into five Subparts. The only complication involves the relatively diffuse nature of Subpart A, but the alignment works smoothly.
- Part C subdivides cleanly into five Subparts. While assignment of Principle C (Limits) to Subpart C raises a few issues, there is sufficient rationale for the assignment.
- Part D subdivides cleanly into five Subparts with only minor questions.

Summary

With this review of the results of the Test of Ambiguous Subdivision now complete, we may summarize our findings in Leviticus:

1. The pattern withstood the Test of Alternate Partition. The proposed alternative partition (in violation of the pattern) resolved into a five-fold partition in ordered alignment with the Shared Principles. This resolution constituted a division into five Parts, thus upholding the Parts Claim. Another configuration lacking Part E could be created,

but it would ignore the concluding blessings and curses as a natural topic.
2. The Test of Point Disparity passed by matching our four division points between Parts against those of Rabbi Honigwachs.
3. The Shared Principles help explain why Leviticus 26:1 need not support the assumption by Source Critics that religious ritual increases in complexity over time.
4. The pattern withstood the Test of Ambiguous Subdivision. Each of the three Parts in Leviticus with five or more *parshiyot* subdivided into five Subparts aligned in order with the Shared Principles. Thus the Subparts Claim was also upheld. Only in one Subpart was there any issue, and the rationale for the alignment was still adequate.

A = respecting Creation; B = loyalty to primary relationship; C = limited access to sanctity/resources; D = duties of testimony/community; E = accepting one's place/status (with ties to land/future)

Section 10

Testing the Pattern in Numbers

Once again, we follow the three-pronged strategy described in Section 7 to test the pattern and provide a special case connected to the tests. Specifically, we proceed through four steps:

1. the Test of Alternate Partition, which proposes a sequence of topics that conflicts with the pattern in regards to Parts;
2. the Test of Point Disparity, which compares our division points for Parts with those of Rabbi Honigwachs;
3. an oddity in Numbers promoting the common perception of the book's disorder; and
4. the Test of Ambiguous Subdivision, which challenges the pattern to progress through Subparts with more layers of themes and without the technique to divide Parts.

A summary will conclude these steps.

i. Test of Alternate Partition

In the Introduction, we highlighted the scholar Martin Noth's comment on the character of Numbers: "There can be no question of… its originating from the hand of a single author. This is already clear from the confusion and lack of order in its contents."[16] Despite this evaluation, two features of Numbers suggest a discernible, though only partial, organization:

- the two large backwards Hebrew letters (each a *nun*) at the end of Chapter 10, which, according to Jewish tradition, divide the earlier text from the transgressions in Chapters 11–18;[17]
- the Red Heifer subtext (Chapter 19) signaling, without any other

marker, the passage of thirty-eight years in the Wilderness to the period of war in the final approach to Canaan.

The break ending Chapter 10 and the subtext of Chapter 19 thus partition Numbers into four components:

- From the beginning through Chapter 10. This component covers the community's count/structure, access issues, Tabernacle dedication, and assembly/movement.
- Chapters 11–18, which report a series of major transgressions.
- Chapter 19, the Red Heifer legal subtext on purifying those touching the dead.
- Chapters 20–36 on wars, inheritance, leadership change, and land borders.

We now move from these four components to a credible alternate partition to test the pattern. Since these components already reflect a natural partition, a credible partition should retain the division points from these components, which means any further topics in the partition would be carved out of the components. Thus, we ask if any of the components lack unity relative to the Shared Principles, for any component with that character should be divided.

Within the first component, the initial ten chapters touch different themes, but all can be interpreted to involve communal infrastructure and thus Principle D. This commonality is clear in matters of the war census, camp layout, communal dedication of the sanctuary, and assembly/movement of the camp. Moreover, community also marks access issues here, such as with camp expulsions and penalties for misuse of dedicated property. The laws of the suspected adulteress, while not as obviously linked to Principle D, could relate to communal responsibility in fidelity questions, and the Nazirite is temporarily subject to certain laws of a priest and cannot go to war.

The second component is unified by the theme of transgression,

---

A = respecting Creation; B = loyalty to primary relationship; C = limited access to sanctity/resources; D = duties of testimony/community; E = accepting one's place/status (with ties to land/future)

which, no matter its type, serves to undermine the special relationship between the Jewish people and God, thus reflecting Principle B (Loyalty). The short third component suggests Principle C (Limits) in the purification of someone defiled by contact with the dead and thus unable to enter the Tabernacle.

That leaves only the fourth component, comprising Chapters 20–36, whose themes coalesce around two Shared Principles rather than one. Roughly the first six of those chapters treat communal matters, generally in the context of war, communal deprivation, or plague, thus reflecting Principle D (Community). While the last eleven chapters also cover several wars, they treat inheritance, leadership change, personal vows, and borders of the land, all related to Principle E (Acceptance). For this reason, the partition in Display 10 below separates the fourth component into those two topics. Again, the notation "~" means approximately.

DISPLAY 10: Alternate Partition of Numbers into Sequence of Topics		
1. Communal census, camp layout, access, dedication, assembly and movement	~Chapters 1–10	D (Community)
2. Series of transgressions in second year in Wilderness	~Chapters 11–18	B (Loyalty)
3. Law of the Red Heifer	~Chapter 19	C (Limits)
4. Wars and communal strife in last year in Wilderness	~Chapters 20–25	D (Community)
5. Inheritance, leadership change, vows, land borders	~Chapters 26–36	E (Acceptance)

The Obvious Problem in the First Topic

This five-topic sequence agrees in number with the pattern. Moreover, the tentative assignment of the five Shared Principles fails to align only with the first topic on communal infrastructure, since the last four topics follow the sequence of Principles B-C-D-E. On its face, the first topic does not seem to bear a clear and substantial enough connection to Principle A (Creation), which is how the pattern must start. Indeed, for several years, I saw this topic as a key problem with the pattern because the possible connections to Principle A seemed ambiguous or insubstantial. Initially, I checked two possible connections. The first failed totally, and while the second was better, it proved inadequate.

First possible connection

One might suggest that a census is a count of human lives, whose importance is stressed in prohibiting murder, thus reflecting Principle A (Creation). Indeed, the language of the census in Chapter 1 features in Numbers 1:2 the term *s'u et rosh* [lift the head], a term used earlier in the text (Genesis 40:19) to mean execution by hanging. Yet, this approach failed in three ways:

1. The present census was carried out for army duty in the upcoming conquest of Canaan, and thus more directly links to Principle D (Community) in the effort of waging war.
2. There is at least one precedent for not considering a census as linked to Principle A (Creation). What about the census in Exodus 30:11–16 that requires a half-shekel head tax for the Tabernacle's operation? That passage also mentions "lifting the head," but we still placed it in Subpart C of Part D, without linking it to Principle A!
3. Even if we could overlook the difficulties listed above, the proposed connection of the census (which is limited to the first two chapters) did not seem adequate to identify the whole of the first topic (and its ten chapters) with Principle A.

Second possible connection

Apart from the consideration of lives within the census, a cluster of textual features may also be viewed as connecting the census and

---

A = respecting Creation; B = loyalty to primary relationship; C = limited access to sanctity/resources; D = duties of testimony/community; E = accepting one's place/status (with ties to land/future)

layout of the camp to Principle A (Creation) by associating these features with ones present at Mount Sinai in the foundational revelation. Ramban takes this approach in his introduction to Numbers, in which he describes the Tabernacle as a mobile Mount Sinai within the camp. In particular, he compares the limitations on access to the Tabernacle within the camp to the limitations on access to Mount Sinai.

The prominence of flags in the first topic (where *degel* [flag] appears, the only thirteen times it is found in the Five Books) also can be read within Ramban's view. The *Midrash Tanchuma* (14) identifies these flags with a vision during the revelation at Sinai of God draped in flags,[18] which the people imagined they themselves would one day carry. In other words, the flags in the arrangement of the camp would remind the people of the foundational revelation (Principle A) they had experienced. In addition, the medieval commentator Seforno calls our attention to another feature that supports Ramban: the litany of the term "according to their families" in the census and camp formation. In his comment on 1:18, he notes, based on the Talmud in *Kiddushin* 70b, that this term stresses the marital purity necessary for the holiness involved in receiving revelation. (The terms *al mishp'chotam* or *l'mishp'chotam* [according to their families] occur twenty-nine times in the first four chapters of Numbers.)

Ramban's picture of a mobile site of revelation is well accepted and presents a much more substantial connection with Principle A than the first possible connection. Nonetheless, it still seemed inadequate to me in two respects:

1. The above-mentioned factors of limited access, flags, and marital purity do not themselves directly correspond to Principle A (Creation). Rather, limited access corresponds to Principle C (Limits), while flags and marital purity both correspond to Principle B (Loyalty). In fact, the correspondence of marital purity to Principle B may promote connecting the law of the suspected adulteress to Principle B as well, which would provide no apparent help in a connection to Principle A.
2. Each of the aforementioned factors occurs in the context of an army

[*tzava*] (first mentioned in 1:3 with heavy repetition) and its encampment for the conquest of Canaan, an activity that should be clearly linked to Principle D (Community). Without a further substantial theme directly connected with Principle A, we lack sufficient cause in the text itself to invoke these three factors for that Principle.

A direct and substantial connection

Thus, before conceding a link to Principle A that would validate the pattern in the first topic, I insisted on a direct and substantial element of this Shared Principle, and none seemed present. As I prepared to decide that the first topic contradicted the pattern, the names of the twelve tribal princes caught my eye. The preponderance of these names suggests belief in God, such as Elitzur [God is my Rock] (1:5) and Shelumiel [My Peace is God] (1:6). Stressing the importance of these names is their complete listing four times in the first topic: in Chapter 1 as the leaders of the census, in Chapter 2 in the arrangement of the camp, in Chapter 7 in bringing the tribal offerings to inaugurate the Tabernacle, and in Chapter 10 in the movement of the camp.

Following the first listing, we also read that these princes were "designated with names" (1:17), a phrase that appears nowhere else in the Jewish Bible.[19] In fact, having God's name within a person's name is very rare before the names of the princes. These names constitute an unmistakable link to Principle A (Creation). Consider three additional points regarding these names:

- the complete listing of these names four times throughout the first topic all the way to Chapter 10;
- the close connection of the names to the flags;[20] and
- to the repeated phrase "according to their families, which are the elements of Ramban's conception of a mobile Sinai.

A = respecting Creation; B = loyalty to primary relationship; C = limited access to sanctity/resources; D = duties of testimony/community; E = accepting one's place/status (with ties to land/future)

These features strongly reinforce the symbolism of revelation and Principle A (Creation), thus bringing me to view the first topic as fitting the pattern.[21]

A Less Obvious Problem in the Second Topic

As for the other topics in the partition, their alignment seemed fairly direct. The only one that offered any further question was the second topic, which covers the transgressions during the second year in the Wilderness. These transgressions range from the people's complaints over lack of meat, showing lack of belief in God in Chapter 11 (Principle A), to the Incident of the Spies with false testimony in Chapter 13 (Principle D), to the Mutiny of Korach over exclusion from the priesthood in Chapter 16 (Principle E). Clearly, several Shared Principles are present, so how does Principle B (Loyalty) include them all?

The answer to this question is twofold. First, as we have already stated, at its most general level (rather than as a specific transgression) sin violates the primary relationship of Man to God. Second, much of the specific transgression in the second topic comes with an element of Principle B (Loyalty), even while the individual transgression ties more closely to another Shared Principle.

In particular, though the first transgression in this topic, the demand for meat, ties directly to Principle A (Creation). That demand is called *taavah* [desire] in 11:4, a term linked to sexual immorality and thus Principle B (Loyalty). This link is indicated in 11:10 with the people crying for their families, which the Talmud in *Yoma* 75a reads as grief over banned intimacy with relatives. Similarly, Miriam and Aaron devalue Moses' prophecy in 12:1–2 as a matter of access, which reflects Principle C (Limits), also reflects Principle B — Moses leaving his wife to have such access. Signs of disloyalty also emerge in the Incident of the Spies (by them publicizing their recount of their travel to discourage conquest, as opposed to reporting to Moses alone and leaving the decision to him) in Chapter 14. Finally, participants in the Mutiny of Korach violated not only Principle E (Acceptance) in not accepting exclusion from the priesthood in Chapter 16, but also B (Loyalty) in challenging Moses' leadership.

All topics in the partition now align with the pattern and thus correspond to five Parts. We now offer Display 10.1 showing that alignment. Note that the first topic has been restated according to our analysis above that ties that topic to belief in God and revelation.

DISPLAY 10.1: Revised Alternate Partition for Numbers (with assignment of Shared Principles)		
1. Foundations of the camp signaling belief in God and symbolizing Sinai revelation	~Chapters 1–10	A (Creation)
2. Series of transgressions in second year in Wilderness	~Chapters 11–18	B (Loyalty)
3. Law of the Red Heifer	~Chapter 19	C (Limits)
4. Wars and communal strife in last year in Wilderness	~Chapters 20–25	D (Community)
5. Inheritance/ leadership change/ vows/ land borders	~Chapters 26–36	E (Acceptance)

ii. Test of Point Disparity

As in Exodus and in Leviticus, this test proceeds in two steps. First, we find the endpoint of each Part (after which the text shifts to the next Part). We then compare these division points with those named by Rabbi Honigwachs in *The Unity of Torah* (pages 78–79) to evaluate the fit.

a. Identifying the Division Points between Successive Parts

Since the end of Part E also ends the book, we need only locate four division points for successive Parts: between A and B, between B and C, between C and D, and between D and E.

A = respecting Creation; B = loyalty to primary relationship; C = limited access to sanctity/resources; D = duties of testimony/community; E = accepting one's place/status (with ties to land/future)

> **Division Point between Part A and Part B**
>
> Part A = foundations of the camp signaling belief in God and recalling Sinai revelation;
>
> Part B = series of transgressions in second year.

Actually, the division point between Parts A and B has already been identified by the second backwards letter *nun* in the Book of Numbers, which coincides with a *p'tuchah* at the end of 10:36. (The first backwards *nun* at the end of 10:34 coincides with a *s'tumah* rather than with a *p'tuchah*.) Thus, we do not need to find a theme related to Shared Principle E (Acceptance) followed by a theme related to Principle A (Creation). However, we note that the last *parshah* in Part A (10:11–36) offers a theme tied to Principle E: Moses' appeal to his father-in-law (renamed Chovav [dear one]) to stay with the Jewish people in entering Canaan. That appeal contains a promise of future good per Commandment 5 and thus is linked to Principle E.

> **Division Point between Part B and Part C**
>
> Part B = series of transgressions in the second year in the Wilderness;
>
> Part C = law of the Red Heifer.

Here, too, identifying the point of division presents no problem. The end of the series of transgressions involves the mutiny of Korach, who would not accept his exclusion from the priesthood. In other words, he did not accept his place, thus violating Principle E. The mutiny story concludes in Chapter 18 with the flowering of Aaron's staff as confirmation of his selection as High Priest, and the law of the Red Heifer begins immediately in Chapter 19. No subdivision of Part C is possible as it consists of a single *parshah*, which means we cannot expect to find a separate theme linked to Shared Principle A. Because a *p'tuchah* follows the last verse in Chapter 18, this *p'tuchah* marks the point of division between Parts B and C at the end of 18:32.

> **Division Point between Part C and Part D**
>
> Part C = law of the Red Heifer;
>
> Part D = wars and communal strife in last year in Wilderness.

Again, Part C coincides with Chapter 19 and consists of a single *parshah*, so we cannot further subdivide it. Thus we would not expect to recognize a theme of Principle E (Acceptance) at its end. However, we do find Principle A (Creation) in Chapter 20 beginning Part D. There we have the Incident of the Rock, and its test of belief over access to water after Miriam's death. A *p'tuchah* closes out Part C, and the division point for Parts C and D is 19:22.

> **Division Point between Part D and Part E**
>
> Part D = wars and communal strife in last year in Wilderness;
>
> Part E = inheritance, leadership change, vows, land borders.

The elevation of Phineas (Pinchas in Hebrew) to the priesthood in *parshah* 25:10–15 represents a change in status with future implications, which relates to Principle E (Acceptance). The next brief *parshah* (25:16–19) presents God's instruction to avenge the damage done by the Midianites, which seems more future-oriented and thus best linked also to that Shared Principle.

The very next *parshah* 26:1–51 reports first a further census, with some of the same signs of Principle A (Creation) found in the census beginning the Book of Numbers, such as counting by families. Individuals' names referring to God also appear, though not as intensely as in the previous census. I sense a shift has occurred, but it is not clear-cut. However, in the next *parshah* 26:52–27:5, we find the census tied to

> A = respecting Creation; B = loyalty to primary relationship; C = limited access to sanctity/resources; D = duties of testimony/community; E = accepting one's place/status (with ties to land/future)

inheritance, over which Moses approaches God to settle a question from the daughters of Zelophchad. This inquiry of God more directly signals Principle A. Thus I would place the division point between Parts D and E following 25:19.

With the four division points now identified, we can display the Parts with their endpoints.

DISPLAY 10.2: Parts of Numbers and Their Endpoints		
Part	Verses	General Description
A (Creation)	1:1–10:36	Foundations of the camp signaling belief in God and recalling Sinai revelation
B (Loyalty)	11:1–18:32	Series of transgressions in second year in Wilderness
C (Limits)	19:1–22	Law of the Red Heifer
D (Community)	20:1–25:19	Wars and communal strife in last year in Wilderness
E (Acceptance)	26:1–36:13	Inheritance/ leadership change/ vows/ land borders

b. Comparing Division Points for Parts with those of Rabbi Honigwachs

In comparing respective division points for Parts, recall from Section 7 that we will consider such points matching if and only if they are no more than two *p'tuchot* apart. (Note that the distance in *p'tuchot* between respective points can be counted from Appendix a.) However, as shown below, each pair of points of division matched identically.

DISPLAY 10.3: Comparison of Respective Division Points in Numbers			
Successive Parts to be divided	Last verse before division Mine	Last verse before division Rabbi Honigwachs'	Distance in *p'tuchot*
Parts A and B	10:36	10:36	0
Parts B and C	18:32	18:32	0
Parts C and D	19:22	19:22	0
Parts D and E	25:19	25:19	0

iii. The Red Heifer and the Thirty-Eight-Year Time Warp

We noted earlier in this unit that Part C is precisely congruent with the single *parshah* consisting of Chapter 19, an exclusively legal subtext that deals with purification of someone defiled by contact with a human corpse. Because such purification requires the ashes of an entirely red heifer, this subtext is popularly known as the laws of the Red Heifer. At first glance, it is not all clear what this subtext has to do with the sequence of transgressions in Part B (which immediately precedes) set in the second year in the Wilderness. But even more puzzling is the chronological position of the laws of the Red Heifer, because Chapter 20 (which immediately follows) presents a narrative set in the last year in the Wilderness, thirty-eight years later. (Our understanding of this passage of time is explained further on.) Why would the laws of the Red Heifer represent such a time warp?

Of course, Source Critics simply view these questions as further proof of multiple authors of the Torah, and of Numbers in particular. According to that view, even if the most important events took place in the first and last years, a single (intelligent) author would surely not insert a disconnected legal subtext between two narratives to mark the passage of a lengthy intervening period. In short, the laws of the Red

---

A = respecting Creation; B = loyalty to primary relationship; C = limited access to sanctity/resources; D = duties of testimony/community; E = accepting one's place/status (with ties to land/future)

Heifer could stand as Exhibit A in Charles Noth's source-critical finding of "confusion and lack of order" in the contents of the Book of Numbers.

However, consider an elaborated explanation of Rabbi Shimon Schwab (d. 1995).[22] The communal transgressions in Chapters 11–18 brought punishments that included immediate death for those most culpable. Such immediate death is reported explicitly with the demand for meat (11:33–34), the Incident of the Spies (14:36–37) and the Mutiny of Korach (16:32–35 and 17:14). In addition, the Incident of the Spies resulted in the men gradually dying off in the Wilderness until the fortieth year. Only two of the men twenty years or older at the time of the Incident were left (see 14:29–34). Thus, there was much need for purification from contact with the dead and so too for the law of the Red Heifer.

In fact, we understand in 20:1 that thirty-eight years have passed since the second year after the Exodus because this verse speaks of "the entire assembly" coming to the Wilderness of Tzin. The use of "entire" indicates that, at this point, the men had finally stopped dying off after the Incident of the Spies (see Rashi here). The entire assembly was the new generation that had buried those who had gone before and that had needed purification as a consequence.

This explanation actually leads to a further structural connection. When we consider the two communal transgressions that precede the law of the Red Heifer — the Incident of the Spies and the Mutiny of Korach — a striking common feature emerges. In both cases, the instigators attempt to use human reasoning to set aside the will of God. Ten of the twelve spies reasoned that their small stature relative to the inhabitants would doom a military campaign despite God's promise. Likewise, Korach sought to establish shared spiritual leadership to replace the alleged nepotism of Moses in designating his brother Aaron as the High Priest. In contrast, the process of the Red Heifer defies human reason in its contradictory effects of purifying the defiled while defiling the purified (the priest who carries out the process). Thus, it provides the perfect antidote to the last two transgressions as it represents the passing of the thirty-eight years and the attendant passing of a generation.

iv. Test of Ambiguous Subdivision

As in the books preceding Numbers, this test checks each Part to see if it subdivides, as asserted by the Subparts Claim, into Subparts aligned in order with the pattern. However, because Part C of Numbers consists of a single *parshah*, it cannot be subdivided, leaving us to check only four Parts: A, B, D, and E. The subdivision of Part E is routine and was covered well enough by Display 4.12 and the paragraph preceding it in Section 4. Thus we limit our analysis to Parts A, B, and D. The underlined headings that follow come from Display 10.2 above.

Subdivision in Numbers of Part A 1:1–10:36: Foundations of the Camp Signaling Belief in God and Recalling Sinai Revelation

Part A occupies nearly a third of Numbers. Its subdivision was originally presented in Display 4.11 in Section 4, but two of the Subparts in Display 10.3A are identified with slight revisions in line with the closer analysis that follows. You will notice that with the question over Principle A (Creation) at the beginning of Numbers having been settled in the Test of Alternate Partition, the subdivision of Part A now proceeds relatively smoothly.

DISPLAY 10.3A: Part A of Numbers Subdivided According to the Shared Principles

Subpart	Verses	Features Related to Shared Principle
A (Creation)	1:1–3:4	Census and camp formation with God's name embedded in names of tribal leaders and with symbols recalling Sinai revelation
B (Loyalty)	3:5–4:49	Roles of Levites who have assumed spiritual mantle of firstborn
C (Limits)	5:1–7:89	Laws of misused consecrated property, suspected adulteress, and Nazirite/ priestly blessing in God's Name/ tribal leaders' offerings

A = respecting Creation; B = loyalty to primary relationship; C = limited access to sanctity/resources; D = duties of testimony/community; E = accepting one's place/status (with ties to land/future)

D (Community)	8:1–10:10	Second Passover/ role of Clouds of Glory in movement of camp/ role of trumpets in war and testimonial observances
E (Acceptance)	10:11–10:36	Future of Moses' father-in-law (renamed Chovav)

Subpart A: Part A begins with the general census of the camp (excluding the Levites) and its layout in roughly the first two chapters. Within this subtext, we have two listings of the tribal leaders whose names reflect belief in God, as well as most of the language symbolizing a mobile version of Sinai where the foundational revelation (reflecting Principle A) took place. Because the focus shifts in 3:5 to God singling out the Levites, Subpart A consists of verses 1:1-3:4.

Subpart B: From 3:5 to the end of Chapter 4, the Levites are designated in place of the firstborn and counted from a month of age and older, as opposed to twenty years and older for the rest of the camp. The duties of the three Levite clans are also specified here, marking a special relationship. Because Chapter 5 turns to matters of access, this Subpart regarding the Levites ends and fits Principle B (Loyalty).

Subpart C: In its opening treatment of temporary expulsion from the camp, misuse of dedicated property, and fraud, Chapter 5 clearly presents themes of access and Principle C (Limits). Next come the laws of the suspected adulteress. The process for testing her fidelity involves erasing God's Name (see 5:23), which also ties to Principle C, but suspected adultery suggests Principle B (Loyalty). However, as we saw in Display 5.1 in Section 5, the subtext of the suspected adulteress actually constitutes the Segment B within a further subdivision of Subpart C, and thus there is no departure from the pattern at all.

Then in Chapter 6 we have laws of the *nazir* [nazirite], someone who by oath denies himself wine, haircutting, and contact with the dead. This denied access reflects Principle C as well. Then, from the end of Chapter 6 through Chapter 8, we have the priestly blessings followed by duties and purification related to the Tabernacle service. Because these subjects involve spiritual access, Principle C (Limits) continues to dominate. This completes Subpart C.

Subpart D: Chapter 9 shifts from Principle C themes in its first subparagraph with an issue arising with the second Passover. As a *moed* [testimonial observance], Passover embodies Principle D (Community), which is reinforced in the latter subparagraph of Chapter 9 with the signals for communal travel and encampment. The first *parshah* of Chapter 10 continues the communal theme (Principle D) with the use of trumpets to signal the camp for various purposes. In all, verses 9:1–10:10 comprise Subpart D.

Subpart E: Seemingly, the second and final *parshah* (10:11–36) of Chapter 10 maintains a communal theme in its first subparagraph with the camp's order of movement in its first journey from Sinai. However, its second subparagraph presents Moses' effort at that time to keep Jethro (renamed Chovav) from leaving the camp and returning home to Midian. That effort includes elements of the land and the future that bespeak Principle E (Acceptance). Right afterwards, we have the two verses enclosed by backward Hebrew letters. No issue remains with the beginning of Subpart E because the initial journey provides context for Moses' appeal that Chovav stay.

Subdivision in Numbers of Part B 11:1–18:32: Series of Transgressions in Second Year

As shown below, Part B of Numbers smoothly subdivides into five Subparts. However, we find an anomaly in one of them that should be noted. While four of the Subparts correspond to specific transgression (such as Subpart D with the Incident of the Spies), Subpart B does not — even though it does reflect Principle B (Loyalty).

A = respecting Creation; B = loyalty to primary relationship; C = limited access to sanctity/resources; D = duties of testimony/community; E = accepting one's place/status (with ties to land/future)

DISPLAY 10.3B: Part B of Numbers Subdivided According to the Shared Principles		
Subpart	Verses	Features Related to Shared Principle
A (Creation)	11:1–15	People craving for meat and doubting God's power to provide it
B (Loyalty)	11:16–22	Special relationship of seventy elders in assisting Moses with people
C (Limits)	11:23–12:16	Access of elders to prophecy and people to quail/ Moses' access to God questioned as reason for his separation from his wife
D (Community)	13:1–15:41	Incident of Spies and related ritual law/ case of Sabbath violation
E (Acceptance)	16:1–18:32	Mutiny of Korach/ selection of Aaron as High Priest confirmed

Subpart A: The people craving meat, and their questioning God's capacity to provide it, clearly involves lack of belief in the first *parshah* in Chapter 11, thus suggesting Principle A (Creation). This *parshah* ends with 11:15 and comprises Subpart A.

Subpart B: Although the second *parshah*, which begins with 11:16, still touches on belief, it focuses on Moses sharing his spiritual responsibility with the seventy elders. This represents a material change in Moses' relationship, thus linking to Principle B (Loyalty). This link mirrors the end of Part B of Exodus where Jethro suggests that Moses appoint individuals to share the load in judging the people. By contrast, we also saw there a stress on the judicial qualifications of the appointed judges that also relates to Principle E (Acceptance), thus placing the subtext about appointed judges in Subpart E of Part B. Here with the seventy elders, however, the sharing of responsibility is stressed — not their qualifications. Thus, we see a shift from Principle A to Principle B in the second *parshah* (11:16–22), which comprises Subpart B.

Subpart C: In the third *parshah* 11:23–35, the seventy elders receive access to prophecy, and the people are given access to meat (Principle C). This shift from Principle B signals the transition to Subpart C. After the punishment over craving for meat, Chapter 12 treats Miriam's criticizing Moses for using his spiritual access as a reason to separate from his wife. Specifically, Miriam (who did not separate from her spouse) equated her own spiritual access to that of Moses. While Miriam was struck with Biblical leprosy,[23] we see the continuing link to Principle C (Limits) through concern with spiritual access. Thus Subpart C consists of verses 11:23–12:16.

Subpart D: The Incident of the Spies spans Chapters 13 and 14, covering three *parshiyot*. The first *parshah* extends to 14:10 and tells of Moses sending twelve spies into Canaan and the improper testimony by ten of them about the land, which discourages the people from fulfilling God's direction to enter and conquer the inhabitants. This testimony clearly reflects a shift to Principle D (Community). Chapter 14 then proceeds with God's punishment: thirty-eight years of wandering in the Wilderness (before entry into Canaan), during which nearly all the men will die. This chapter concludes with a defiant and ultimately disastrous effort by some to enter Canaan anyway. Principle D continues with war, which constitutes communal activity.

In its first two *parshiyot*, Chapter 15 states two new requirements that follow the Incident of the Spies: additions to individual sacrifices and the separation of dough in making bread. The commentary of Seforno on 15:3 provides grounds to view the sacrificial additions in testimonial terms,[24] and thus Principle D (Community). The final two *parshiyot* of Chapter 15 present first an account of Sabbath violation (gathering wood in a public place) and then a law recalling the Incident of the Spies (wearing fringes on four-cornered garments). The violation suggests Principle D through both Sabbath and communal contexts. In words mirroring the spies' mission, the law of wearing fringes warns in 15:39 not to explore [*lo taturu*] things after one's own hearts and eyes as the spies did.[25] This completes Subpart D (13:1–15:41).

Subpart E: In recording the Mutiny of Korach, Chapter 16 shifts from

---

A = respecting Creation; B = loyalty to primary relationship; C = limited access to sanctity/resources; D = duties of testimony/community; E = accepting one's place/status (with ties to land/future)

Principle D (Community), since the mutineers did not accept their exclusion from the priesthood and violated Principle E (Acceptance). This account runs through the end of Chapter 18, when God has Aaron's staff blossom to confirm his selection as High Priest. Thus Subpart E consists of verses 16:1–18:32.

Subdivision in Numbers of Part D 20:1–26:1: War and Communal Strife in Last Year

The subdivision of Part D of Numbers goes smoothly in all but one respect. Each shift to the next Subpart is routine, but the linkage of Subpart D to Principle D (Community) is not clear. As shown below, this linkage finds support in the text, but so does linkage to Principle B (Loyalty).

DISPLAY 10.3D: Part D of Numbers Subdivided According to the Shared Principles

Subpart	Verses	Features Related to Shared Principle
A (Creation)	20:1–21:3	God doubted after Miriam dies/ Aaron and Moses fail to promote belief at rock/ Aaron dies/ God's help sought against Arad
B (Loyalty)	21:4–20	Complaints over quality of food and punishment with serpents
C (Limits)	21:21–24:25	Passage through Emorite land denied/ Balaam's failed effort to use God's name to curse the Jewish people
D (Community)	25:1–25:9	Public immorality with Midianite women/ communal judgment fails/ Phineas kills offenders and stops deadly plague
E (Acceptance)	25:10–26:1	Covenant of peace and priestly status for Phineas for his actions

Subpart A: This Part opens in Chapter 20 with the death of Moses' sister Miriam and the people's lack of belief (Principle A), reflected in their complaints over lack of water. The second *parshah*, which runs from

20:7 through 20:21, remains concerned with belief because God tells Moses and Aaron after the incident at the Rock that they did not believe in Him (see 20:12). At the same time, the second *parshah* also reflects Principle B (Loyalty) in Israel's brotherhood with Edom (20:14) and Principle C (Limits) in denial of passage through Edomite land (20:21).

The same sense of Principle A (Creation) along with other Shared Principles also holds in the third *parshah* (20:22–21:3). To wit, this *parshah* recounts the people's public mourning, reflecting Principle D (Community), after Aaron's death. They also promise in line with Principle E (Acceptance) to dedicate certain Canaanite cities to the Tabernacle for God's help in defeating Arad's army. Thus, the first three *parshiyot* in Part D reflect Principle A but also show an ordered sequence of the other Shared Principles. In the end, verses 20:1–21:3 comprise Subpart A.

Subpart B: The next *parshah* (21:4–20) opens with complaints over water and food, but a close look at the text shows that God's ability to provide essentials is not in doubt. Rather, the people see their food as lacking substance (21:5). Thus, they complain about God not fulfilling His part in their relationship as they would like, an idea signaled in the punishment of serpents. From its first appearance in Genesis 2, the serpent represents the evil inclination opposing Man's relation to God and Principle B (Loyalty). The *parshah* 21:4–20 is identified with Subpart B.

Subpart C: Right after Subpart B, in subparagraph 21:21–22:1, the text takes up yet another refusal of passage, this time involving the Emorites, who are then defeated by the Jewish people. The long subparagraph 22:1–24:25 completes the *parshah*, telling of Balaam, the Canaanite prophet hired by Balak, king of the Midianites, to curse the Jewish people (and thereby shield his land from conquest). Balaam's failed efforts to curse also reflect Principle C (Limits), in seeking access to God's Name for an improper purpose. This completes Subpart C (21:21–24:25).

A = respecting Creation; B = loyalty to primary relationship; C = limited access to sanctity/resources; D = duties of testimony/community; E = accepting one's place/status (with ties to land/future)

Subpart D: In the next *parshah* 25:1–9, we find an account of Jewish men involved in immorality with Midianite women, with the resulting plague stopped only by Phineas' zealous execution of the instigating tribal leader and his Midianite consort. On the basis of this initial description, we would link this story to Principle B because forbidden sexual acts violate loyalty to a primary relationship. The mention here of worship of Midianite gods also signals Principle B (Loyalty), instead of Principle D (Community), which the pattern would have predicted.

Yet, two vital factors do in fact reflect Principle D. First, the text places extreme stress on the tribal leader and his consort sinning in public "before the eyes of the entire assembly," (25:6). The same verse says that the entire assembly cried before the Tent of Meeting. Second, the judges clearly did not act or act quickly enough to sentence the idolatry's instigators to death as they had been ordered to do in 25:4. The court system represents the community, reflecting Principle D.

Though I accept the authority and credibility of the Talmud and recognized *Midrashim*, the pattern has been expected to withstand the various tests on the basis of the Torah's text alone. While we will continue this expectation, there are two further factors outside the text suggesting Principle D that bear noting. According to *Sanhedrin* 106a, the process of the Midianite women seducing the men first required their oral disavowal of the Torah (improper testimony). In addition, a common reading of *Nazir* 23b allows some sort of communal motivation for the tribal leader publicly consorting with one of the Midianite women.[26] With the only the strength of two factors in the text, however, it is hard to say they outweigh the factors arguing for Principle B (Loyalty). This lack of clear alignment is where we must leave Subpart D (25:1–9).

Subpart E: The *parshah* 25:10–16 shifts to Principle E (Acceptance) through the covenant of peace given to Phineas and through his elevation and that of his offspring to the priesthood. The ensuing brief *parshah* halts in the middle of verse 26:1 and serves to cap the story of Phineas. Thus verses 25:10–26:1 comprise Subpart E.

Summary

Having analyzed the Test of Ambiguous Subdivision in detail, we can now summarize our overall findings in Numbers involving the pattern:

1. For the Test of Alternate Partition, unusual textual features in Numbers limited the choices for alternate partitions that would offer a natural sequence of topics. These features already determined three points dividing any such topics. Using these division points and adding a fourth based on thematic differences, Numbers divides into five topics aligned in order with the five Shared Principles. The only question had occurred in aligning the first topic with Principle A (Creation), but this question was resolved through unusual references to God in the names of leaders listed four times in the topic. These lists, along with other features, support the idea of the camp being structured as a mobile Sinai, thus recalling revelation.
2. The Test of Point Disparity resulted in no failures in matching our division points to those of Rabbi Honigwachs.
3. Though the placement and surrounding chronology of the Red Heifer subtext may seem arbitrary, that subtext aptly signals the passing of thirty-eight years and a generation's demise. This signal comes through the use of the ashes of a red heifer to purify those defiled by contact with the dead.
4. The Test of Ambiguous Subdivision found no ambiguity at all in subdividing three of the four Parts in Numbers with at least five *parshiyot*. Only in subdividing Part D was there ambiguity, which was limited to one subtext. That subtext presented signs of both adhering and not adhering to the pattern, without clear dominance by the signs of adherence.

A = respecting Creation; B = loyalty to primary relationship; C = limited access to sanctity/resources; D = duties of testimony/community; E = accepting one's place/status (with ties to land/future)

Section 11
Concluding Evaluation and Broader Implications

This section first condenses the results of Sections 6, 8, 9, and 10, which scrutinized the pattern in the first four books. We proceed here in the order of the three tests generally applied to each book (though we did not need an alternate partition of natural topics in Genesis).

1. Test of Alternate Partition — to challenge the division of each book into five Parts aligned in order with the pattern (i.e., the Parts Claim).
2. Test of Point Disparity — to challenge reliable replication of division points between Parts.
3. Test of Ambiguous Subdivision — to challenge the subdivision of each Part with at least five *parshiyot* into five Subparts (i.e., the Subparts Claim).

In each case above, we review how the pattern stood up to scrutiny in the first four books. Through that review, we can determine how well the pattern fared overall on the test in question. In reading these analyses, note that underlying details, if needed, can be found as shown below:

Test	Sections with Underlying Details (by book)
Alternate Partition	6 and 15 (Genesis), 8 and 16 (Exodus), 9 (Leviticus), 10 (Numbers)
Point Disparity	Same as above, plus 17 (all of the first four books)
Ambiguous Subdivision	Same as for Alternate Partition

The balance of this section will address three essential matters:

1. Revisiting Deuteronomy — in light of Section 14 and of tests applied to the first four books. This discussion will provide a more definitive sense of how Deuteronomy differs from the other books in relation to the Shared Principles.
2. Issues for Further Exploration — regarding the structure of the Torah.
3. Completing the Evaluation — with broader implications for the authorship debate.

i. Test of Alternate Partition

The test challenges the Parts Claim, which asserts that each book of the Bible is made up of five continuous subtexts (Parts) corresponding in order to the Shared Principles.

Genesis

Because Genesis offers a natural fivefold division (universal history, focus on Abraham, focus on Isaac, focus on Jacob, and focus on Joseph and his brothers), scrutiny of the Parts Claim in Genesis began with that division. Specifically, we checked whether those five subtexts aligned in order with the five Shared Principles, and in the end verified the alignment.

In this verification, the correspondence for four of the subtexts was straightforward. Even a simple reading shows, for example, that the universal history subtext corresponds with Principle A (Creation) and that, with all the attention on dreams, the subtext focused on Joseph and his brothers, corresponding with Principle E (Acceptance). Only in the case of the subtext that focused on Abraham did we find that correspondence with Principle B (Loyalty) required a deeper analysis. This analysis involved recognizing that the two covenants during Abraham's life (Covenant between the Parts in Chapter 15 and Covenant of Circumcision in Chapter 17) define a primary relationship in line with Principle B.

A = respecting Creation; B = loyalty to primary relationship; C = limited access to sanctity/resources; D = duties of testimony/community; E = accepting one's place/status (with ties to land/future)

In contrast to Genesis, the next three books present no natural fivefold partition into subtexts aligning with the pattern. Thus, for each of Exodus, Leviticus, and Numbers, we offered an alternate partition into topics that, on their face, do not align with the Shared Principles. With this approach, we began to test the Parts Claim in each of those books. For the Claim to stand, each such alternate partition would have to resolve into a fivefold sequence aligned in order with the Shared Principles.

Exodus

In Exodus, our alternate partition into seven topics offered three potential conflicts with the pattern. The first potential conflict had the alternate partition beginning with a topic linked to servitude and Principle B (Loyalty), rather than Principle A (Creation). However, we could not ignore the presence of infanticide (murder) and the midwives' belief in God (both being themes of Shared Principle A) in the opening of the book. Thus, the opening of Exodus combined with our second topic (the revelations to Moses and Aaron) to form a single topic linked to Principle A (Creation). Our next three topics (the Plagues and the Exodus, the Ten Commandments and civil law, and directions for building the Tabernacle) then aligned with Principles B through D.

But we had linked our sixth topic (Incident of the Golden Calf) to Principle B (Loyalty) as idolatry. This linkage would have contradicted the pattern since the preceding topic gave the directions for building the Tabernacle, reflecting Principle D as a communal task. Closer scrutiny of the Golden Calf subtext showed heavy signs (especially in the intense repetition of the less common terminology *am* for the people) of Principle D (Community). Finally, our effort to deny linking the last topic (the actual building of the Tabernacle) to Principle E (Acceptance) also failed because that subtext included fulfillment of promises of revelation from the previous subtext. Thus, our partition did resolve into a fivefold sequence aligned in order with the Shared Principles, and the Parts Claim in Exodus withstood the Test of Alternate Partition.

Leviticus

In Leviticus, we also proposed an alternate partition of seven topics. However, unlike the alternate partition for Exodus, this one began with a topic (the description of the sacrifices) linked to Principle A (Creation). Moreover, our Leviticus partition ended with the last four topics (sexual matters and atonement; laws associated with holiness; Sabbath, holidays, and release years; and blessings and curses for the future) linked respectively to Principles B through E. In these respects, the alternate partition in Leviticus lay closer to the pattern than did the alternate partition in Exodus.

In fact, the sole obstacle to alignment lay in the second and third subtexts (located between the first subtext and the last four), creating an apparent conflict with the pattern. The second topic (priestly ritual, the strange fire, and the dietary laws) seemed to link to Principle C (Limits) through limited access, and the third (laws of leprosy) to Principle D (Community) through the leper's separation from the camp. However, upon closer examination, it turned out that these two topics, together with the first topic, include a full progression through the five Shared Principles. Thus those three topics would be combined to form Part A, with the internal progression forming its Sections. The shortest label we could offer for Part A would therefore be "Types of Sacrifices and Sacrificial Ritual with Application to Certain Circumstances."

While the pattern withstood the Test of Alternate Partition in Leviticus, there were two points of modest qualification. First, Part A is an amalgamation of topics without a relatively simple description (such as had applied up to now for other Parts in the Five Books). Beneath this point of qualification lies the fact that sacrifices still are mentioned beyond Part A into Part B, thus complicating any distinction of Part A based on its unique content. At the same time, this point of qualification may reflect more about semantics than the validity of the pattern.

The second point involves Part E (blessings and curses for the future)

A = respecting Creation; B = loyalty to primary relationship; C = limited access to sanctity/resources; D = duties of testimony/community; E = accepting one's place/status (with ties to land/future)

— more specifically, whether there must be a fifth Part in Leviticus. This issue actually arose within the next test (the Test of Point Disparity), and we will cover it in more detail in evaluating the results of that test. However, the Parts Claim is also involved in that, technically, we could have divided Leviticus into four Parts with Part E absorbed into the end of Part D. This absorption could have occurred because Part E only contains three *parshiyot* and does not subdivide into Sections. In this absorption, Part E could be attached to and could enlarge Subpart E of Part D.

What keeps us from doing this is that our original Subpart E of Part D concerns the Sabbatical and Jubilee years and redemption of slaves. Thus this Subpart has, at least on its face, little if anything to do with blessings and curses for the future. Still, we have seen in the previous paragraph that Part A contains somewhat disparate topics, though they do have the element of sacrifices in common.

Numbers

This brings us to Numbers, where our alternate partition into a natural sequence of topics was guided by two key textual features:

- the pair of large reversed Hebrew letters framing the end of Chapter 10, which, according to Jewish tradition, purposely divide the earlier text from the major transgressions that follow; and
- the Red Heifer subtext (Chapter 19) signaling, without any other account, the passing of thirty-eight years in the Wilderness to the period of war as the Jewish people approached Canaan.

The inverted letters marked the end of the first topic covering the foundations of the community; the beginning of the Red Heifer subtext immediately followed the second topic of the transgressions in the second year in the Wilderness; and the Red Heifer subtext constituted the third topic. That left the remainder of Numbers, which split naturally into two topics.

The last four of the resulting five topics aligned in order with the last four of the Shared Principles (B through E). Yet the first topic in Numbers seemed to be more tied to Principle D (Community) than to A (Creation). A strong argument for a link to Principle A could be Ramban's well-accepted symbolic interpretation of the first topic as describing a mobile Sinai and thus an environment for revelation. But, at first blush, key aspects of this symbolism did not link directly to Principle A. Only when I rediscovered Rabbeinu Bachya's insight on the tribal leaders, whose names are fully listed four times, did Ramban's explanation gain a sufficient direct link to Principle A. Those names contain names of God within them, an unusual feature signaling belief. Moreover, the text specifies those leaders as having been "designated by name," a phrase unique in Torah.

Summary

In summary, among the first four books, only Leviticus presented some difficulty in its division into Parts according to the pattern. The difficulty involves whether there are five Parts to that book, or only four in alignment with the first four Shared Principles. Even so, the division into five appears more natural. With that qualification noted, I conclude that the pattern passed the Test of Alternate Partition, thus satisfying the Parts Claim overall for the first four books. As noted in Section 1, Deuteronomy need not fulfill the Parts Claim to validate the pattern, though, as shown in Section 14, there is nonetheless limited fulfillment in the last book.

ii. Test of Point Disparity

This test was developed in Section 7 to challenge the replication of the pattern identified by Rabbi Honigwachs under an independent determination of division points between Parts. In other words, we would see how close our division points came to his. To make this comparison stringent, we would use the minimum number of *p'tuchot* [occurrences of opening spacing] in each of the first four books to set the standard for matching.[27] Through this consideration, an individual division point between Parts would count as matching the

---

A = respecting Creation; B = loyalty to primary relationship; C = limited access to sanctity/resources; D = duties of testimony/community; E = accepting one's place/status (with ties to land/future)

corresponding point of Rabbi Honigwachs if and only if it fell no more than two *p'tuchot* away.

To set the standards for our analysis, we must still account for expected differences in different trained observers and the probabilities of random matching (as detailed in Section 17). In other words, reasonable replication would still occur with a very limited number of failures. In the end, we decided to accept no more than two cases of non-matching points within the first four Books. Let us now review the outcomes Book by Book within the first four.

- Genesis: All four points of division matching
- Exodus: Three points of division matching, one non-matching
- Leviticus: All four point of division matching
- Numbers: All four points of division matching

Because only one case of non-matching points occurred in the first four Books, the pattern passed the Test of Point Disparity, thus validating the pattern in this respect. Again, Deuteronomy need not be considered for validation, but, for completeness, we will report that there are two division points that match and two that do not.

iii. Test of Ambiguous Subdivision

The Test of Ambiguous Subdivision challenges the Subparts Claim, which asserts that each Part with at least five *parshiyot* is made up of five continuous subtexts aligned in order with the Shared Principles. In Genesis, each Part meets the condition on the minimum number of *parshiyot*, with Parts B, C, and D (corresponding to the three Patriarchs Abraham, Isaac, and Jacob) having exactly five each. We confirmed that the Subparts Claim holds remarkably well in Parts A, B, D, and E. In Part C, however, there is uncertainty with the subtext that should identify with Subpart B and so link to Principle B (Loyalty). This subtext (22:20–24) gives an account mainly of lineage with, at best, an implicit link to that Shared Principle, though no other Shared Principle seemed evident. Otherwise, Part C subdivides in alignment with the pattern.

In Exodus and Leviticus, the Subparts Claim held firm overall. All five Parts of Exodus contain five or more *parshiyot*, but only three of the

Parts in Leviticus satisfy this condition. For the eight Parts combined, all subdivisions were smooth, and only Subpart C of Part C had an issue in alignment, with its wide-ranging legal character touching several Shared Principles. Still, in the end, the strongest case could be made for Principle C, thus preserving the alignment.

Numbers presents four Parts (all but C) with five or more *parshiyot*. In these four Parts, no serious issues emerged except in Part D. There, the subtext of verses 25:1–9, i.e., Subpart D, seemed from the text alone to be at least as connected to Principle B (Loyalty) through sexual misconduct and idolatry as to Principle D (Community). The other subtexts in the subdivision of Part D clearly aligned in order with the pattern.

Success or Failure?

Looking at the first four books of the Bible then, we see that the Subparts aligned with their respective Shared Principles cleanly in all but three cases, with predominant alignment in one of the three. Let us weigh this level of performance in regard to the total number of Subparts in question. Each of the first four Books has five Parts, amounting to twenty Parts. Since only three of those Parts (two in Leviticus and one in Numbers) have fewer than five *parshiyot*, there are seventeen Parts with five or more *parshiyot* in the first four Books. In turn, each of these seventeen Parts has five Subparts. This means there are 17x5 = 85 Subparts in the first four Books.

Three cases with incomplete resolution among eighty-five constitute about 3.5%, which reduces to 2.4% if only two of them are counted. We cannot confuse these rates of incomplete resolution with what might be termed "rates of failure," since even the worst two cases cannot be termed failures per se. Recall that in the first of the two, the link to the respective Shared Principle is implicit but likely the only link with any Shared Principle. And in the second, resolution would be much closer were I willing to weigh authoritative sources outside the actual Torah text.

A = respecting Creation; B = loyalty to primary relationship; C = limited access to sanctity/resources; D = duties of testimony/community; E = accepting one's place/status (with ties to land/future)

While the rate of incomplete resolution is already quite low, it becomes even more impressive in being achieved without using the "standard opening" (see Section 7) to find shifts between Subparts. In this light, the pattern passes the Test of Ambiguous Subdivision, and the Subparts Claim is upheld in the first four Books. When we revisit Deuteronomy below, we will find though that the Subparts Claim does not hold in Deuteronomy.

iv. **Revisiting Deuteronomy**

We first discussed Deuteronomy in relation to the pattern in Section 3. There we saw that while the last book presents an initial context that links to Principle E (Acceptance), it has no single dominant Shared Principle tied to its overall content. This lack of a dominant Shared Principle for its content differentiates Deuteronomy from each of Genesis through Numbers. For the first four Books, the dominant Shared Principle matches the initial context: Shared Principle A (Creation) for Genesis, Principle B (Loyalty) for Exodus, and so forth.

In Section 3, Rabbi Honigwachs' explanation of this difference in Deuteronomy was also brought forward: the Jewish people's arrested development through transgressions in Numbers. According to this explanation, the people had successfully advanced through the first three Shared Principles as Leviticus ended. But, in light of the transgressions recounted in Numbers, Moses reviewed many laws in Deuteronomy to prevent further transgression, especially regarding the last two Shared Principles, which the people had not mastered.

We also learned how this explanation dovetails with Ramban's view of why there are changes in the laws in Deuteronomy in relation to their earlier statements. In fact, the four major variations in the Ninth and Tenth Commandments in Chapter 5 of Deuteronomy (with respect to the same commandments in Exodus, Chapter 20) correspond to four major communal sins in Numbers. In Section 14, this approach extends to non-communal sins in Numbers, which fit the variations between the Fourth and Fifth Commandments as stated in Exodus and Deuteronomy. In sum, the Fourth, Fifth, Ninth, and

Tenth Commandments correspond to Principles D (Community) and E (Acceptance), exactly those not mastered by the end of Numbers, according to Rabbi Honigwachs.

This strongly suggests that the pattern's validity does not depend on subjecting Deuteronomy to the tests applied in the first four books. Still, it is useful to consider the three elements of our strategy here. As shown in Section 14, Deuteronomy does not divide into Parts in complete alignment with the Shared Principles. The lack of complete alignment occurs in not finding a clean break at a *p'tuchah* between the components that would presumably correspond respectively to Parts B and C. Thus, in Deuteronomy, the pattern does not withstand the Test of Alternate Partition and does not satisfy the Parts Claim.

When it comes to the Test of Point Disparity, it turns out that of the four points identified in my partition of Deuteronomy, only the first two fall close enough to those of Rabbi Honigwachs to be considered matching.[28] This lack of a fit is striking, especially with only thirty-four *p'tuchot* in Deuteronomy, even less than the forty-three in Genesis. We would have expected a better fit with so few *p'tuchot*, so this level of fulfillment proves plainly inadequate — not just incomplete.

Finally, for the Test of Ambiguous Subdivision, the pattern falls even shorter in Deuteronomy. Rabbi Honigwachs and I agree on what would correspond to Part A (1:1–4:49), which contains only four *parshiyot* (and thus cannot be subdivided into Subparts and is not subject to the Subparts Claim). That leads us to what would be Part B (5:1–10:11), which has seven *parshiyot* and is therefore susceptible to subdivision. As we can see from these *parshiyot* summarized below, they cannot be configured to align in order with the Shared Principles.

A = respecting Creation; B = loyalty to primary relationship; C = limited access to sanctity/resources; D = duties of testimony/community; E = accepting one's place/status (with ties to land/future)

DISPLAY 11.1: *Parshiyot* within Part B of Deuteronomy and Suggested Shared Principles

Parshah	Description	Shared Principle(s)
5:1–6:3	Covenant of Sinai revelation restating Ten Commandments	A (Creation), B (Loyalty);
6:4–7:11	Promise in the land of Canaan/fulfillment of covenant	B, E (Acceptance)
7:12–26	Promise to remove enemies/demand to destroy idolatry	B, E
8:1–18	Promise in land of Canaan/warning not to forget God	B, E
8:19–20	Threat in future if the people fall into idolatry	B, E
9:1–29	Exhortation to enter Canaan/ Golden Calf, Spies recounted	A, B, E
10:1–11	Account of 2nd Tablets (forgiveness)/elevation of Levites	B

In line with Display 11.1, there appears no material suggestion of Principle C (Limits) or Principle D (Community). If you were to argue that the Incident of the Spies violated Principle D (within the next to last *parshah*), you would be correct, but in that context the verses are clearly stressing the people's lack of belief rather than the improper testimony of the Spies. The absence of components aligned with Principles C and D makes for a general failure of the Subparts Claim and therefore a general failure to withstand the Test of Ambiguous Subdivision. And lest you think that Rabbi Honigwachs' version of Part B would work better, keep in mind that his version consists of exactly the first five *parshiyot* as mine. In fact, Rabbi Honigwachs lists no Subparts within Deuteronomy in his overall outline of Parts and Subparts.

This state of affairs in Deuteronomy regarding the pattern — lack of a dominant theme within the Shared Principles and the pattern's failure to withstand any of the three tests applied in the other books — leads us to further inquiry. Beyond the rationales of Rabbi Honigwachs and

Ramban for the differences, is there some other reason why the previous structure would not continue in Deuteronomy? There is, indeed.

Unique Quality of Deuteronomy

According to a dictum dating from Talmudic times, the first four Books were spoken by the Divine Presence *mitokh g'rono* [from within his (Moses') throat],[29] while Deuteronomy was spoken by Moses *mipi atzmo* [from his own mouth]. This mention of the throat calls to mind another recognized reference in *Sefer Yetzirah*, a sacred text known at least since the sixth century. Even in its great antiquity, this text (see 2:1) manages to list the five physiological sources of speech (throat, palate, teeth, tongue, and lips), though these sources' exact vocal contributions were not well recognized until a few centuries ago. More remarkably, when rendered in the original Hebrew, these five parts of the anatomy correspond naturally to the five Shared Principles as shown below.

DISPLAY 11.2: Sources of Speech and Corresponding Shared Principles

Sources of Speech	Corresponding Shared Principle: Rationale
1. *garon* [throat]	A: *Garon* is a noun form of *gimel-resh-hei* [to give cause] (see Deuteronomy 2:9, *lo titgar*) and relates to *garmi* [culpable causation]. *Garon* is the first cause of speech and links to respecting Creation.
2. *cheikh* [palate]	B: *Cheikh* is the part of the mouth most associated with pleasure and is related to *chiki*, a metaphor for sexual intimacy in Song of Songs 2:3.

A = respecting Creation; B = loyalty to primary relationship; C = limited access to sanctity/resources; D = duties of testimony/community; E = accepting one's place/status (with ties to land/future)

3.	*shinaiyim* [teeth]	C: *Shein* [tooth] is the paradigm of damage through an animal's improper access to someone's property. See *Bava Kama* 19b–21b.
4.	*lashon* [tongue]	D: *Lashon hara* [evil tongue] is associated with improper testimony of the Spies. Rashi on Numbers 14:36–37 says the Spies set the people's tongues [*l'shonam*] against Moses, with the Spies dying by a plague on the tongue.
5.	*s'fataiyim* [lips]	E: The Hebrew root of *s'fataiyim* is *safah* [speech], which first occurs with the Tower of Babel in Genesis 11:1. The purpose of the Tower was to aggrandize the name of its builders, who did not accept their place.

Consider now the alignment of the components of speech with the Shared Principles, together with the earlier dictum of the first four Books coming from the Divine Presence *mitokh g'rono* [from within his (Moses') throat]. Because the first four Books come directly from the First Cause of speech, we suggest that they fully embody the potential of each vocal component. On the other hand, Deuteronomy, which came from Moses himself, does not. And just as human beings represent the highest form of animal in their power of speech, the Torah's voice in the first four Books represents the highest form of speech in its expression, i.e., in the Shared Principles.

v. Issues for Further Exploration

While the highly synchronized character of the Torah has been demonstrated in many respects, the investigation of the pattern of Shared Principles is far from complete. Here are three specific questions that intrigue me (in no particular order), followed by a matter of broader speculation.[30]

Three Intriguing Questions:

1. Almost everywhere before Deuteronomy, the pattern proceeds through a division of a Book and then to a subdivision of the Book into Subparts. However, three Parts in the first four Books lack

enough *parshiyot* to be subdivided into Subparts (Parts B and E of Leviticus and Part C of Numbers). These three Parts clearly reflect different Shared Principles, and, while the first and third are mainly legal in nature, the second is mostly blessings and curses. Is there some common feature or some unified rationale to explain why these three Parts, in particular, should have too few *parshiyot* for subdivision?

2. While Rashi and Ramban together guide the traditional understanding of the text, they do disagree at times, with perhaps the most pervasive disagreement involving chronology. Ramban holds that whenever possible the order of events should be understood as the order in the text, but Rashi is not so constrained and, for example, takes the Incident of the Golden Calf as occurring before the instructions for the Tabernacle (which appear earlier). Does the pattern of Shared Principles shed any light on this disagreement?

3. The one place in the first four Books where my division point was not close enough to match that of Rabbi Honigwachs is between Parts A and B in Exodus. Is there a different method from the one I used for division points that would resolve that discrepancy? Such a method would presumably be able to distinguish changes in themes at the level of Parts from those at the level of Subparts.

A Matter of Broader Speculation

The *Midrash Rabbah* (1:1) on Genesis is often paraphrased as "God used the Torah as a blueprint for Creation." However, the *Midrash* does not say what the Torah contributed to the design. One answer involves the explanation of the word *b'hibaram* [in creating them (Heaven and Earth)] in Genesis 2:4 found in *M'nachot* 29b. Focusing on the smaller than normal *hei* as the second letter of the word, the Talmud interprets the word as: with a *hei*, Heaven and Earth were created. This interpretation stresses the shape of the *hei* to specify the possibility of repentance

---

A = respecting Creation; B = loyalty to primary relationship; C = limited access to sanctity/resources; D = duties of testimony/community; E = accepting one's place/status (with ties to land/future)

within Creation.[31] Because repentance is a Torah concept that occurs explicitly in Deuteronomy 30, we can resolve the meaning of the *Midrash Rabbah*: the Torah served as a blueprint by placing repentance into the design of Heaven and Earth.

Perhaps, however, the Torah's contribution to Creation is more physically detectable than the spiritual concept of repentance. There may be more to the word *b'hibaram* that hints at another contribution from the Torah. More specifically, we note that the numerical value of *hei* is five, so the Talmud's rendering of *b'hibaram* could be read as "with five, they were created." Might this rendering also hint at the "fiveness" of the Shared Principles as a property of Torah reflected in nature?

We have already seen the correspondence between the five sources of speech (an element of nature) and the five Shared Principles (which characterize the Torah's structure). But nature expresses itself numerically in ways other than "fiveness"; we also have two eyes and two ears. Thus, it would take something more pervasive in nature that is rooted in the number five to suggest a link between nature and the Torah on the basis of the Shared Principles.

The Golden Ratio

It turns out that the Golden Ratio, a physical constant first described in the Introduction, is found in countless phenomena of growth and is rooted in fiveness. Let us elaborate.

The Golden Ratio is the ratio of lengths of two lines considered most pleasing to the eye by the early Greeks. They held that such visual pleasure occurs when the ratio equals the ratio of the sum of longer and shorter lengths to the length of the longer. In Euclid's *Elements* (ca. 300 BCE), the Golden Ratio, denoted by ϕ (the Greek letter phi), was defined by the equation $\phi = (\phi + 1)/\phi$, where ϕ is the longer length, and 1 is set as the shorter. (The left side of this equation is the ratio of length of the longer to that of the shorter = $\phi/1$, and the right side is the ratio of the sum of lengths to the length of the longer.) With the quadratic formula to this equation, Euclid found $\phi = \frac{1}{2}(1 + \sqrt{5}) = 1.61803...$ (a non-repeating and non-terminating decimal).

To see how ϕ is rooted in five, consider its original construction in

Euclid's *Elements*. Euclid constructed φ in a regular pentagon (a five-sided figure with equal angles and equal sides) where the longer line is a diagonal (from point A to point B) in the figure below and the shorter line is one of its sides (point B to point C).

For about two millennia, the Golden Ratio was viewed exclusively in this way — as the geometric embodiment of the number five. Not until the seventeenth century did the astronomer Kepler find the key that would also link φ to natural phenomena.

Ironically, Kepler found this key in a numerical sequence devised in the thirteenth century to solve a recreational puzzle. This sequence is known as the Fibonacci series whose first two entries are the number 1 (repeated) and whose further entries proceed as follows:

2=1+1, 3=1+2, 5=2+3, 8=3+5, 13=5+8, 21=8+13, 34=13+21, 55=21+34,...,

where any entry in the sequence other than 1 is the sum of the previous two entries.

It can be shown that the ratio of each number in the Fibonacci series to its predecessor approaches φ as we go further and further out. The actual proof is a bit far afield, but we can illustrate the idea by looking at the first eight ratios of Fibonacci numbers to their predecessors. (As a point of reference, φ rounded to four decimal places is 1.6180.)

A = respecting Creation; B = loyalty to primary relationship; C = limited access to sanctity/resources; D = duties of testimony/community; E = accepting one's place/status (with ties to land/future)

Fibonacci numbers	1	1	2	3	5	8	13	21	34
Ratio to predecessor			1/1	2/1	3/2	5/3	8/5	13/8	21/13	34/21
Value of ratio (to four decimals)			1	2	1.5	1.6667	1.6	1.625	1.6154	1.6190

Though the Fibonacci series is based solely on a progression of numbers and intrinsically suggests no physical construct, Fibonacci numbers and their consequent ratios are found pervasively in nature, especially in growth phenomena. One of the most striking cases is the leaf arrangement of single-stem plants, as explained and illustrated by the scientist Mario Livio.[32]

The constant angle between successive leaf extensions from the stem allows lower leaves optimal access to sun and moisture (without too much blockage by the upper leaves). This angle is specific to the plant, but only certain angles can occur, with these angles related to Fibonacci numbers as follows. First, count the number of turns about the stem from the lowest leaf extension until the next leaf extension directly above it, and then count the total number of leaf extensions until that point. These two counts are the Fibonacci numbers before and after their difference, which is also a Fibonacci number.

To summarize, Fibonacci numbers characterize leaf arrangements and are intrinsically related to ϕ, itself a reflection of fiveness, and fiveness is intrinsic to the structure of the Torah. In this light, does the Torah serve as a blueprint for Creation by contributing its structure, which we see manifested everywhere in nature through the physical constant ϕ?

vi. Completing the Evaluation

The pattern of Shared Principles has withstood my three tests in the first four Books. Each of these tests confronted the pattern in a fundamental way.

- The Test of Alternate Partition challenged the Parts Claim: each Book divides into five Parts aligned in order with the Shared Principles;

- The Test of Point Disparity challenged the reliable replication of Book divisions with comparisons of division points;
- The Test of Ambiguous Subdivision challenged the Subparts Claim: each Part with five or more *parshiyot* subdivides into five Subparts aligned in order with the Shared Principles.

Despite the pattern's success here, we must recognize that the first test, with which the entire strategy begins, relies on a specific choice of an alternate partition. Someone may point out that a different alternate partition could result in a different outcome, i.e., non-alignment with the pattern. While that observation cannot be dismissed, there is good reason to doubt that such a different partition will be found. In particular, the credibility of an alternate partition demands that it follow an informed, direct reading of the text, a notion deserving further context.

Rashi and Ramban vs. Wellhausen and the Source Critics

In seeking an informed, direct reading of the Torah, the great medieval commentaries of Rashi and Ramban have guided me. The original versions of these commentaries accompany the text in standard editions of *Mikraot G'dolot*, the elaborated Hebrew Pentateuch that accompanies traditional Jews from middle school throughout their lives. Though both commentaries have been translated into English from Hebrew, the translations are relatively recent, leaving most English speakers outside the traditional Jewish community with limited access. At the same time, trying to parse the text from a traditional Jewish perspective without knowing Rashi and Ramban would be like trying to practice medicine without knowing anatomy and physiology.

Nonetheless, in academic quarters, the use of Rashi and Ramban as guides generally runs counter to the accepted (but unfortunate) characteristic "conceit of originality" [my terminology]. While the natural and applied sciences still expect new ideas or methods to prove themselves

---

A = respecting Creation; B = loyalty to primary relationship; C = limited access to sanctity/resources;
D = duties of testimony/community; E = accepting one's place/status (with ties to land/future)

against the past, other fields — and notably the humanities — often prefer original approaches to established ones. In fact, it seems at times that the more an idea can be distinguished from the past, the more honored (and likely to be published) it may be, without weighing real questions of effectiveness or validity. This does not mean to dismiss the value of true scholarship in the humanities, but rather to call attention to a bias against traditional understandings.

Let us return now to Source Criticism and its Documentary Hypothesis. That approach clearly distinguishes itself from what it considers the backwards mindset of traditional religious acceptance of the Five Books of Moses. It asserts that the Torah was compiled over time from multiple sources — typically, at least the four popularized by Julius Wellhausen toward the end of the nineteenth century. Section 12 explains the development of these supposed sources, along with the main points of opposition previously made against Source Criticism. Those points of opposition have yet to be convincingly answered, but the Documentary Hypothesis still flourishes, largely on the strength of the perceived lack of a logical organization of the text.

The Pattern vs. Multiple Authorship of the Torah

How does the assertion of multiple authors with compilation over time now square with the pattern of Shared Principles? Imagine a scene from the past that Source Critics must paint to accommodate the pattern's precise division and then subdivision of the text. In this scene, we emerge in a previous age beside one of the compilers central to the Documentary Hypothesis. He has just received the latest installment of (self-serving) ideas to be integrated into the existing text. This task requires him to preserve the intricate framework of parallel sequences of topics and subtopics followed by his predecessors. (For some reason, the compiler's predecessors had switched from symmetric sequences to parallel ones.[33])

He begins work and quickly finds that preserving the framework with the new insertions means keeping track of more pieces of text than is reasonable on his own.[34] Without access to a laptop, he does the best he can, finally finishing Genesis after ten years. He shows the product to his colleagues, who then demand assurance that this version be able to accommodate the next installment in several centuries. An honest man, the compiler cannot provide that assurance, and so a new compiler is named.

The picture is plain: the level of synchronization in the pattern would be next to impossible to sustain within a compilation over time — especially without modern software.

And why would we look for a compiler if a single author is a more direct explanation? Perhaps someone will say we need a compiler because of the various discrepancies (consistency challenges) alleged by Source Critics. However, he will then need to explain how the compiler was clever enough to arrange the synchrony in the text but lacked the sophistication to eliminate the purported discrepancies. In fact, we have already dispatched three of the main groups of purported discrepancies: those between versions of laws in Deuteronomy versus earlier versions, those involving different names of God, and those involving so-called doublets (narratives with certain similarities).

In this light, future discussion of the origin of the Five Books ought to begin with the realization that it is a unified, highly synchronized text. If some wish to treat it as not originating from God, they may surely do so — though not as a matter of evidence from the text itself. Good people need not believe in God, but neither can advocates of direct Divine authorship of the Five Books be dismissed as blind or unthinking. This would mean a marked shift in how the Five Books are taught in most colleges and universities in the Western World. That is why we must read the Five Books for their own meaning and not for what the academy says they are.

A = respecting Creation; B = loyalty to primary relationship; C = limited access to sanctity/resources; D = duties of testimony/community; E = accepting one's place/status (with ties to land/future)

Notes

1 The individual rationales for assigning Shared Principles in Display 8 are as follows:

In assigning Principle B (loyalty) to enslavement of the Jewish people in Chapters 1–2, enslavement is seen as imposing a master other than God, showing disloyalty to a primary relationship.

Because Divine revelation associates naturally with belief in God, Shared Principle A (Creation) is tentatively assigned to revelations at or relating to the Burning Bush (~Chapters 3–5).

Liberation from slavery again signals loyalty to a primary relationship and thus Shared Principle B for the Plagues and the Exodus (~Chapters 6–17).

Law inherently sets limits and limits access, so T4 (~Chapters 18–24) fits Shared Principle C.

The directions for making the Tabernacle (~Chapters 25–31) involve communal responsibility, which accords with the tentative assignment to Principle D (Community).

Actually making the Tabernacle is certainly a communal task, or it could suggest Principle E (Acceptance) through the limiting of certain work to those with particular talents.

2 One might try to link this *parshah* to Shared Principle A using the Talmud's statement that purity of lineage is a precondition for revelation (*Kiddushin* 70b). However, this link assumes that simply reciting the names implies such purity. Though the *Mekhilta* (5:28) lists the retention of both Jewish names and Jewish marital standards among the people's virtues in Egypt that granted redemption (and therefore the subsequent revelation on Sinai), no clear implication of the latter by the former appears.

3 In Book Three, Chapters 45–46, Maimonides described many specific idolatrous practices, showing how these practices are changed in the Tabernacle and in the sacrifices so as to redirect the passion for the worship of the physical. However, many other authorities rejected any consideration of compensation for idolatrous tendencies in Jewish ritual. Notably, Ramban (see his comment on Leviticus 1:9) questioned Maimonides' linking of sacrifices with idolatry by noting Cain and Abel's sacrifices in Genesis 4:3–4 before the recorded emergence of idolatry in

Genesis 4:26. While several worthy rejoinders have upheld Maimonides, his approach here is simply not broadly accepted.

4   To appreciate the lack of acceptance of Maimonides' approach of ritual compensation for idolatry in the Tabernacle and offerings, we can be guided by the classic thirteenth century work *Sefer HaChinnukh*. This work gives reasons for each of the 613 laws in the Torah in the order they appear, noting that the author relies on Maimonides' stated count and designation of laws. As you would expect from that note, *Sefer HaChinnukh* gives much credence to Maimonides throughout in offering reasons. However, in giving the reason for the law of building the Tabernacle (the ninety-fifth law), Maimonides' approach is not mentioned. Instead, there is praise for the rationale of Ramban, a leading critic of Maimonides' approach. This rationale involves the thoughts of a person who comes to the Tabernacle to offer an animal for a sin committed in the correspondence between the components of sin and those of sacrificial ritual. It is found in Ramban's comments on Leviticus 1:9, where he also castigates Maimonides (See note above.)

5   Interpreting the necessarily metaphysical meaning of God's back is extremely difficult (as is that of any term that seemingly attributes human features to God) and goes well beyond my own ability. However, in the interest of illustrating what Moses may have seen in the revelation, I will paraphrase two of the better known interpretations from popular Jewish sources:

the reward in the Hereafter (*achorai* = Hereafter); *C'li Yakar*, eighteenth century;

the Godly pattern in what has passed (*achorai* = what has passed); *Chatam Sofer*, eighteenth and nineteenth centuries.

6   There are many famous interpretations of "we will do and we will understand" in Exodus 24:7, though, interestingly, neither Rashi nor Ramban chose to comment. Among the interpretations and commentaries most often cited to explain this passage are the following:

We will observe the laws already given and pay attention to others that will be given (Rashbam, eleventh century).

We will carry out the positive laws and understand (and therefore not do) what is prohibited (*Panim Yafot*, eighteenth century).

A = respecting Creation; B = loyalty to primary relationship; C = limited access to sanctity/resources; D = duties of testimony/community; E = accepting one's place/status (with ties to land/future)

We will not only observe the laws, but also understand them (*Chatam Sofer*, eighteenth and nineteenth centuries).

We will follow the Written Law and hear (in order to follow) the Oral Law (Rabbi Samson Raphael Hirsch, nineteenth century).

We will observe the laws first before we understand them, i.e., we don't have to have reasons for the laws before doing them (Malbim, nineteenth century).

We will observe the laws in order to understand them, i.e., we will learn by doing (*Mikhtav M'Eliyahu*, twentieth century).

7   Rabbi Honigwachs' identification of the Plagues and the Splitting of the Sea with Part A can be understood through references in those accounts to knowing or believing in God. In regard to the Plagues, such references occur, for example, in Exodus 7:5 and 8:6. The first of these verses is included in my Subpart A of Part B, which also reflects Principle A, while I consider the second verse more focused on God's uniqueness and thus linked to Principle B. Similar comparisons can be drawn regarding the Splitting of the Sea.

8   The connection between the four cups and the "four terms of redemption" comes from the Jerusalem Talmud (which does not follow the format of the Babylonian Talmud), *Pesachim* 10:1. In that source may also be found other less familiar rationales for the Four Cups at the Seder.

9   For more background on the fifth cup, see M. Kasher, *Israel Passover Haggadah* (New York: Shengold Publishers, 1964), p. 333.

10 For example, *Or HaChaiyim* of the eighteenth century and Rabbi Samson Raphael Hirsch of the nineteenth century.

11 See Chapter V ("The Endowment of the Clergy") in the English version of Julius Wellhausen's work, *Prolegomena to the History of Israel*, translated by Black and Menzies (Edinburgh: A & C Black, 1885). There Wellhausen asserts that the priests set up the system for their own financial support, to which they attributed a Divine imprimatur.

12 The adjective *zarah* shares its root with the noun *zar* [non-priest] common in Torah (cf. Exodus 29:33). Thus, *zarah* connotes "outside the priesthood," implying the strange fire violated Aaron's sons' special relationship with God and Principle B (Loyalty). It may also be argued that any linkage of the strange fire to Principle C (Limits) comes from Leviticus, which is that book's overall association.

13 As noted in the preface to the English version of his work, *Prolegomena to the History of Israel*, Wellhausen adopted the idea of increasingly complex

ritual from Karl Heinrich Graf. This idea is found in Graf's *Die Geschlichten Bucher das Alten Testaments* (Leipzig: T. O. Weigel, 1866).

14   This approach follows Ramban, who understood the imperative to be holy in Leviticus 19:2 as requiring adherence not just to the formal legal demands of the Torah, but also to the spirit of the law. In his comments there, he famously characterized one who acts to meet only the bare minima as "a jerk with the permission of the law."

15   See Rashi on Leviticus 19:2.

16   M. Noth, *Numbers: a Commentary* (London: SCM Press, 1968), p. 4.

17   What this marking of the text means is debated in *Shabbat* 115b–116a, but both sides would agree that the second of the two letters *nun* divides the prior text from the major transgressions in the second year in the Wilderness after the Sinai experience. One side does say the Jewish people leaving Sinai, which is recounted in 10:33 before the first *nun*, is considered a sin in the way they left. In particular, Ramban comments on 10:33 that the Jewish people left Mount Sinai "like a child running from school," i.e., to flee further duties. Yet, Ramban notes that unlike the subsequent sin, there was no punishment.

18   Rabbi Matis Weinberg connects the vision of the Divine flags with the words "saw the voices" (Exodus 20:15) in the account of the Sinai revelation. This connection appears in *FrameWorks: Au Desert/ Numbers* (Boston: Foundation for Jewish Publications, 2002), pp. 31–32, where the *Midrash* is quoted.

19   This observation came from my teacher Rabbi Kalman Worch, who also noted the precedent for interpreting names of tribal leaders in *Sotah* 34b, which discusses the names of several of the twelve spies as harbingers of disaster.

20   In particular, the commentary of Rabbeinu Bachya (d. 1340) notes that the princes with whom the flags were associated all have names that incorporate one of God's names.

21   Although the reasons stated here are sufficient to link the first topic in the partition to Principle A (Creation), there is another possible linkage that merits mention. Typically, the word *l'gulg'lotam* is translated as "according to their headcount" (or something equivalent). Yet neither Rashi

---

A = respecting Creation; B = loyalty to primary relationship; C = limited access to sanctity/resources; D = duties of testimony/community; E = accepting one's place/status (with ties to land/future)

nor Ramban view this census as actually being conducted by headcount, since Numbers 1:2 states that the count is to take place by names. Neither commentator provides an alternative meaning for *l'gulg'lotam* based on anything other than a headcount, so perhaps they understand a count of names equating to being skull by skull. However, there may be a hint of a different meaning in the initial use of the word *gulgolet* [skull] in Exodus 16:16, which speaks of the manna falling in a certain measure, literally, per skull. *Yoma* 75a adds that the quality of someone's faith determined how close the specified measure of manna fell to him (thereby reflecting the test of faith implied in 16:5). Thus, the term *gulgolet* may suggest the skull as the seat of faith, which relates to Principle A. This same relationship is also reflected in a root *giluy* [revelation], from which *l'gulg'lotam* may itself be derived (with the skull being revealed when the skin is removed from the head). Although the prefix *l'* can mean "according to," it can also mean "for the purpose of." Thus, *l'gulg'lotam* may suggest revelation (the most direct sign of Shared Principle A), but one could also argue that it comes from *l'galgeil* [to roll], because a skull is round.

22 *Maiyan Beit Hashoeivah* (Brooklyn: Mesorah Publications, 1996), p. 351.

23 Although Miriam is the only one stricken with leprosy, the text actually says both Miriam and Aaron spoke (in 12:1). However, Rashi explains on this verse that Miriam initiated the conversation, which is borne out by the use of the singular feminine verb *vat'daber* [and she spoke], as noted by the commentary of Rabbi David Kimchi. In this light, a close reading of the next verse 12:2 (in which the plural verb form "and they said" is used) suggests that Aaron did not actually criticize his brother Moses.

24 As noted by Seforno on 15:3, the additions of the flour offering and the oil and wine libations were first required only for communal sacrifices after the Golden Calf (before which they were not required at all). This link to the Golden Calf finds support in 15:22–32, regarding sacrifices for unintentional idolatry and punishment for intentional idolatry. Although idolatry itself connects to Principle B, its mention here seems to mark the additions as testifying to the Incident of the Spies being connected to the Golden Calf.

25 Rabbi Samson Raphael Hirsch's commentary on the Torah elaborates on this linkage based on the charge to the spies given in 13:16 by Moses: *latur* [to explore] the land. See Rabbi Hirsch's comment on 15:39.

26 *Nazir* 23b compares Zimri to Tamar, who disguised herself as a prostitute

to seduce her father-in-law Judah in Genesis 38 when he denied her his last son in levirate marriage. Her act is viewed as a "sin for the sake of Heaven," so Zimri's act is seen by many (but not all) as well-intentioned (though misguided); see S. Bornstein, *Shem MiShmuel*, tr. Z. Belovski (Southfield, MI: Targum Press, 1998), p. 361. I have seen two communal motives given for Zimri: to take his tribe's punishment on himself and to absorb the surrounding peoples, thus speeding conquest and establishment of the Jewish kingdom.

27 In Section 7, we briefly considered the approach of using 5% of the smallest number of verses in any book, which turned out to be 859 in Leviticus. That approach would allow a maximum of forty-three verses between respective division points but would not take into account the relative density of *p'tuchot* within each book. However, in the interest of completeness, I checked the distances against the forty-three-verse maximum and found that it made a difference in matching in only one case. Thus, the pattern would also pass the Test of Point Disparity under the forty-three-verse maximum.

28 Rabbi Honigwachs' points for dividing Parts in Deuteronomy are the *p'tuchot* that follow 4:49, 8:18, 28:69, and 32:47, while mine are the *p'tuchot* that follow 4:49, 10:11, 26:19, and 30:20. The distances in *p'tuchot* between our respective points of division are 0, 2, 3, and 3, which means that only our first two points match.

29 *Mitokh grono* [from within his (Moses') throat] is the common Hebrew expression adopted from the longer Aramaic phrase *v'Shechintei m'dabeir al pumoy* [and the Divine Presence speaks through his (Moses') mouth] in the *Zohar*, *Pinchas* 232a. (The *Zohar* can also be found in a format with numbered paragraphs, rather than folio and side as cited. Thus the following reference specifies a version with the folio and side format: D. Porish, *Matuk MiD'vash* (Jerusalem: Makhon Daat Yosef, 2004). This work presents the *Zohar's* text, with the modern Hebrew commentary *Matuk MiD'vash* of Rabbi Porish underneath. Special thanks go to my teacher Rabbi Aron Rosenberg for locating this source in the *Zohar* and the further reference. Rabbi Rosenberg also pointed out Rabbi A. Grossman's citation of the *Tikunei Zohar* basing the *Zohar's* phrase on Exodus 19:19.

A = respecting Creation; B = loyalty to primary relationship; C = limited access to sanctity/resources; D = duties of testimony/community; E = accepting one's place/status (with ties to land/future)

30   A more extensive treatment of this matter appears in the author's article "Greenway and the Torah Blueprint for Creation," 24 *B'Or Ha'Torah* 2016-2017, pp. 7–19.

31   According to the Talmud, the shape of the Hebrew letter *hei* (think of an inverted letter "u" with a small gap between the top of the left leg and the roof of the letter) suggests repentance. This shape features a full opening at the bottom symbolizing man's easy fall into sin from the surrounding structure of holiness. However, by clinging to the outside of the left leg of the *hei* and pulling himself up and away from sin, a person may still reach the narrow gap at the top and reenter the structure of holiness.

32   M. Livio, *The Golden Ratio* (New York: Broadway Books, 2002), which provides many cases of growth phenomena exhibiting the physical constant ϕ.

33   As noted in Section 5, many academic scholars are quick to show the Torah follows the same patterns as other ancient writings (without intrinsic sanctity). In particular, there is stress on symmetric patterns found in other ancient writings. Such patterns show a mirror image in a sequence of themes, such as A-B-C-D-E-D-C-B-A, instead of the parallel sequence A-B-C-D-E-A-B-C-D-E... in the Shared Principles. There are certainly symmetric sequences in the Torah, but that is not the pattern of the Shared Principles.

34   To make the divisions and subdivisions just to the level of Subparts within the first four books would require some 100 separate operations, with corresponding textual breakdowns that need to be coordinated. Drilling down to the level of Segments would require even more complexity.

ELABORATION ON STAGE I

Section 12

The Wellhausen Hypothesis: Origins, Development, and Points of Opposition

Section 1 of Stage I introduced the Wellhausen Hypothesis, which argues that the Torah was compiled from four separate source documents. The theory takes its name from Julius Wellhausen (1844–1918), a German theologian who popularized this view of authorship of the Mosaic Text. Widely translated, his 1878 book *Prolegomena zur Geschichte Israels*[1] synthesized major ideas up to that time within Source Criticism, i.e., Biblical analysis that explains apparent textual irregularity as the result of multiple authors.

Gradually, Source Criticism has itself come to raise questions on Wellhausen's presentation and thus to promote the more inclusive notion of a "documentary hypothesis," which extends beyond the particular theory of source documents in the Wellhausen Hypothesis. Still, this broader notion draws heavily on the ideas in the *Prolegomena*. As noted in the Introduction, Source Criticism has grown so pervasive on campuses that it is often cited in literary analyses of the Biblical text, even when the study itself need not involve multiple authorship. These gestures of fealty to Source Criticism have led to its confusion with Biblical Criticism, though Bible Critics need not be Source Critics.

The aim here is to provide an overall grasp of the components of Source Criticism, as well as the flaws perceived in that approach. This will require at least a working sense of the development of the Wellhausen Hypothesis. Towards that end, we now elaborate in the following subunits.

1. Original doubts over textual authenticity, with Rashi's explanations in key cases.
2. Distortion by Spinoza of Ibn Ezra's view of questioned passages.
3. Key elements in the development of the Wellhausen Hypothesis.
4. Major points of objection to the Wellhausen Hypothesis.

i. Doubts over Textual Authenticity, with Rashi's Explanations in Key Cases

With the Enlightenment came the first publicly sustained expressions of doubt over the authenticity of the Pentateuch, i.e., as the Mosaic transcription of God's words. Several seventeenth century philosophers, notably Thomas Hobbes and Benedict Spinoza, questioned the traditional acceptance of such authenticity. Specific verses in the text were held to be incompatible with Mosaic transcription, including Genesis 12:6 and Deuteronomy 34:5–6, which were cited by both Hobbes and Spinoza.

The perceived incompatibility of Genesis 12:6 involves the passage "and the Canaanites (descendants of the man named Canaan) were then in the land," meaning in the days of Abraham, hundreds of years before Moses. Because the text also reports the Canaanites inhabiting the land at the time of Moses (cf. Deuteronomy 7:1), the word "then" would seem to have been written when the Canaanites were no longer there, i.e., after Mosaic times. As for the verses in Deuteronomy, they record Moses' death and the concealment of his burial site "until this day," which apparently reflect the perspective of a later period, as well.

While both Hobbes and Spinoza raised these questions, their overall approach to Divine authorship differed markedly.

Hobbes

To Hobbes, though the questions signaled specific pieces of the text Moses probably did not write, there was room for discussion. For example, regarding the question on the verses in Deuteronomy, Hobbes stated in Chapter 33 of the *Leviathan* (1651), "but it may perhaps be alleged that the last chapter only, not the whole Pentateuch, was written by some other man, but the rest not."[2] Though Hobbes went on from this statement to name several perceived incompatibilities appearing earlier in the text, we see his willingness to consider the traditional view when it could reasonably be defended. In fact, Hobbes concluded that the existence of such incompatibilities remained consistent with Moses' transcription of the vast majority (as opposed to the entirety) of the Five Books.

Spinoza

In contrast, Spinoza held the traditional view to a standard designed for total rejection. As he declared in Chapter 8 of *Theological-Political Tractate* (1670), "we must not accept what is reasonably probable."[3] (Later in this unit, we will revisit the standard of reasonable probability, for it has come to haunt the Wellhausen Hypothesis.) From this standard, Spinoza arrived at what has become the normative position of Biblical Criticism: "...as there are many passages in the Pentateuch which Moses could not have written, it follows that the belief that Moses was the author of the Pentateuch is ungrounded and even irrational."[4] Indeed, Spinoza concluded in the same chapter that it was the prophet Ezra (fourth century BCE) who compiled and edited the text into the form that we use today. This notion of Ezra as the grand redactor became the first tenet of what eventually emerged as the Wellhausen Hypothesis.

Before we explore the origins of the Wellhausen Hypothesis further, let us see what the standard eleventh century Torah commentary of Rashi had to say about the two passages discussed so far. Keep in mind that sustained doubt over Divine authorship had not emerged in Rashi's time, so he was not defending the traditional view from attack by opponents. Rather, he simply addressed potential anomalies or redundancies in the text. Please also note that when Rashi had no explanation (cf. Genesis 28:5 with the seemingly unnecessary familial identification of Rebecca), he said so.

Rashi on the Canaanites

In the case of the verse 12:6 in Genesis, Rashi explained the use of the word "then" relative to a later verse in Genesis that would otherwise be difficult to understand. In particular, that later verse (14:18) would cast doubt on the presence of the Canaanites in the land as early as Abraham. Thus, in

Rashi's view, the word "then" means "already" and does not imply a writer's time frame beyond that of Moses. Rather than connoting a different time frame, "then" stresses the discomfort of Abraham's environment, since the Canaanites were to be particularly avoided. (Their ancestor Canaan had been cursed by Noah [10:25], and Abraham had his servant swear that he would not find a wife for Isaac from among the Canaanite women [24:2–4].)

Let me now outline why verse 14:18 would cast doubt on the presence of Canaanites. That verse mentions Melchizedek as the ruler of Shalem, a region of the land to which Abraham had come. Since Melchizedek is associated with Noah's son Shem, he could not have been a Canaanite, i.e., he could not have descended from the man Canaan, who was the son of Ham, the brother of Shem.[5] Had the text not told us that Canaanites were already there, we might have thought rule by a non-Canaanite would preclude any substantial presence of Canaanites. After all, the Canaanite presence became so pervasive as to have the land take the name Canaan. Therefore, Rashi has explained the confusing statement about the Canaanites in a way that does not raise doubts to its authorship as Spinoza asserted it does.

Rashi on Moses' Burial

As for the two verses questioned in Deuteronomy, Rashi offers two possible explanations. First, he says that these verses and the remaining seven verses in the Torah were written by Moses' successor Joshua as an epilogue, which would not take away from the overall notion that Moses transcribed the words of God. (Note that this explanation conforms to the one envisioned by Hobbes.) Alternatively, Rashi offers another explanation, saying that the concluding verses were still transcribed by Moses, but with great sadness in recognition of his own imminent demise. In both of Rashi's explanations, the final subtext accords with the full authenticity of the Five Books.

ii. Distortion by Spinoza of Ibn Ezra's View of Questioned Passages

We cannot say for sure how many of the seventeenth century philosophers who questioned Divine authorship were, in fact, aware of Rashi's explanations, and we certainly cannot say how many would have accepted his explanations. However, we can say that one among those philosophers was certainly aware of them. That would be Spinoza himself, an apostate Jew whose first name Benedict was Latinized from his original Hebrew name Baruch. Spinoza had been educated traditionally in Amsterdam before parting ways with Judaism. Though his family had fled the Iberian Peninsula with its Sephardic (Mediterranean) Jewish legacy, he would have been schooled in the already standard commentary of Rashi from nearby France.

Yet, in Spinoza's *Theological-Political Treatise* (Chapter 8, where the difficult textual passages are listed), neither Rashi nor any of his explanations appear. While we would not expect Spinoza to promote particular opposing views, the *Treatise* made it appear that there were no other explanations, not even ones to be disputed. Moreover, in its key reference to traditional interpretation, the *Treatise* attributed doubts over textual authenticity to a recognized Sephardic authority of the twelfth century, Abraham Ibn Ezra. This Spinoza did by reading Ibn Ezra's comments on two verses in ways that were plainly not intended. Inasmuch as Spinoza's reading of Ibn Ezra has been taken as authoritative by Source Critics (who repeat it to this day), we will examine those two comments with some care.

These comments of Ibn Ezra are those on Genesis 12:6 and Deuteronomy 1:2. Because Spinoza portrayed the first of these comments in the context of the second, we begin with Ibn Ezra's comment on Deuteronomy 1:2. That verse gives the specific location of Moses' final addresses before the Jewish people entered Canaan. Ibn Ezra observed that the previous verse had described this location in more general terms as "the other side of the Jordan (River)." Since the Jordan had to be crossed to enter the land, this reference to "other side of the Jordan" would seem to have come from someone in Canaan, rather than from Moses. Noting this problem, Ibn Ezra listed a few other passages, among them Genesis 12:6 and the last twelve verses of the Torah (including Deuteronomy 34:4–5 on Moses' death), that are also hard to view as transcribed in Mosaic times.[6] Then Ibn Ezra said of these passages, "If you understand *sod* [a level of insight hidden below the surface]...you will recognize the truth."

Though nothing in Ibn Ezra's words here (on Deuteronomy 1:2) identifies any specific hidden insight, he did give a sense, in the introduction to his Torah commentary, of his use of *sod*. There he wrote:

> *If something (in the Torah) is not supported by the intellect or if it contradicts the (normal) sense of connections, then we must ask for sod — because intelligence is the foundation (of Torah) and because the Torah was not given to those who cannot understand. A person's wisdom acts as the messenger between himself and his God. Thus, wherever it (the text of the Torah) does not contradict the intellect, it should be interpreted logically according to its plain meaning.*

Clearly, Ibn Ezra's notion of *sod* assumed that any hidden meanings in the text were fully compatible with the giving of the Torah by God! In addition, the introduction makes plain that his commentary deals primarily with *p'shat* [the plain meaning of the text], as opposed to *sod*. Thus, Ibn Ezra's more than 100 references in the commentary to *sod* generally identify matters that are not resolved by *p'shat*.[7]

Notwithstanding this notion of *sod* that bolsters authenticity of the text, Spinoza disingenuously asserted that Ibn Ezra was alluding to a contradictory hidden meaning in his comments on Deuteronomy 1:2 — that all the listed passages were written well after Mosaic times. This assertion also flew in the face of Ibn Ezra's subsequent comments on the last twelve verses in the Torah (which are among the passages he listed in Deuteronomy 1:2). On those verses, Ibn Ezra gave the same explanation as the first of Rashi's: that Joshua wrote them. Ibn Ezra went on to say that Joshua did so through prophecy, which would address the perceived incompatibility (with transcription in Mosaic times) of the phrase "until this day" in Deuteronomy 34:5. Thus, these comments reflect belief both in textual authenticity and in prophecy, an idea Spinoza repeatedly disparaged.

However, Ibn Ezra didn't only confirm his view of the text as written in Mosaic times on the last twelve verses. His comments on Genesis

36:31 characterize as "laughable" the idea that this verse was written later (as had been suggested by an individual whose first name was identified by Ibn Ezra as Isaac). Ironically, Spinoza listed this verse among other passages (beyond those mentioned by Ibn Ezra) as incompatible with Mosaic transcription. He specifically prefaced the listing with the observation that Ibn Ezra had not found these passages, thus suggesting that, had Ibn Ezra found them, he would have also mentioned them.

Yet Spinoza's misunderstanding and misrepresentation did not stop here. The most bizarre distortion came in his portrayal of Ibn Ezra's comment back in Genesis on 12:6 itself. There (but not on Deuteronomy 1:2) Ibn Ezra wrote, "He who is enlightened will keep silent." This kind of comment (discouraging further explanation) appears many times in his commentary and generally signals that a deeper treatment (i.e., involving *sod*) would be confusing, beyond the level of many of his readers, or outside the scope of his relatively brief approach.[8] However, Spinoza included this comment within the scope of remarks on Deuteronomy 1:2, thus suggesting Ibn Ezra's own need to be silent over textual authenticity. This linkage then suggested Ibn Ezra had been afraid to challenge the traditional view openly.[9]

Contrary to Spinoza's suggestion, however, Ibn Ezra did differ openly on occasion from established explanations. In fact, the thirteenth century authority Nachmanides (referred to earlier in this book as Ramban) devoted much space in his own commentary on Torah to opposing such views of Ibn Ezra, whom he named individually.[10] It is noteworthy that Nachmanides, as he is known to a larger body of Bible students, clearly stated his personal belief in Mosaic transcription (in his introduction to Genesis) but did not dispute Ibn Ezra's comments on Genesis 12:6 or Deuteronomy 1:2. Thus, Nachmanides, who had read Ibn Ezra from the same Sephardic tradition and from a point much closer in time, saw no challenge over the authenticity of the text.

Such was the character of Spinoza's use of Ibn Ezra's commentary to support his own views. Yet one may ask why this matter is so critical. Might Spinoza still have influenced Biblical Criticism without claiming such support? Perhaps, but consider the likelihood that, in the Enlightenment, the typical student of the Bible without a strong background in Hebrew would have relied on Spinoza for understanding Ibn Ezra and other Jewish commentaries. With this advantage over Hobbes, Spinoza emerged with his approach (and, notably, the broad rejection of Mosaic transcription) ingrained in Source Criticism and ultimately in the Wellhausen Hypothesis.

As a result, today's Source Critics often begin with Spinoza's analysis, with little mention, much less weighing, of possible explanations that support textual authenticity. Routinely, such analysis includes the purported doubts of Ibn Ezra, and when these doubts are denied by Ibn Ezra's own words, the investment in the Documentary Hypothesis is too great to accept such evidence. Instead, books like Brettler's *How to Read the Jewish Bible* (Oxford: Oxford University Press, 2007) imply that Ibn Ezra's condemnation of a challenge to textual authenticity on Genesis 36:31 was meant to conceal his own doubts (see page 2). We can but guess how literary analysis of the text might have developed had it been guided by Hobbes's more open and objective approach, since we see scant re-examination of Spinoza's premises in our time.

iii. Key Elements in the Development of the Wellhausen Hypothesis

We have traced in some detail the origins of doubt over Divine authorship and the misrepresentation of Ibn Ezra's commentary to fuel that doubt. Now that we are entering into the further developments leading to the Wellhausen Hypothesis, we will focus on certain key elements that connect most clearly with the four "source documents" framing the Wellhausen Hypothesis. It is these elements that, along with Spinoza's redactor concept, account for the major points of objection to Source Criticism.

"J" and "E" Sources Based on "Doublets"

From its roots in the seventeenth century, what became the Wellhausen Hypothesis drew heavily on a succession of ideas beginning with those of the eighteenth century French scholar Jean Astruc. Ironically, Astruc sought to defend Moses' writing of the Five Books but was troubled by what he perceived as two separate accounts of Creation: Genesis 1:1–2:3 (the seven days of Creation) and second in 2:4–3:21 (scene in the Garden of Eden). As noted in Section 6 of Stage II, these two accounts do not use the same name of God and differ in other respects. Astruc was also concerned with other so-called "doublets" (such as two different rulers having designs on Abraham's wife Sarah at different times). To rationalize what he viewed as inconsistent or unlikely repetitions of narrative text, Astruc introduced the idea of two pre-existing subtexts (one using the E-Name of God and the other using the J-Name) from which Moses compiled Genesis.

During the first quarter of the eighteenth century, the German theologian J. G. Eichhorn extended Astruc's model to apply throughout the entire Mosaic text, not just within Genesis. But, more importantly, following the ideas of Spinoza, Eichhorn also transformed the subtexts into source documents written after Moses. At this point, there were then two source documents, E and J, which were largely designed to accommodate the occurrence of the perceived narrative doublets.

"D" Source Based on Josiah's Discovery

At roughly the same time as Eichhorn, another German scholar, W. M. L. de Wette, took a special interest in Deuteronomy. Spinoza had already noted the specific variation between the Ten Commandments in Deuteronomy 5 and the Ten Commandments in Exodus 20, but de Wette looked at the general character of the discrepancy between laws stated in Deuteronomy and those stated earlier in the text. Just as the Deuteronomic version of the Fourth Commandment provides more detail than the version in Exodus, so too do the Deuteronomic versions of other laws (e.g., those involving the return of lost objects and use of fair weights[11]) in relation to their counterparts in earlier books. Moreover, certain laws in Deuteronomy cover totally new topics — e.g., divorce (in Chapter 24) and levirate marriage (in Chapter 25).

Thus, De Wette concluded that Deuteronomy was drawn mainly from a source document (labeled D) separate from E and J, with D reflecting more extensive legal enactments of a later period. He placed the actual writing of D during King Josiah's reign (seventh century BCE), as described in Kings II 22-23. Specifically, Kings II 22:8 tells of a scroll being found during that reign, which de Wette asserted was actually the then newly created Book of Deuteronomy.

Among the evidence cited for this assertion is the resemblance of the obligation in Deuteronomy 7:5 to love God "with all your heart, and with all your soul, and with all your might" to the characterization of King Josiah in Kings II 23:25 as having repented, as no other King, "with all his heart, and with all his soul, and with all his might." That characterization suggested to de Wette that Deuteronomy's author (labeled as the "Deuteronomist") was both a contemporary and an admirer of King Josiah. According to this approach, Deuteronomy was added to the other Mosaic Text to give more standing to the new and extended versions of the law implemented in King Josiah's time.

Another link between Deuteronomy and the reign of King Josiah lay for de Wette in Deuteronomy 16:2 where a place of central worship is mentioned: "in the place that God will choose to have His name dwell there." De Wette noted that Exodus 20:21 speaks of "in every place that I (God) cause My name to be mentioned," which suggested that people had more choice at that point in where to worship. And, inasmuch as Kings II tells of Josiah's destruction of *bamot* [private altars] and his centralizing of sacrificial rites, Deuteronomy 16:2 was thus created to support the King's actions. In viewing Deuteronomy as promoting an author's agenda, De Wette heralded an attitude toward the text that became more pronounced as the Wellhausen Hypothesis took final form.

"P" Source Based on Ritual Complexity

The last major development in the Wellhausen Hypothesis grew out of the ritual matters that make up most of Leviticus (e.g., sacrifices, priestly duties, and dietary laws) and that occupy substantial subtexts in Exodus (e.g., the Sabbath and the building of the Tabernacle) and Numbers (e.g., the dedication of the Tabernacle and Nazirite vows). As proposed by H. Hupfeld in the mid-nineteenth century, the fourth documentary source included these matters and was labeled "P" to suggest that priests wrote it. Especially as interpreted by yet another

German scholar, K. H. Graf, the P source came later than King Josiah. To understand Graf's dating order, consider that Deuteronomy (which repeats so much from the previous books) only briefly deals with details of ritual — though, as we saw before, it does mention a central site for worship. Thus, if P had been written at the same time or before D, Deuteronomy would have, according to Graf's perspective, included a more extensive treatment of ritual matters.

Within this analysis, two critical assumptions took hold:

1. First, cultural forms grow more complex as they mature, with the greater complexity of later Jewish practice illustrating this principle; and
2. Second, the detailed ritual in the P source had been designed by the priests so as to solidify their communal authority.

Denigrating Religious Practices and Attributing Political Agendas

Not only did this second assumption wrap P with a distasteful political agenda, but also it pointedly denigrated many vital aspects of traditional Judaism (notably, the Sabbath and dietary laws) still being practiced. This feature of Source Criticism made the Wellhausen Hypothesis especially attractive to more liberal forms of Judaism that have forgone traditional observance. This feature also appealed, not surprisingly, to anti-Semites and, along with denial of the Divine authorship of the Five Books, formed an essential underpinning for Nazi "religious" doctrine.[12]

The development of P also created an opening for those who would attribute political agendas to J and E. To those individuals, the division into two subtexts reflected the splitting of the Jewish nation into a southern and northern kingdom after King Solomon's death in roughly 800 BCE. Specifically, the J source reflected the view of the southern kingdom, in which control by priests, as descendants of Aaron, continued from Solomon's times. Meanwhile, E aligned with the northern kingdom where Moses' descendants, the Levites, dominated. Thus, the presumed existence of the two subtexts (with J first and E slightly later) was interpreted as a struggle involving competing authorities: the priests and the Levites.

Prior to P, this interpretation of priest-Levite competition was challenged in explaining large pieces of J and E that seem to favor neither Aaron nor Moses and do not fit stylistically with other parts of J and E. The so-called first account of Creation (Genesis 1:1–2:3), which uses only the E-Name of God, provides an easy example of a subtext that cannot be said to favor either purported side. Yet, by attributing this account to P, advocates of the competition model could distinguish it from other parts of E with a supposedly less formal narrative.

The J Name of God in the "J" and "P" Sources

Beginning in Exodus, however, the J-Name occurs much more frequently than the E-Name, especially after Exodus 6:3, where God states that the patriarchs Abraham, Isaac, and Jacob did not know Him by the J-Name. Thus, from that point on, subtexts using the J-Name could be allocated to J or P depending on the circumstances. Among the circumstances most important for allocating such subtexts to P is a clear involvement with ritual, which was considered more formal. In particular, this ritual involvement (with the simultaneous use of the J-Name) dominates

- virtually all of Leviticus,
- major pieces of Exodus (notably, Chapters 25–31 and 35–49), and
- major pieces of Numbers (notably, Chapters 1–10, 15–19, and 25–36).

Thus forerunners of the Wellhausen Hypothesis assigned these portions to P. In contrast, Chapters 21–23 of Exodus also use the J-Name but deal with civil law rather than ritual. These portions were assigned to J.

Synthesis of J, E, D, and P

At this point, Wellhausen synthesized the foregoing elements and presented his hypothesis of the four sources in the chronological order of J, E, D, and P, with the final redaction attributed to Ezra. In light of Graf's contribution to the perceived order of the sources (and therefore to their synthesis), some scholars give him equal billing by referring to the "Graf-Wellhausen Hypothesis." Since the publication of the Wellhausen Hypothesis, many variations have been advanced, including an earlier fusion of J and E and further subdivision of the four sources into separate subtexts with their own distinctive authors. In addition, objections (to be discussed next) and further analysis (often based on later archaeological work) have brought many scholars to markedly revise the Wellhausen Hypothesis or to retain only certain parts. Thus, the term "documentary hypothesis," which encompasses all such adjustments, takes in a wide range of views.

iv. Major Objections to the Wellhausen Hypothesis

In tracking the major points of objection, we will not touch on more specialized issues that can be found in other sources.[13] This approach permits placing each major point within the context of one of the three key developments of the Wellhausen Hypothesis, as outlined below:

a. Text divided into two sources J and E, reflecting doublets (perceived variants of the same events); sources identified according to different names of God: the four-letter Hebrew name starting with transliterated J and the five-letter name starting with transliterated E.
b. Deuteronomic text (D) split off from the preceding text, reflecting the perceived later redaction of D in times of King Josiah.
c. Priestly text (P) supposedly written in Ezra's time and drawn from law/ritual in first four Books and from other narrative parts of J and E; narrative portions of P drawn from J and E are those that promote neither Aaron nor Moses individually.

The compilation over time and the final editing of the whole of the five Books, which the Wellhausen Hypothesis associates with Ezra, figure into each one of these developments.

Objections to J and E

Let us focus on (a) above: the text divided into two sources in response to doublets with different names of God.

In Section 6 of Stage II, we explored Wellhausen's perception of two conflicting versions of Creation (Genesis 1:1–2:3 and 2:4–3:24), as well as the traditional explanation of Rashi that the first subtext plays the role of a summary. In that explanation, the details of the second version (e.g., the creation of man before woman) would not be expected to match the broader statements in the first. Many Source Critics grant that the first version looks like a summary but attribute this appearance to the redactor's editorial skill in fusing conflicting texts.[14]

The Wellhausen Hypothesis also views the use of different names of God (E alone in the first version and a combination of E and JE in the second) as evidence of separate authors. Yet, as we noted in Section 6 of Stage II, there is ample cause to distinguish between the Names through context rather than authorship. To wit, the E-Name marks God in the distant role of Creator and Judge, while the J-Name connotes direct interaction/intervention with Man or the Jewish people.

Further into Genesis, additional doublets are detected, such as in two different covenants made with Abraham: the Covenant between the Parts (Gen. 15:1–21) and the Covenant of Circumcision (Gen. 17:1–14). In the first, only the J-Name is used, while the E-Name predominates in the second. Hence Wellhausen concluded that these two subtexts were drawn from different sources. However, the traditional distinction in Divine Names cited above can be seen to fit the case at hand. In particular, the Covenant between the Parts reflects direct Divine intervention and such intervention focused on the Jewish people, while the Covenant of Circumcision involves only indirect intervention and applies to all descendants (not just Jewish descendants) of Abraham, as the father of nations.

Other perceived doublets (for example, the abduction of Sarah by Pharaoh's officers in Genesis 12 and the abduction of Sarah by Abimelekh in Genesis 20) employ different Divine names whose distinction can be explained accordingly.[15] Yet, proponents of the

Wellhausen Hypothesis insist that such pairs of narratives (which give accounts of similar events) must have different authors. This insistence was lampooned in Walter Kaufmann's hypothetical analysis of Goethe's classic nineteenth century work *Faust* from the viewpoint of Source Criticism.[16] From that viewpoint, the protagonist Faust's involvement first with a heroine named Gretchen and then with Helen of Troy would require authorship of the first account to be different from the second.

Until now, we have been dealing with doublets formed from two distinct subtexts with no overlap. However, divisions based on different Names of God have also led Source Critics, in various cases, to fragment what reads in the Torah as a single continuous account, thus creating a doublet. We see, for example, the Flood story (Genesis 6:9–8:22) where both the J-Name and the E-Name appear as follows:

	Verses where J-Name occurs	Verses where E-Name occurs
Chapter 6		9, 12, 13, 22
Chapter 7	1, 6, 16	16
Chapter 8	20, 21	1, 15

This distribution of Divine names means (for Source Critics) that the redactor assembled this subtext from separate verses in variable order. Verses using the J-Name came from one source; verses using the E-Name came from another source; and verses using neither came from whichever source seems more likely according to subject or language. Moreover, Genesis 7:16 must have come from two sources because both names occur there.[17] While proponents of the Wellhausen Hypothesis accept a contorted compilation along these lines,[18] they do not accept what they perceive as anomalous features of the text itself.

Objections to D

Let us now examine (b), the Deuteronomic text, as purportedly written in the time of Josiah, and split off from preceding text.

As we noted above, the perception of D as written separately comes in large part from variation in the laws found in Deuteronomy in relation to those in previous Books. This perception ignores the traditional explanation by Nachmanides (1194–1270) of these variations. Writing in the introduction to his comments on Deuteronomy, Nachmanides noted that the laws in Deuteronomy typically carry further details and further justification than those of their counterparts in the preceding text. Such elaborations, he said, were intended to avoid past transgressions in the Wilderness and to overcome new challenges in the Land of Canaan.

Failing to address traditional explanations is a major objection to the Wellhausen Hypothesis that could also be associated with other key developments of the Wellhausen Hypothesis besides D. (We have, for example, already mentioned Rashi's understanding of the two accounts of Creation, which is also ignored by Wellhausen.) Here, however, with Nachmanides' explanation for the variation in the laws in Deuteronomy, we have a single rationale that could obviate the separate identification of an entire purported source document. It is a rationale clearly rooted in the text, since Deuteronomy begins by focusing on transgressions committed in the Wilderness and follows with challenges (such as intermarriage — see 4:25–28) to be faced in Canaan. Only after addressing these subjects does the main body of law in Deuteronomy commence.

While the literature of Source Criticism is far too vast to guarantee that Nachmanides' explanation has never been addressed, its omission both from the Wellhausen Hypothesis and from recognized contemporary works is quite telling.[19] Perhaps one might argue that Source Critics should not be expected to choose Nachmanides from the large body of traditional commentators for particular refutation. Nachmanides' commentary is not simply one among many, however. Popular versions of the Hebrew printed Pentateuch have long carried Rashi and Nachmanides as the two standard commentaries that accompany the actual text (with a few other commentaries sometimes present, but not consistently). Ironically, when Nachmanides disagreed with an interpretation of another commentator, he still described the interpretation and identified its proponent (especially Rashi or Ibn Ezra). Proponents of the Wellhausen Hypothesis have typically not met this standard of discourse.

Returning to the specifics underlying the separation of D, we find that its dating by the Wellhausen Hypothesis relies primarily on several factors beyond the variation in legal material. First, as we saw earlier, there is a perceived conflict in two particular verses, one in Exodus and another in Deuteronomy, which address possible locations of altars for offerings. From this perceived conflict comes the idea that the second of these verses was written at a later time. This later time was fixed by the second factor, a verse in Kings II noted above, which speaks of a scroll being found in the time of King Josiah, which the Wellhausen Hypothesis proposes was a newly written Deuteronomy. Finally, according to this view, the extolling in Kings II of certain qualities in King Josiah that are demanded in Deuteronomy indicates that Deuteronomy was written, at least in part, to legitimize what is perceived as Josiah's adjustment of law and religious practice. Let us examine these factors more carefully.

In discussing altars in Exodus 20:24, the Torah refers to their locations thusly: "***b'khol ha-makom*** *asher azcir et sh'mi* — **in each place** where I will have my name recognized." Meanwhile, Moses speaks in Deuteronomy 16:2 of offering sacrifices: "***ba-makom*** *asher Yivchar* — **in the place** that He (God) will choose..."

The variance (as highlighted by the bold characters) tells us, claimed Wellhausen, that people were allowed, in the time of Exodus, to bring offerings any place they felt called on to do so, but that by the time of Deuteronomy (purportedly during King Josiah's reign), worship was centralized.

The problem with this approach, as pointed out by Rabbi David Tzvi Hoffmann,[20] lies in a distortion through translation. The presence of the definite article prefix *ha* in *ha-makom* means a designated place, which precludes the more permissive interpretation in the Wellhausen Hypothesis. While offerings were brought in different locations in the Wilderness, they were brought only in the Tabernacle (as the designated place). On the other hand, when the verse in Deuteronomy speaks of a single location God will choose, it means in the future, after the conquest of Canaan when the Temple stood in Jerusalem. Thus, there is no inconsistency at all between the verses in question, and the perception of inconsistency results from a misreading of Hebrew. In fact, errors by the Wellhausen Hypothesis in translation and syntax occur elsewhere,[21] but this error concerning the choice in sites for offerings may be the most critical.

We have already mentioned the use of Kings II 22:8 by proponents of the Wellhausen Hypothesis to suggest that Deuteronomy was actually created during the reign of King Josiah, even though the verse actually speaks of a scroll being found at that time. Then, in contrast, the same proponents take at face value the report (in Chapter 23) of Josiah's destruction of private altars. In other words, where the text supports their theory of the first centralization of worship in Josiah's time, it is accepted; but where the text doesn't support that theory, it is simply reinterpreted. If that approach to proof strikes you as arbitrary, you are not alone.

Finally, there is the description of Josiah upon his death as having returned to God, "as no other king, with all his heart, with all his soul, and with all his might" (Kings II 23:25). Because the character of his return matches the language in Deuteronomy 7:5, Wellhausen asserted that D was written by an admirer of Josiah who sought to give Josiah's additions to the law more standing. In weighing the merits of this approach, just think of the many eulogies that praise the deceased in terms of lines taken from famous books or speeches. Following the lead of the Wellhausen Hypothesis, we could then ascribe the writing of the famous books or speeches to the eulogist to give more honor to the deceased.

Objections to P

Let us now examine (c), the Priestly text (P) supposedly written in Ezra's time and used as source of law/ritual in the first four books and as source for more "formal" narrative formerly ascribed to J or E.

The separation of P from the subtexts in the first two major components of the Wellhausen Hypothesis involves three primary perceptions:

1. The details of ritual reflect later development of religious practice, consistent with the premise that key elements of culture grow more complex over time.

2. There is a discernible formality that objectively distinguishes certain parts of the narrative in the first four Books.
3. In the first four Books, some narrative seems to favor Aaron over Moses or Moses over Aaron, while some narrative favors neither.

Increasing Complexity over Time

We begin with the first premise mentioned above — that key elements of culture grow more complex over time. At the very outset of our journey, in Section 1 of Stage I, we introduced this premise, along with the devastating counterexamples offered by Oxford Professor Reverend George Rawlinson. Drawn from major languages, these counterexamples represented key elements of culture whose complexity diminished rather than grew as they developed. Rawlinson's argument not only rendered the premise untenable, but also raised doubts over Wellhausen's purportedly scientific approach.

Undeterred by Rawlinson, proponents of the Wellhausen Hypothesis clung to the premise restricted to religious practice and obligation. Though this restricted assertion of growing complexity can itself be directly challenged, it is even more enlightening to assume its truth and then follow the consequences for the consistency and credibility of the Wellhausen Hypothesis. As will be seen below, the restricted assertion cannot coexist with the terms of the second major component, the separation of the source D. In particular, if the restricted assertion holds, then D could not have been written at the time of King Josiah in the seventh century BCE. Here is why:

Let us recall that the laws repeated in Deuteronomy are typically more detailed than their preceding versions. For example, consider two such laws as shown below:

Subject of Laws	More Detailed Treatment	Less Detailed Treatment
Returning lost objects	Deuteronomy 22:1–4	Exodus 23:4
Using fair weights	Deuteronomy 25:13–16	Leviticus 19:35–37

In light of this added detail in Deuteronomy, in accepting the focused assertion about growing complexity in religious practice and obligation, we must conclude the passages in Deuteronomy came later than the corresponding versions in the earlier Books. In particular, Deuteronomy 25:13–16, which the Wellhausen Hypothesis assigns to D, came later than Leviticus 19:35–37, which is assigned to P.

But wait! This conclusion runs counter to the Wellhausen Hypothesis tenet that P was written in the time of Ezra (fourth century BCE), three centuries later than King Josiah (when D was supposedly written). Either Wellhausen failed to grasp this consequence of the premise underlying P, or else he saw nothing wrong in applying it selectively. In any event, this dilemma makes for another major objection.

The preceding paragraphs have focused on the subtexts of P that predominantly involve ritual law and practice and that occur chiefly in Leviticus and in certain chapters of Exodus and Numbers. We saw particular difficulties in placing the authorship of the legal subtexts in P at a later time than certain legal subtexts in Deuteronomy. Now, let us turn to the narrative portions of P.

As you will recall from our discussion in (iii) above, the Wellhausen Hypothesis distinguishes these portions from the narrative portions of J and E in two ways. Specifically, P uses more formal language than J or E, and P favors neither Aaron over Moses nor Moses over Aaron. Because Moses and Aaron do not appear in the text until Exodus, and because Genesis is essentially all narrative, the subtexts of P in Genesis can be separated from J and E, according to the Wellhausen Hypothesis, purely through their purportedly greater formality.

However, in the *Prolegomena*, Wellhausen simply stated this principle without providing many specific assignments of particular subtexts to J, E, or P. Thus, it was left to those who followed to make the assignments explicitly, frequently with wide differences among themselves. Even in subtexts that, according to Source Critics, involved only J and E (and not P), such differences were well known.[22] When P was added to the mix, the new dimension of choice exacerbated the lack of agreement among proponents of the Wellhausen Hypothesis and the growing appearance of subjectivity. Yet Source Critics insisted on the scientific certainty of their work. They were, ironically, following Spinoza's approach, which denied the acceptance of what was only reasonably probable.

Statistical Linguistics vs. Source Criticism

This brings us to the work of Y. T. Radday and H. Shore in *Genesis: An Authorship Study* (Rome: Biblical Institute Press, 1985). Radday and Shore applied statistical linguistics to one of the more respected allocations of Genesis to J, E, and P, as presented by Sellin and Roth.[23] This particular allocation is the one used by the Encyclopedia Judaica, and like most mainstream allocations assigns no subtexts in Genesis to D. The basic research question was this: when obvious controls (to be identified shortly) are applied for the type of text, is there any statistically valid difference among J, E, and P as regards certain standard linguistic indicators? These indicators include the relative frequency of, for example, various word lengths, number/states of verbs, the definite article, prefixed prepositions, suffixed prepositions, and marks of possession.

It should be noted that this type of analysis reliably distinguishes works written by different authors and has been used forensically to help determine whether the same person wrote two different messages. This capacity for distinction results from the involuntary nature of such indicators in an individual's style. To control for natural differences in text (that would not be attributable to different authors), Radday and Shore separated each of the J, E, and P subtexts into three categories: narrative (N), Divine speech (D), and human speech (H). In this way, the researchers were able to make comparisons among NJ, NE, and NP; among DJ, DE, and DP; and among HJ, HE, and HP. The data showed J and E were indistinguishable and that the difference between N and D+H was significantly stronger than the difference between P and J+E.

You will recall that Wellhausen viewed P as more formal than J or E. Because formality might also be a function of vocabulary, as opposed to style, Radday and Shore also analyzed the use of vocabulary in the various subsets. They found that the differences among N, D, and H were at least as strong as the differences among J, E, and P. In other words, it makes as much or more sense to attribute differences in vocabulary to whether the text is narrative, Divine speech, or human speech. Of course, this statistical analysis does not guarantee certainty, but it does raise large questions over the purportedly objective allocation of the text by Source Critics. And perhaps the most vital question is whether such allocation of the text meets the standard posed by Spinoza and embraced by his followers in dismissing the single authorship of the five Books. In particular, if Spinoza's standard for acceptance requires more than reasonable probability, how can Source Critics now accept the differentiation of the text into J, E, and P in the face of another more objective method with the same or greater statistical validity?

In summary, we have seen striking logical flaws in the three major facets of the Wellhausen Hypothesis, as well as evidence that its classification of text is statistically unfounded.

Section 13
Textual Integrity and Role of the Ten Commandments

i. Authenticity of the Text and the Placement of P'tuchot

Section 2 of Stage I spoke of the demarcation of *parshiyot* [paragraphs] within the Five Books of Moses through *p'tuchot* [open spacing]. This presumes the consistent placement of *p'tuchot* from one scroll to another. Consider however the potential for scribal error over thousands of years, since Torah scrolls, as a matter of Jewish Law, must be written by hand. How could one treat any designated placement of *p'tuchot* without at least some skepticism? And even if we find the demarcation of *parshiyot* consistent among current Torah scrolls, is it not possible that some corruption of the original version crept in over time?

Let us begin with the issue of the consistency among different scrolls. There are three different traditions in writing Torah scrolls: Ashkenazi (European), Sephardic (Mediterranean), and Yemenite. When examining today's scrolls written under any of the three traditions, only one variation occurs in the placement of the *p'tuchot*: whether a *p'tuchah* appears just after Leviticus 7:21 or just after Leviticus 7:27. Torah scrolls of the Ashkenazi (European) and Sephardic (Mediterranean) tradition show the latter placement, while those of the Yemenite tradition show the former.

Perhaps that singular difference seems unremarkable in our world of photocopiers and digital scanners, but the general level of agreement in the placement of *p'tuchot* can be traced back to the twelfth century and the great code of Maimonides, the *Mishneh Torah*. There, Maimonides actually lists the exact location of every *p'tuchah*, as shown in Appendix a, and every *s'tumah* [closed spacing] in the Five Books of Moses. He also summarizes the numbers of *p'tuchot* (that do not open or close a Book) and *s'tumot* as follows:

	Genesis	Exodus	Leviticus	Numbers	Deuteronomy
p'tuchot	43	69	52	94	34
s'tumot	48	95	46	66	124

Today's print version of the *Mishneh Torah* follows the Ashkenazi/Sephardic placement of the *p'tuchah* ending Leviticus 7:27. However, Yemenite scholars contend, with some evidence, that the listing in the original manuscript of Maimonides was tampered with.[24] The importance attached to correct placement of spacing is evident in the *Mishneh Torah*'s requirement that any scroll with an omitted or misplaced *p'tuchah* or *s'tumah* is invalid and must be buried. Actually, such absolute insistence on textual integrity goes back much further than the *Mishneh Torah*. As noted in Section 2 of Stage I, many scribal rules presented by Maimonides appeared in *Masekhet Sof'rim*, a work commonly dated in the eighth century. However, because these scribal rules typically bear no attribution, many consider them centuries older, possibly pre-Talmudic.

The reader may be convinced by now that such limited variance in our document of 79,847 words and 304,805 letters would at least allow for the discussion of a pattern in the text. At the same time, however, there is still the second issue of authenticity. Granted that scrolls written after the *Mishneh Torah* should be expected to maintain a high degree of consistency in *p'tuchot* and *s'tumot*, how did Maimonides know what was authentic? How could he be sure that nowhere before him had corruptions been introduced? The answer is the Masoretic tradition and its culminating document, the codex of Aaron ben Asher, which is mentioned explicitly in the *Mishneh Torah*.

Masoretic Text

The Hebrew word *masorah* means "transmission." While the Babylonian destruction of the First Temple 586 years before the

Common Era led to some dispersion of the Jewish people, that dispersion proved quite limited in comparison with what occurred after the second destruction some 650 years later at the hand of the Romans. The early sages of the Talmud recognized that the Oral Law (which informs the Written Law in the Five Books of Moses) would not be accurately transmitted simply by mouth amidst the dislocation and so took part in the redaction of the Oral Law under the editorship of Rabbi Judah the Prince. In a similar way, certain scribes (known several centuries later as the Masoretes) dedicated themselves to faithful textual transmission of the original Five Books of Moses.

Underlining the importance of accurate transmission, the sages of the Talmud sometimes relied on peculiarities of spelling in the Five Books of Moses to make judgments in Jewish Law. One example involves the requirement for a Jewish man to bind his arm during certain times of prayer, a requirement alluded to in Exodus 13:16. In that verse, the Hebrew word *yad'khah* [your arm] is spelled anomalously, with its possessive suffix resembling the Hebrew word for "weak." From that spelling, the Talmud derives (in *M'nakhot* 37a) that a man should bind his weaker arm, i.e., the left for a right-handed person. This reliance on exact spelling notwithstanding, the sages of the Talmud also acknowledged (in *Kiddushin* 30a) that not all sages were sufficiently expert in variant spellings in the text. These Talmudic references date back to the fourth and fifth century.

In support of their special mission, the Masoretes developed various forms of annotation alongside, beneath, and within the text of the Five Books of Moses. The annotated text was recorded on separate sheets, more like notebook paper than a scroll. A scribe's full collection of such sheets covering some or all of the sacred texts is known as a codex (plural: codices). The annotations addressed various matters of textual integrity, including placement of *p'tuchot* and *s'tumot* and insertion of vowels and syllabic accents (since the words of a Torah scroll appear with consonants only). The annotations also specify whether the spelling of a given word, which may occur in more than one place, is at that point *malei* (i.e., includes silent consonants) or *chaseir* (lacks such consonants) and whether the word should be read differently from its spelling. A third important function was the inclusion of cantillation symbols, which indicate how verses are to be chanted, with implications for how words are grouped. In particular, the cantillation symbols identify the ends of verses in a text with no visible signs of punctuation other than *p'tuchot* and *s'tumot*.

While Masoretic codices encompassed all the sacred texts (including the Prophets and the Writings), more attention was paid to the Five Books of Moses as the most basic and holy document among them. Special effort went into systematizing the annotations, and the format attributed to the ben Asher family of Masoretes gained wide acceptance. In addition, the judgment of a tenth century descendant of that family, Aaron ben Asher, in choosing the correct nuance of text from competing versions was deemed superior. And so it was that Maimonides relied on a codex available to him in Alexandria, Egypt, that he described as having been personally checked by Aaron ben Asher. This codex, which covered the entire Jewish Bible (including the Prophets and Writings), is thought by many to be the Aleppo Codex, named for the town in Syria to where it was moved in the fourteenth century. There it was housed and guarded by the local Jewish population until a large part of the codex (including nearly all of the Five Books of Moses) was destroyed or stolen during anti-Jewish riots in December 1947 following the United Nations vote to partition Palestine.

With but a small remnant of the Five Books of Moses left physically present in the Aleppo Codex, Rabbi Mordechai Breuer still compared the Aleppo Codex with five other recognized Masoretic codices using notes made by scholars in Aleppo before the 1947 riots.[25] His study showed that for the five other codices (four recognized manuscripts and the earliest printed version),[26] there were more than 200 words in the text with a disagreement in spelling, but, for the preponderance of them, four of the codices agreed (so the single outlier could be ignored). Of the twenty remaining cases (with a more balanced disagreement than four-to-one), fourteen were resolvable by looking to the Masoretic notations themselves, which sometimes clearly determined the actual spelling. The Aleppo Codex, it turned out, is fully consistent with this analysis: it was on the majority side on each of the four-to-one disagreements; it agreed with the notation-based determination in the additional fourteen cases; and it presented one of the two variant spellings arising in the six cases of balanced disagreement among the other five versions.

Because the *Mishneh Torah* was written as a code of law, it provided only certain highlights of the codex — such as the list of *p'tuchot* and *s'tumot* in the Five Books of Moses, which were well known and accepted. It did not, however, provide details of possibly variant spellings. Amidst the Crusades and other persecutions in medieval Europe, there was scant access to a reliable codex and spelling variance did creep in. This prompted one of the chief arbiters of Jewish law in the thirteenth century to issue a guide for words with possibly variant spelling, which eventually led to elimination of discrepancies, especially among Ashkenazi scrolls.[27]

Modern Torah Scrolls

Today, the total visible disparity in Torah scrolls among the three traditions (Ashkenazi, Sephardic, and Yemenite) is quite limited, not only in the placement of *p'tuchot*, but also in all respects other than distinctions in the size or design of letters. Between scrolls of the Ashkenazi and Sephardic tradition (which constitute the vast majority), there is but one distinction — the spelling of the fourth word in Deuteronomy 23:2. The Ashkenazi version ends in the silent Hebrew letter *hei*, while the Sephardic version ends in the silent letter *aleph* (in both versions, the word means "crushed" and is pronounced identically as *dakkah*).

The Yemenite version agrees with the Sephardic version on this point but also differs in a few other ways. The most pronounced of these further differences involves the passage of "the Song of Moses" (Deuteronomy 32:1–43) that appears in a poetic format with an extra (non-*s'tumah*) space in the middle of each line. Ashkenazi and Sephardic scrolls present this poem on seventy lines, as opposed to sixty-seven in the Yemenite version. A second further difference occurs in **Genesis**

9:29, which begins with a singular past tense verb in the Ashkenazi and Sephardic versions, but the plural past tense in the Yemenite. However, within the context of the verse there is no effective change in meaning. The nine other differences involve spelling only, with no effect on pronunciation. Appendix b provides a full list of spelling and spacing differences.[28]

In summary, none of the differences in the recognized Hebrew texts of the Five Books of Moses affects the meaning. This statement holds true even for those scholars who, despite Rabbi Breuer's definitive study, argue for the greater accuracy of a codex (e.g., the Leningrad Codex[29]) other than the Aleppo Codex. Inasmuch as the matter of placement of *p'tuchot* permits only a single and tiny variation, we can rely on the faithfulness of our current text to consider a pattern in the original Five Books of Moses based on that placement.

ii. The Ten Commandments as Guidance for Other Laws

In developing the Ten Commandments as a framework for textual organization, Section 2 of Stage I noted that they are actually viewed in Jewish tradition not merely as individual laws, but rather as broader guidance from which other laws in the Five Books of Moses derive. This section will explain a traditional source for this view within Exodus and, in so doing, will illustrate the reliance on the exactness of language in the Five Books of Moses.

Before we turn to this source, let us carefully read the Torah's actual Hebrew term for the Ten Commandments: *Aseret HaD'varim*. The word *Aseret* means "ten," while *HaD'varim* means "the statements," and it is precisely the term "the Ten Statements" that appears each of the three times the biblical text refers to what we call the Ten Commandments (Exodus 34:28, Deuteronomy 4:13, and Deuteronomy 10:4). If the intended translation had been "the Ten Commandments," the text would have read *Aseret HaMitzvot*, since *mitzvot* is the Hebrew word for "commandments." Especially because the Torah often refers to its own individual laws as *mitzvot*, it must be that the Ten Commandments constitute something different from simply ten particular commandments among the 613 traditionally counted in the Five Books as a whole. Indeed, within the complete text of the Ten Commandments, there are commandments (such as the prohibition against making a graven image) that go beyond the recognized ten.

The Biblical term *Aseret HaD'varim* changed slightly by the fifth century in the redaction of the Talmud to the term *Aseret HaDibrot* (cf. B'rakhot 12a) instead. The word *dibrot* [pronouncements] shares the same three-letter Hebrew root *dalet-beit-reish* as *d'varim* and thus bears a close relation. However, *d'varim* can refer equally to written or spoken statements, while *dibrot* refers only to spoken statements. It may be that Talmudic usage reinforced the conviction that the Ten Commandments were Divinely spoken before they were written. Or it may be that the context of the occurrence in Tractate *B'rakhot* (involving a daily recitation in the Temple service) suggested the word *dibrot* instead of *d'varim*. In any event, the notion of something beyond regular commandments still accompanies the term *Aseret HaDibrot*.

With this understanding that the Ten Commandments are somehow distinguished from ten ordinary commandments, we come to Exodus 24:12. We show below both in transliteration (see the Introduction for pronunciation) and in translation the key excerpt from that verse. There, after the oral presentation of the Ten Commandments (as recounted in Exodus 20:1–14), God tells Moses:

...*Alei eilai v'etnah l'cha*	Ascend to Me and I will give you
et Luchot HaEven	the Tablets of Stone,
v'HaTorah v'HaMitzvah	and the Torah and the Commandment,
asher catavti l'horotam.	which I wrote to instruct them.

As the translation appears here, the third and fourth lines excerpted above serve as an appositive phrase modifying "the Tablets of Stone." In other words, with the tablets there is the Torah, as well as the actual Commandment written on the tablets. The word "Torah" is thus taken as all of the commandments in the Five Books of Moses, while "Commandment" signifies the Ten Commandments as specific law, as stressed by the singular *mitzvah* (as opposed to the plural *mitzvot*). Finally, the pronoun "them" in the fourth line refers to the Jewish people.

This rendering of the excerpt follows the understanding of the standard commentator Rashi, as explained by his super-commentary Mizrachi.[30]

You will recall, however, that the only visible punctuation on a Torah scroll is the spacing, and no spacing occurs in the middle of this verse. So how did Rashi know that "the Torah and the Commandment..." constitute an appositive phrase, as opposed to the second and third elements of a series with "the Tablets of Stone" as the first element? The answer is the first word *et* on the second line of excerpt above. This word, which is never translated, precedes a direct object. Thus, if a series were intended, then the words *HaTorah* and *HaMitzvah* would have each been preceded by *et*. Accordingly, the third line of Hebrew would have read *et HaTorah v'et HaMitzvah* instead of *v'HaTorah v'HaMitzvah*. But since the third line does appear in the latter form, Rashi took the prefix *vav* (transliterated as *v'* and meaning "and") before *HaTorah* and *HaMitzvah* as explicative, thus making the third and fourth lines into an appositive phrase.[31]

The final conclusion that all 613 commandments derive from the Ten Commandments takes two further steps. First, since the tablets contained the Ten Commandments alone and since most of the Torah had not even been presented at that point, the relative clause of the fourth line ("which I wrote to instruct them") must refer exclusively to "the Commandment." Inasmuch as the narrative (i.e., non-legal) portion of the Five Books of Moses cannot reasonably be derived from a collection of laws, we must now read the third and fourth lines as "the legal part of the Torah (i.e., the 613 commandments) and the Commandment, which I wrote to instruct them." And because "the legal part of the Torah" forms an appositive for "the Tablets of Stone," which includes only the Ten Commandments, the Ten Commandments must form the basis for all 613 commandments in the Five Books of Moses.

This notion of all Torah law deriving from the Ten Commandments may explain why the passage from *Midrash Rabbah* on Song of Songs was not seen earlier as linking the Ten Commandments to the order of the text. If you will recall the discussion in Section 2 of Stage I, that passage speaks of the *parshiyot* [paragraphs] and the syntax [*dikduk* in Hebrew] of the text being written from the Ten Commandments. The word *parshiyot* could suggest the scope or breadth of law (rather than the order of paragraphs), while the word *dikduk* could refer to the details or depth of the law (rather than syntax). Thus, the passage in *Midrash Rabbah* could be read as confirmation of the idea explained by Rashi in Exodus 24:12. If read this way, there would be no special connection to an overall textual pattern.

Section 14
Mastery and Failure with the Shared Principles and Deuteronomy's Pattern

Section 3 of Stage I discussed the Jewish people's progression in the Torah through the Shared Principles until the Book of Numbers. We observed that although Principle D (duties of testimony/community) forms both the primary theme and context for that Book, this Shared Principle was not fulfilled — owing to transgressions in the Wilderness. We also stated that at the end of Leviticus, the first three Shared Principles had been fulfilled. Thus our approach in the present section will proceed as follows:

1. a demonstration of fulfillment of the first three Shared Principles in the first three Books;
2. further connections between the variations in the two versions of the Ten Commandments (in Exodus 20 and Deuteronomy 5) as a function of transgressions in Numbers;
3. division of Deuteronomy in relation to the Shared Principles.

i. Fulfillment of the First Three Shared Principles in the First Three Books

The first three Shared Principles, we will show, are fulfilled Book by Book in Genesis, Exodus, and Leviticus. In other words, fulfillment comes for

- Principle A (Respecting Creation) by the end of Genesis;
- Principle B (Loyalty to a Primary Relationship) by the end of Exodus;

- Principle C (Limited Access to Spiritual/Physical Resources) by the end of Leviticus.

In establishing these three points, we will identify transgression within each Book reflecting its respective Shared Principle and mark where such transgressions were overcome in that Book. We will also find an indication each time that the next Shared Principle was not attained.

Genesis

Murder, as forbidden in the Sixth Commandment, reflects Principle A (respecting Creation) and is pervasive in Genesis. This pervasiveness emerges in the following content:

- Cain's murder of Abel (Gen. 4:8);
- The role of *chamas* (violence) in bringing the Flood (6:11);
- Abraham's fear that he would be murdered for Sarah (12:12);
- The test of Abraham's willingness to slaughter Isaac (Chapter 22);
- Isaac's fear that he would be murdered for Rebecca (26:7);
- Esau's desire to murder Jacob (27:41);
- The intended murder of Joseph by his brothers (37:20).

One can name occurrences in Genesis (e.g., the rape of Dinah in Chapter 34) involving the violation of Shared Principles other than respecting Creation, but the more central role of murder seems clear. At the same time, Joseph's life was spared because the brothers changed their minds in response to the plea of Reuben, the eldest brother (37:21–22). While Judah, the eventual leader of the brothers, embraced the decision to forgo murder, he suggested and the brothers agreed to sell Joseph to a passing caravan (37:27). This was tantamount to making Joseph a slave, a violation of Principle B (loyalty to a primary relationship), since Joseph would have a master other than God. Thus, by forgoing murder, the brothers demonstrated fulfillment of Principle A in Genesis, but non-fulfillment of Principle B by selling Joseph.

Exodus

This Book displays key elements connected with Principle B (loyalty to a primary relationship), including:

- The enslavement of the Jewish people, i.e., imposing a master other than God (Exodus 1–5)
- Moses' repeated demands for Pharaoh to let the people go to serve God (5:1, 7:16, etc.);
- The Jewish people's need to show, by sacrificing the Paschal lamb, abandonment of the idolatry practiced in Egypt (12:21);
- The incident of the Golden Calf (Chapter 32).

Though circumstances occur in Exodus related to other Shared Principles, notably murder (in the form of infanticide) in 1:16, Principle B dominates, as reflected in the refrain of "Let my people go" and in the repeated references to servants or service..

We see in the bulleted items above two aspects of an improper primary relationship: bondage to human beings and worship of idols. As we examine the role of the Jewish people in Exodus in relation to bondage, we see relative passivity in their own liberation. True, we have Moses' involvement in seeking freedom in the second bullet, but we see no broad participation in this pursuit, apart from the willingness of those who left Egypt to sacrifice the Paschal lamb and follow other Divine directions for the Exodus. In light of this limited activity, one might demand evidence the Jewish people actually progressed beyond a slave mentality (and thus demonstrated fulfillment of this aspect of Principle B). Yet, as I read the early nineteenth century commentary commonly known as the *Chatam Sofer*, such evidence does appear later in Exodus.

Specifically, a vital change in the Jewish people's attitude took place in Exodus 24:7. There we find the people's signature promise to follow the teachings of the Torah: "We will do and we will hear," where "hear" is interpreted as "understand." Twice earlier in Exodus, the text reports promises by the people solely of "we will do" (19:8 and 24:3). Those promises from the former slaves signaled obedience to a new master, but clearly obedience was not sufficient in itself. Only after the declaration in 24:7 is the covenant sealed in 24:8.

In fact, God had already declared to the Jewish people in 19:5, "…if you will **hear** My voice and keep My covenant, you will be My treasured possession among all the peoples." In other words, a commitment to understanding God's teachings was also needed. And it is this understanding of God's teachings that would make it improper to accede to any form of permanent or abusive servitude. Thus, in the case of a servant who wished to remain in the service to his master beyond the period necessary to repay an unsettled debt, the Torah writes that the ear of the servant was to be bored with an awl (Exodus 21:6). Rashi explains that this ear had **heard** from Mount Sinai (where the Torah was given) that the Jewish people are to serve God. Therefore, in taking a human master, the ear should be bored as a mark of failure to understand.

With this background, we now see how the promise to both obey God and understand His teachings finally reflected abandonment of unthinking servitude, an abandonment that demonstrated fulfillment of the first aspect of Principle B (loyalty to a primary relationship). This brings us to the second aspect, which would be fulfilled by abandoning idol worship. The initial abandonment was expressed in the slaughtering of the Paschal lamb, since the lamb was an Egyptian god. (How do we know the lamb was worshipped? A primary source can be found in the first century Aramaic translation of the text known as Onkelos. In that translation, the justification given by Moses to Pharaoh in Exodus 8:22 for leaving Egypt to worship is that Egyptians would regard the sacrifice of their deity as a *toeivah* [abomination]. Similarly, a variant of *toeivah* is applied to the work of shepherds in Genesis 46:34.)

Of course, the people regressed from this abandonment of idolatry with the Incident of the Golden Calf. In its aftermath, Moses successfully pleaded to turn aside God's intended destruction of the people (Exodus 32:11–14). When Moses returned to the camp, he broke the tablets, forced the drinking of the ashes of the Golden Calf, promoted the killing of those responsible, and rebuked the nation for its sin (32:15–30). While the Levites carried out the killing of those responsible, the only contrition of the people as a whole seems to be their mourning the loss of God's direct presence (33:4), which was ultimately restored. One may then ask what the people did that demonstrated their actual abandonment of idol worship. This demonstration will be required to show fulfillment of the second aspect of Principle B.

What the people did as a whole was to contribute resources to the Tabernacle and to build it (in Exodus 35–39). Though much of the character of the Tabernacle was specified by God, a great deal was voluntary. One can understand that the people's engagement in this activity indicated their intent to show loyalty to God. As we noted in Section 3 of Stage I, the settling of the cloud of God's presence in the Tabernacle in 40:34 marked the completion of the redemption of the Jewish people. This completion could be attained only through full repentance from idolatry, thus fulfilling Principle B (loyalty to a primary relationship).

While the fulfillment of the second Shared Principle was demonstrated in the Book of Exodus, it turns out that Principle C (limited access to spiritual/physical resources) was not fulfilled. We see this in the behavior of the seventy elders as Moses prepared to ascend Mount Sinai to receive the full law. In 24:11, they are reported as eating and drinking while having a vision of God. This behavior represents improper access to spiritual resources. The same verse also reports that they were spared punishment, presumably because most of the laws concerning how to approach God were not made known until the next Book, Leviticus.

Leviticus

This Book focuses on laws and events reflecting Principle C (limited access to spiritual/ physical resources). Large portions of the text are devoted to sacrifices, priestly rites, and ritual cleanliness, as in Chapters 1–16 and 21–23, thus showing concern with access to spiritual resources, while Chapters 19 and 25 show a concern with physical resources. As for actual transgressions in Leviticus, there are but two to speak of: the offering of a strange fire by Aaron's sons Nadab and Abihu (10:1); and the uttering of blasphemy by a Jew with an Egyptian father (24:11).

Clearly, both transgressions involve improper access to spiritual resources. In the first case, we have two priests who did not perform their ritual duty as expected, for which they were consumed by God (10:2). In the second, we have someone outside the priesthood (because he had an Egyptian father and Jewish mother) who misused God's name. In response to this deed, he was first imprisoned (24:12) and then stoned by the people (24:23) after seeking and receiving direction from God. When we study the aftermath of these transgressions, we see Principle C in Leviticus fulfilled, but not Principle D (duties of testimony/community).

In the aftermath of the deaths of Nadab and Abihu, the text reports an exchange on the same day between Moses and Aaron and his remaining sons in Leviticus 10:16–20. Moses began by berating those remaining sons over them burning a certain sacrifice instead of eating from it as they were commanded. Aaron answered that he and his sons did not view themselves as eligible to partake in such a meal given the circumstances of their bereavement. In the end, Moses understood and approved of the priests' limiting their access to spiritual resources, thereby marking fulfillment of Principle C.

In the case of blasphemer, the people recognized that misuse of the Divine name could not be allowed to pass. This recognition also showed fulfillment of Principle C (limited access to spiritual/physical resources). At the same time, the proper final response from the community in this situation was not clear. As a result, the blasphemer was imprisoned until God could be consulted. While the people's approach was understandable and not without merit, it still demonstrated unreadiness for full responsibility in matters of punishment. This unreadiness showed a lack of fulfillment of Principle D (duties of testimony/community).

ii. Numbers and Variations in the Ten Commandments

Section 3 of Stage I notes that the substantial variation in the two versions of the Ten Commandments (Exodus 20 vs. Deuteronomy 5) occurs in the Commandments tied to Principles D (duties of testimony/community) and E (accepting one's place/status), i.e., Commandments 4, 5, 9, and 10. We then linked four key communal transgressions in Numbers with the four material changes in Commandments 9 and 10, with these changes making the prohibition of the four transgressions more explicit in Deuteronomy.

Let us briefly review that linkage between communal transgressions and changes in the last two Commandments:

- The Incident of the Spies (Numbers 13–14) linked to change from "false witness" to "vain witness" in Commandment 9;
- Korach's Rebellion (Numbers 16–17) linked to change from "Thou shalt not covet" to "Thou shalt not desire" in Commandment 10.
- Improper sexual relations with Midianite women (Numbers 25) linked to a change in order of what is covered under prohibited coveting in Commandment 10.
- The request by the tribes of Reuben and Gad to settle outside Canaan (Numbers 32) linked to inclusion of a field in prohibited coveting in Commandment 10.

Before we relate transgressions to the two versions of Commandments 4 and 5, let us return to the two failures in Numbers that we cited in Section 3 of Stage I (but did not link to the differences in the last two Commandments). As you will recall, these failures were the episodic complaints by the people about food and water and the shortcoming of Moses — and probably Aaron as well — in drawing water from the rock at Kadesh. Like the four transgressions linked to differences in the Commandments, these further failures both occurred in a communal context.

Sometimes the episodic complaints by the people are explicitly identified as sinful by the text (e.g., the complaints in 21:5 after the victory over Arad) and but not always (the complaints in 20:3–5 after the death of Miriam). To the extent that the complaints were sinful, they surely demonstrated the people's discontent with their circumstances, and this discontent reflected a failure to fulfill Principle E (accepting one's place/status). At the same time, no specific change in the last Commandment seems to mark the episodic complaints by the people. Later in this section, when we speak of the change in the Fifth Commandment to honor one's parents, we will suggest a possible relationship between these complaints and that change.

As for the failure at the rock (20:6–13), we should note that one important body of commentary views this failure as a substantial personal shortcoming, but possibly not a transgression in the same sense we have discussed until now. According to Ibn Ezra and others,

Moses and Aaron did not exercise sufficient initiative in the face of the people's complaints over the lack of water. Instead of fleeing from the complaints (see 20:6), the leaders should have, according to this view, taken immediate steps to bring water. As it was, the failure to do so showed a lack of resolve on behalf of God and was accounted in 20:12 as not sanctifying God in the eyes of the people. In line with this view, the problem was one of inadequate leadership, thus showing non-fulfillment of Principle D (duties of testimony/community).

There are, however, at least three other major opinions that do view the failure at the rock as a direct violation of a specific prohibition.

1. Rashi took the command in 20:8 to speak to the rock as meaning not to hit the rock, which Moses did in 20:11.
2. Rambam said Moses lost his temper causing him to publicly (and unjustifiably) call the people "rebels" in 20:10.
3. Ramban pointed to another word in the statement by Moses in 20:10: "…shall **we** (meaning Moses and Aaron) bring forth water…?" The miracle should have been attributed to God.

While both the second and third of these opinions directly involve testimony, the opinion of Ramban presents an especially rich connection with Principle D (duties of testimony/ community). By attributing the bringing forth of water to himself and Aaron, Moses did not actually bear false witness (as it is termed in the first version of Commandment 9) in the sense that he and Aaron did play a role. At the same time, he was bearing vain witness (as it is termed in the second version) by not acknowledging God's role as more vital than his own. In line with Ramban's interpretation, the change in Commandment 9 could also reflect the failure at the rock.

Having treated the transgressions in Numbers of a communal nature, let us now consider two other transgressions in Numbers that were committed in a less public manner. We will see that they relate to changes in Commandments 4 and 5. The transgressions in question are

- the private criticism of Moses by Miriam and Aaron without him present in 12:1–2; and

- the gathering of wood by one of the people in violation of the Sabbath in 15:32.

a. *The private criticism of Moses by Miriam and Aaron*

What was the actual transgression? At first glance, we might view the criticism of Moses as flawed testimony, but the private nature of the conversation between Miriam and Aaron discourages this view. Furthermore, when we consider their criticism as it is usually understood, other features also argue against placing the transgression within testimony. According to the standard meaning, Miriam and Aaron did not regard their brother Moses' relationship with God as just cause for divorcing his wife (see Numbers 12:1). Because Moses' divorce was likely well known, there would be no need (or use) for testimony. The key to the disapproval by Miriam and Aaron lay in their keeping their spouses while God also spoke to them (see 12:2). Thus, they focused on whether their brother's behavior should be respected in relation to their own, which was not a matter of testimony per se.

In this light, it seems that Miriam and Aaron saw something amiss in how Moses handled his relationship with God, and it was God Himself who dispelled them of this misconception (see 12:6–8) by declaring Moses' spiritual relationship closer than theirs. It seems that God placed Moses in a position of respect relative to his siblings on account of this relationship. This is not unlike the position of a parent relative to his or her child, as set forth in the Talmud in *Kiddushin* 30b. There the Talmud says that the parents form a partnership with God in conceiving the child. (For this reason, incidentally, the Fifth Commandment, that of respecting parents, is on the same side of the Tablets as the other Commandments between Man and God.)

If we understand the transgression of Miriam and Aaron as not giving proper respect, then we may begin to look at the Fifth Commandment as what was violated. However, it would be fair to argue that the object of respect in this Commandment seems limited to parents, while Moses was only a brother. This protest must be

ELABORATION ON STAGE I 281

answered first by examining the actual Hebrew statement of the Fifth Commandment in detail.

In both versions (in Exodus and in Deuteronomy), the Commandment opens as follows:

*Cabeid **et** avikha v'**et** imekha — Honor your father and your mother.*

Note the inclusion of the bolded direct object marker *et* preceding both *avikha* [your father] and *imekha* [your mother]. While this marker carries no specific translation, a general Talmudic principle in *Pesachim* 24b guides the interpretation of *et*. The principle states that the presence of *et* signifies an expansion of the direct object that follows beyond its literal meaning. In other words, because the Fifth Commandment uses the term *et avikha*, there is an obligation to respect those other than a father who share certain paternal functions.

One such function is exercising authority. Indeed, the Egyptians' name for Joseph (as Pharaoh's viceroy) was *avreikh*, which contains *av* [father] (see Gen. 41:43). Interestingly, the same connection surfaces in "Father," the form of address used for a Catholic priest as a religious authority. Even the maternal function arises with Moses, as well, as he complains in 11:12–13 about being put in the role of a mother who is responsible for feeding her demanding offspring.

From the preceding paragraphs, we see that there was an obligation to respect Moses in line with the Fifth Commandment. That still leaves us with one issue: how do the changes in this Commandment (from Exodus to Deuteronomy) suggest more specifically that Moses should be respected? The changes come following the simple imperative to honor one's parents that opens the Commandment. In Exodus, the single result of fulfilling this imperative is stated immediately afterwards:

l'maan yaarikhun yamekha	in order that your days will be lengthened
al haadamah...	on the land (meaning the Land of Canaan).

In contrast, the second version first inserts after the opening imperative the phrase "as God commanded you" before stating two results of honoring parents:

l'maan yaarikhun yamekha	in order that your days will be lengthened
ul'maan yitav lakh	and in order that it will be good for you
al haadamah…	on the land (meaning the Land of Canaan).

The link to Moses in these changes will emerge more clearly if we begin with the added result of honoring one's parents: ul'maan **yitav** lakh [and in order that **it will be good** for you]. I have bolded the word yitav to stress its connection with the word tov, which is associated with Moses in Exodus 2:2. There it speaks of his mother's sense of him at birth:

| …vateireh oto ci **tov** hu… | and she saw in him that he was **good.** |

Thus, we can understand the added result in Deuteronomy as the good presence of Moses (and, by extension, succeeding leaders) that will follow from the people properly respecting religious authority. In fact, Moses was punished with not entering Canaan as a result of his failure with the rock (see Numbers 20:6–13). This failure (whatever it was — see the earlier discussion of communal transgression in this section) was precipitated by the complaints of the people after the death of Miriam. As part of those complaints, the people exhibited disrespect for Moses, asking him (in 20:5), "Why have your brought us up from Egypt to bring us to this evil place?" As a result of this disrespect, Moses was not with them in the land of Canaan. In later cases, the Jewish Bible reports other leaders unable to persist successfully after their authority was not accepted — for example, the prophet Elijah (see I Kings, Chapters 18–19).

The other change, the inserted phrase "as God commanded you," fits very well with this interpretation. God Himself clarified that Moses was to be respected and then publicly demonstrated the punishment for failure to do so with Miriam's leprosy (see Numbers 12:10). It is this explicit clarification that corresponds to the inserted phrase. And when God announced the duration of Miriam's affliction, He likened Himself to a father disciplining his daughter (see 12:14). With this metaphor, we have reinforced the connection between the changes in the Fifth Commandment and the criticism of Moses by Miriam and Aaron.

Let us summarize the points of this connection.

- Miriam and Aaron did not fully appreciate Moses' unique function, especially regarding his religious authority, which extends a parent's role.
- The Fifth Commandment in Deuteronomy (but not in Exodus) refers to the necessity of its observance to enjoy "good" in the land, a term associated with Moses' presence.
- Whatever Moses' failure at the rock, it was surely promoted by the lack of respect for his authority, thus depriving the Jewish people of his presence (and "good") in Canaan.
- The language of Miriam's punishment suggests parental rebuke of a child.

b. *The gathering of wood in violation of the Sabbath*

Clearly, this transgression involves the Sabbath, which is the subject of the Fourth Commandment, but how does it fit with changes from the version of the Commandment in Exodus to the one in Deuteronomy? Let us identify the aspects of the Commandment affected by the change, as well as the level of difference, as we compare the two versions verse by verse.

Both versions occupy four verses (Exodus 20:8–11 and Deuteronomy 5:12–15) and treat the same aspects of the Commandment in order of the verses. Thus, in the chart below, the term "first verse" refers to Exodus 20:8 in the first version and Deuteronomy 5:12 in the second; "second verse" refers to Exodus 20:9 in the first version and Deuteronomy 5:13 in the second; and so on.

	Aspect of Commandment	Level of Difference between Versions
First verse	General command	Limited difference
Second verse	Time that work is permitted	No difference

Third verse	Parties affected by its cessation	Limited difference
Fourth verse	Reason for cessation	Extensive difference

The largest difference between the versions occurs in the fourth verse (with the reason for the obligation), so we focus on that verse in each version. However, we now briefly note the differences in the first and third verses. The Commandment's first verse in Exodus states: "**Zakhor** *et yom haShabbat l'kad'sho* [**Remember** the Sabbath day for its holiness]," while the first verse in Deuteronomy opens, "**Shamor** *et yom haShabbat l'kad'sho* [**Guard** the Sabbath day for its holiness]." This language exhausts the first verse in Exodus, while Deuteronomy's first verse goes on, saying "as God commanded you." As for the third verse, the version in Deuteronomy also adds a final phrase, "in order that your man-servant and maid-servant will rest like you."

According to the traditional Jewish understanding, the command *zakhor* [remember] refers to the positive action of sanctifying the Sabbath by reciting the account of the Sabbath of Creation with a blessing over wine. In contrast, the command *shamor* [guard] refers to the extensive prohibitions of the Sabbath, which are keyed to the activities of building and operating the Tabernacle. (Some of these activities, such as kindling a flame, are not particularly laborious, so the popular general understanding of "work" as what is prohibited on the Sabbath often misses the mark.)

According to the same traditional understanding, both commands were spoken together by God. However, in the written form of the Commandments, the different commands accord with the differing reasons found in the respective fourth verses. The final phrase that appears only in the third verse of the version in Deuteronomy can be explained in the same way. As for the final phrase "as God commanded you" in the Commandment's first verse, it will turn out to reflect a specific Divine intervention (to be identified shortly).

Our brief treatment of differences in the first three verses of the Fourth Commandment strengthened the focus on the very different reasons given in the fourth verses of the Commandment. In Exodus the reason involves Creation, which the Sabbath completed (hence the testimony from Genesis associated with *zakhor*). In Deuteronomy, the reason involves the liberation from Egyptian slavery (hence the prohibited activities associated with *shamor*). As we noted earlier, the people's role with the Tabernacle atoned for idolatry, also associated with Egypt, which explains the link between Sabbath prohibitions and the activities of the Tabernacle.

Why Observe the Sabbath?

Now let us look more carefully into the reason given in Deuteronomy for observing the Sabbath. God's role in the liberation from Egypt is stated as follows in 5:15: "*v'yotziakha...misham...* [and He brought you out...from there...]."

As noted by the great nineteenth century commentator Rabbi Samson Raphael Hirsch, the verb *v'yotziakha* shares its root with the term *hotzaah*, the act of carrying in a public place, which is prohibited on the Sabbath. In other words, through not carrying (i.e., taking something out), the Jewish people were to recall that they were taken out of Egypt by God — and not by themselves.

This prohibition of *hotzaah* is, according to most Torah commentaries, the law violated by the gathering of wood in Numbers 15:32. The act of carrying then does much more than correspond to the act of moving the Tabernacle from place to place; it corresponds to the final decree in the Egyptian bondage, the decree that the Jewish people gather their own straw for making bricks in Exodus 5:11–12. If anyone doubts the correspondence between gathering wood and gathering straw, consider the striking commonality in language between *m'kosheish eitzim* [gatherer of wood] in Numbers 15:32 and *l'kosheish kash l'teven* [to gather straw for bricks] in Exodus 5:12. *Kosheish* does not appear anywhere else in the Mosaic text. Thus, the change in the Fourth Commandment's reason in Deuteronomy to *v'yotziakha* [and He brought you out] is directly linked with the transgression of *hotzaah* [carrying] in Numbers. This link may be understood as forgoing carrying on the Sabbath to remember our ancestors having been carried out of Egypt and spared the necessity of gathering straw for bricks.

The only other difference that still needs explanation is the addition in Deuteronomy of the phrase "as God commanded you." In fact, God became directly involved with this transgression because the people (and Moses) did not know how to punish the perpetrator. Thus, we find in Numbers 15:35 the Divine command to stone him, completing the connection between the changes in the Fourth Commandment (as it appears in Deuteronomy) and the Sabbath violation of gathering wood.

iii. The Character of Deuteronomy in Relation to the Parts Claim

Let us take stock of the developments in this section so far:

- We saw earlier that the major transgressions of Genesis, Exodus, and Leviticus comport in order with Principles A (Creation), B (Loyalty), and C (Limits), which were attained respectively by the end of each of the first three books.
- We also saw that transgressions in Numbers line up with changes in the different versions of the Ten Commandments linked to Principles D (Community) and E (Acceptance). Specifically, changes in Commandments 4 and 5 correspond to private transgressions and changes in Commandments 9 and 10 correspond to communal transgressions.

Taken together, these developments reinforce Rabbi Honigwachs' conception of the spiritual and ethical growth of the Jewish people. In that conception, the people succeeded in the first three books in conquering the challenges of Shared Principles A, B, and C. Yet, in Numbers they often stumbled in trying to build a community in the Wilderness. These failures, along with those involving the necessity of accepting their place or status, reflected non-fulfillment of Principles D and E. This non-fulfillment prompted Rabbi Honigwachs' term "arrested development" in the people's progression through the Shared Principles.

In line with that analysis, the arrested development then gave rise in Deuteronomy to additional laws and refinements of previous laws, particularly the Ten Commandments. Accordingly, these additional laws and refinement of previous ones were given by Moses to get the people back on track before entering the Land of Canaan, just as had been suggested by Ramban in the thirteenth century. In fact, as we will soon see, Deuteronomy first refers to several failures in Numbers before presenting the main legal text. All these factors support our understanding of the differences in Deuteronomic law, rather than Wellhausen's understanding that such differences reflect inconsistencies introduced by another author from another time.

Deuteronomy

Let us now examine the content and structure of Deuteronomy itself. As we have observed earlier, law predominates in Deuteronomy. This legal content includes both

- repetition of laws given in the previous Books, often with variation or further explanation; and
- laws that have no counterpart in the previous Books.

According to the Torah's account, these laws were given as the Jewish people prepared to enter the Land of Canaan. While this initial context aligns with Principle E (in accepting the destiny and responsibility of inheriting the land), the legal topics range too broadly to assign the overall focus to one Shared Principle alone.

At the same time, Deuteronomy's internal progression still connects (though imperfectly) with the Shared Principles in that the Parts Claim seems fulfilled to some extent. The last book offers an almost natural division into five Parts that begin and end with *p'tuchot* as shown below:

DISPLAY 14.1: Parts of Deuteronomy and their Endpoints		
Part	Verses	General Description
A (Creation)	1:1–4:49	Account of major events after revelation at Sinai, stressing God's role and failures in belief
B (Loyalty)	5:1–10:11	Presentation of general laws and other ideas to guide the special relationship with God

C (Limits)	10:12–26:19	Presentation of laws for more specific situations
D (Community)	27:1–30:20	Account of the testimonial covenant in plains of Moab
E (Acceptance)	31:1–34:12	Moses' final song and the account of his death

General Laws vs Specific Laws

However, fixing the precise point where the laws shift from general (Part B) to more specific (Part C) gave me real trouble. The twentieth century scholar Rabbi Joseph Hertz, who served as Chief Rabbi of Great Britain, distinguishes between general ideas/laws and specific laws in his commentary on the Pentateuch, but he places the point of shift at the end of Chapter 11 (where there is no blank space of any kind).

While we cannot use this point of shift for the Shared Principles, we can understand his thinking. There is a long *parshah* opening with 10:12 and ending with 13:1, which includes both general ideas/laws and specific laws, and Rabbi Hertz clearly sees the more specific laws as reaching dominance over the general in Chapter 12.

At the same time, some of the more general ideas between 10:12 and 12:1 may actually explain the specific laws, rather than stand independently of them. In particular, as I read the obligation to pray ("service of the heart" in 11:13), the next several verses seem to suggest how this specific law connects to the more general idea of God providing sustenance. Thus, it is largely through prayer that rain comes in its season (11:14). With this thought in mind, I placed the point of shift just before the obligation for prayer. Still, the alignment with the Shared Principles that is discussed below seems forced in setting the break between Parts B and C. A distinction between general and specific is just harder to make cleanly.

Alignment of Parts A and B

Let us examine the alignment with the Shared Principles part by part. The clear message of Part A is that God had been with the people through both the good and the bad times. This message reinforces belief in God, in fulfillment of Principle A (respecting Creation). Within this message, we find reference to three of the failures in Numbers: the Incident of the Spies (in 1:22–36), the materialism of the Tribes of Reuben and Gad (in 3:16–20), and Moses' own failure at the rock (in 3:23–27).[32]

In entering Part B, we find language early on (in Deuteronomy 5:1) introducing laws that will follow, first among them the Ten Commandments (in 5:6–18). Now, as stressed in Section 2 of Stage I, the Ten Commandments are actually broad principles that guide one's relationship with God (the first five Commandments) and with Man (the second five). The Commandments lead into the signature standard of "you shall love God with all your heart, with all your soul, and with all your might" (6:5), along with general expectations and consequences of relating to a "jealous God" (6:15), including how one should explain the resulting obligations to one's children (6:20–25). In summary, Chapters 5 and 6 provide a foundation for more detailed laws that appear in the third portion, while reflecting Principle B in framing a primary relationship.

The subsequent chapters (7–10) in Part B present several more specific laws in the context of what will be needed for success in the Land of Canaan, which was about to be entered. Some of these laws (e.g., not to intermarry in 7:3) themselves link directly with Principle B. However, quite apart from the linkages of the laws themselves, there are also repeated warnings about sliding into the idolatry of the land, so that these laws are connected with avoidance of idolatry. Such general warnings about idolatry, suggestive of Principle B, can be found in 7:4 and 8:19, along with an extensive treatment of the Golden Calf in 9:12–21.

Alignment of Part C

This brings us now to Part C. The verse 12:1 refers (as does 5:1 at the beginning of Part B) to *mishpatim* (laws between man and man) and *chukim* (laws between man and God) that will follow, thus suggesting yet another beginning. However, in 12:1 we find an additional identification of the succeeding laws not found in 5:1. The laws that follow 12:1 are described as ones whose implementation must be guarded *"in the land God gave you to possess all the days you live on the land."* In other words, there is a particular obligation to keep such laws, an obligation linked to being given the Land of Canaan and living there. Keep in mind that Principle C involves limited access to spiritual/physical resources. Since the language in 12:1 ties access to the land to fulfillment of the laws in Part C, those laws reflect Principle C.

Moreover, Part C is virtually all legal, encompassing both expanded versions of laws given previously and laws in such areas as warfare and divorce not previously addressed. According to the most familiar enumeration of the laws in the Torah,[33] the combination in Part C of entirely new laws, and of separately counted refinements of previous laws, amounts to 175 of the total number of 613 — well over one-quarter. Thus, because the laws of Part C connect to Principle C, so does Part C as a whole. One further connection to Principle C may be found by examining the location in earlier Books of the preceding versions of laws in Part C. The preponderance of those preceding versions occurs in Part C of Exodus (19:1–24:18) and Part C of Leviticus (17:1–21:24).

While the preceding paragraphs present a strong case for linking Part C with Principle C, one feature of this subtext in Chapter 11 should raise a question. The Mutiny of Korach, which we have already connected to coveting under Principle E (accepting one's place/status), is cited in 11:6 through a reference to Korach's co-conspirators Dathan and Abiram. Thus one might ask how that event connects to Principle C (limited access to spiritual/physcal resources).

The key distinction here lies in the event being identified with Dathan and Abiram rather than with Korach (the mutiny's recognized leader, whose acts fell just shy of coveting). The text cites an act of defiance on their part that even Korach did not engage in. Specifically, their refusal to meet with Moses (see 16:12) constituted an improper denial of access (Principle C). Thus it makes sense in Part C to associate Dathan and Abiram, as opposed to Korach, with the mutiny against Moses. (We note that there may also be grounds in associating them as two Reubenites with the mutiny under Principle B as a failure in loyalty.[34])

Alignment of Parts D and E

There is a clear shift in entering Part D in Chapter 27. Until that point, the text represents the speech of Moses alone. However, 27:1 identifies what then follows as the command of Moses and the elders of Israel. In fact, they command erecting great stones on which to inscribe the text of the Torah (27:2–3). As distinct from the laws in Part C that apply continuously, this command applies once and just when the people will cross into Canaan. On the heels of this testimonial act will come the full participation of the people in specific blessings and curses (27:11–26), each punctuated by the testimonial "Amen." Chapter 28 constitutes an elaboration on these blessings and curses, which are labeled a covenant (28:69).

The themes of covenant and testimony continue in Chapters 29 and 30. Adding to the sense of community (Principle D) in Chapters 27 and 28, the two subsequent chapters describe an expectation that the covenant set with the people at that time extends to those not yet born (29:13–14). There is also a clear expectation of responsibility of the individual to the community (29:15–20). Finally, the theme of testimony (Principle D) reaches a climax in the next to last verse of Chapter 30: "I call as witnesses today Heaven and Earth in the life and death I have put before you..." In all of Part D, only one new law or refinement of a previous law occurs — that in 28:9 — thus distinguishing Part D from the intensely legal Part C.

Part E begins with Moses' statement in 31:2 that he can "no longer go out and come in." In referring to his condition and to the imminence of death, a new tone emerges in the text, which switches to a narrative voice soon after in 31:12. Not since the beginning of Deuteronomy had a true narrative voice been found. Part E then turns in Chapter 32 to the Song of Moses, a poetic forecast of the future, which precedes Moses' blessings to the tribes in Chapter 33. In actuality, those statements to the tribes are more aptly read as a description of their individual capabilities, thus closely reflecting Principle E (accepting one's place/

status).

Part E, and Deuteronomy for that matter, ends in Chapter 34 with the narrative account of Moses' demise. That account includes two further points particularly reflective of Principle E: Moses being shown the land of Canaan and the description of him being unique among the prophets. This completes our examination of the limited alignment of Deuteronomy's Parts with the Shared Principles.

Summary

In summary of this section, we can now recognize three major aspects of the pattern culminating in or related to Deuteronomy:

1. Each of the first three Shared Principles were fulfilled respectively in the first three Books, but the Jewish people failed to fulfill either of the last two Shared Principles in Numbers;
2. The individual changes in Deuteronomy's Ten Commandments, as compared with those of Exodus, can be understood as a response to the specific public and private transgressions in Numbers;
3. Deuteronomy divides into five Parts in limited alignment with the Shared Principles, with the problem occurring in distinguishing subtexts on the basis of generality versus specificity.

Notes

1. The English version used here is *Prolegomena to the History of Ancient Israel*, tr. Black & Menzies (Edinburgh: A and C Black, 1885), as reprinted in paperback by Kessinger Publishing.
2. An online version of the reprinted 1651 edition (Oxford: Clarendon Press, 1909) is available at http://oll.libertyfund.org/titles/869.
3. An online version of the translation by R.H.M. Elwes of the 1670 work (London: George Bell & Sons, 1891) is available at http://oll.libertyfund.org/titles/1710.
4. Ibid.
5. The Talmud in *Nedarim* 32b states this association, which is based on *Midrash Tanchuma* 15 concerning a descendant of Melchizedek who was killed when Abraham rescued Lot. The association also involves an appreciation of what it meant to be a priest at that time and why the priestly service was not passed along to Melchizedek's children.
6. The other three passages cited by Ibn Ezra are as follows: Deuteronomy 31:9, Genesis 22:14, and Deuteronomy 3:11.
7. For a discussion of the relationship among the four categories of interpretation, see I. Lancaster, *Deconstructing the Bible: Abraham Ibn Ezra's Introduction to the Bible* (Abingdon, GB: Routledge, 2003).
8. With a straightforward search with software from the Bar-Ilan University Responsa Project, we find seventy-three occurrences of the precise word *sod* [deep insight hidden below the surface] in Ibn Ezra's commentary on the Torah. If we add in occurrences of *sod* with the prefixes for the definite article and for the conjunction "and," we turn up forty more. In reviewing many of these 113 cases, we see that further explanation is discouraged and that the context suggests the reasons I have cited. As pointed out by Rabbi Kalman Worch, this analysis accords with the explanation of Ibn Ezra's use of *sod* by the eighteenth century supercommentary *Avi Ezer* on Genesis 7:23.
9. Indeed, had Ibn Ezra meant his advice on Genesis 12:6 to conceal a challenge to the traditional view, he would have given that advice in Deuteronomy 1:2 for all the passages listed there. Since he made no

comment regarding any of the other passages listed in Deuteronomy 1:2, this suggests his concern in Genesis 12:6 involved something other than textual authenticity. I would speculate that Ibn Ezra discouraged further explanation specifically for Genesis 12:6 because greater complexity was involved. For those other passages, the issue is largely limited to the appearance of a perspective later than Mosaic times. However, in Genesis 12:6, there are the further complications mentioned in note 5 above.

10 See, for example, Nachmanides' comment on Genesis 9:18, in which he castigates Ibn Ezra for departing from the clear sense of the text.

11 For lost objects, the version in Exodus occupies the single verse 23:4, while the Deuteronomic version, comprising the four verses 22:1–4, adds the obligation to announce that something has been found. The version in Leviticus occupies the three verses 19:35–37, while Deuteronomic version comprises the four verses 25:13–16 and further prohibits possession of discrepant weights.

12 Under the German Christian Movement (symbolized by the combination of a cross and swastika), any connection between Judaism and Christianity was strongly denied, and all references to the Old Testament in Protestant liturgy were eliminated. A few Christian leaders did rise to challenge this approach, cf. M. Faulhaber, *Judaism, Christianity, and Germany*, tr. G. Smith (New York: Macmillan, 1934). An avowed opponent of Hitler, Faulhaber was Archbishop of Munich when this book was written.

13 Cf. Y. Etshalom, *Between the Lines of the Bible* (Brooklyn: Yashar, 2006), pp. 72–121.

14 Cf. R. E. Friedman, *Who Wrote the Bible?* (New York: HarperCollins, 1997), p. 227.

15 In the first abduction, where God intervenes directly with a plague, the J-Name is used; in the second, where God is only seen in a vision and does not act directly, the E-Name is used.

16 *Critique of Religion and Philosophy* (Princeton, NJ: Princeton University Press, 1978), p. 377.

17 The verse in question, Genesis 7:16, works out according to the classical distinction between the J-Name and E-Name, since the use of the J-Name refers to God closing the door of the Ark (and thus intervening directly), while the use of the E-Name refers to God as the source of a command.

18 R. E. Friedman, op. cit., pp. 54–59.

19   Nachmanides is not mentioned at all in J. Kugel's *How to Read the Bible* (New York: Free Press, 2007). The single reference in R. E. Friedman's *Who Wrote the Bible?* (New York: HarperCollins, 1997) simply describes Nachmanides, along with Rashi, as "especially skillful at seeking explanations to reconcile...contradictions," without identifying any of these explanations (or indicating why they should be rejected). M. Brettler in *How to Read the Jewish Bible* (Oxford: Oxford University Press, 2007) also mentions Nachmanides only once, but only to dismiss him as out of step with modern scholarship in his perspective on situations that recur in the Five Books.

20   The explanation presented here slightly extends that in the *Hertz Pentateuch and Haftorahs* (London: Soncino, 1995), the most recent edition of Rabbi Joseph Hertz's commentary on the Five Books. The Hertz commentary in question appears on Exodus 20:21. My elaboration follows Rabbi Hoffman's original work, *Die Wichtigsten Instanzen Gegen die Graf-Wellhausensche Hypothese* (Berlin: Rabbinerseminar zu Berlin, 1902/03), translated privately from German by H. Weiss.

21   For a short treatment of such blunders, see Lecture 4 in U. Cassuto, *The Documentary Hypothesis*, tr. I. Abrahams (Jerusalem: Shalem Press, 2006).

22   The work of Radday and Shore cited in the next paragraph refers (on page 261) to the discrepant assignments of various pieces of Genesis 27:27–29 by different Source Critics, as recounted originally in a 1933 article by the German scholars P. Volz and W. Rudolph.

23   The actual assignment to different sources can be found in the English translation and revision of Sellin's work by G. Fohrer, *Introduction to the Old Testament* (Nashville: Abingdon Press, 1968), pp. 146–173.

24   The twentieth century scholar Rabbi Yoseph Kapach reported the existence of other manuscripts of Maimonides' work that place the *p'tuchah* in question according to the Yemenite version. This report appears in Rabbi Kapach's introduction to his Hebrew commentary on *Mishneh Torah* (Jerusalem: Machon Mishnat HaRambam, 2002). As further evidence of the Yemenite placement, Rabbi Kapach noted this placement agrees with other ancient manuscripts of the Torah text, such as the Leningrad Codex.

25 M. Breuer, *The Aleppo Codex and the Accepted Text of the Bible* (Jerusalem: Mossad HaRav Kook, 1976). See the English introduction pp. VII–XLV.

26 The four standard recognized manuscripts covered in that analysis were the Leningrad Codex (B 19a), British Museum Manuscript (Or. 4445), and two Sasoon Manuscripts (507 and 1053). The earliest printed version is the 1525 Venice edition compiled by Jacob ben Hayyim from a number of manuscripts.

27 *Masoret Seyag laTorah* by Rabbi Meir haLevi ben Todros Alufia. As noted by Rabbi Mordechai Breuer (op. cit., p. XXIV), it remained for Rabbi Menachem di Lonzano in *Or Torah* to resolve several points not decided in *Masoret Seyag laTorah*.

28 M. Breuer, op. cit., p. XXIV, where the footnote cites the book *Sa'arot Teiman*, pp. 103–105, as presenting an explicit list of the variant Yemenite spellings.

29 The Leningrad Codex is a codex in the style of ben Asher that covers the entire Jewish Bible. It was made more available than the Aleppo Codex (even before 1947) and became the basis for the *Biblia Hebraica Stuttgartensia* (*BHS*), the standard Masoretic text in most academic circles. Consequently, the Leningrad Codex was among the recognized codices analyzed by Rabbi Mordechai Breuer. An excellent self-contained explanation of Masoretic notations can be found in relation to the BHS: P. Kelley, D. Mynatt, and T. Crawford, *The Masorah of the Biblia Hebraica Stuttgartensia* (Grand Rapids, MI: Eerdmans, 1996).

30 Rashi's very terse style spawned a number of super-commentaries, i.e., commentaries on his commentary, to explain such matters as to what in the text instigated his comment and what distinction his comment was intended to make. Among Rashi's super-commentaries, the one by Rabbi Eliyahu Mizrachi (d. 1525 or 1526) of Turkey is one of the best known.

31 Our explanation follows the approach of Rabbi A. M. Silbermann in his annotated translation *Chumash with Rashi's Commentary*, (Jerusalem: Silbermann, 1934), as republished and distributed by Feldheim in 1985. See Appendix to Volume 2, Note 3 to page 130, pp.257–258.

32 For the Incident of the Spies and the materialism of the tribes of Reuben and Gad, the explicit connections appear in the passages cited. However, Moses' failure at the rock is not actually mentioned in 3:23–27, only God's anger at Moses. Noting how this anger differs in description from anger against Moses on account of the Spies, Spain's classic fifteenth century commentator Abarbanel links this passage to the rock.

33 The *Sefer HaChinnukh* of the fourteenth century, which is often ascribed to Rabbi Aaron HaLevi of Barcelona. A convenient Hebrew-English version is C. Wengrov (tr.), (New York: Feldheim, 1978).

34 One may also interpret the behavior of Dathan and Abiram as violating Shared Principle B for failing to recognize God's special relationship with the Tribe of Levi, which supplanted the previous primacy of their tribe (Reuben) as descendants of the firstborn. As described in the eighteenth century Torah commentary of Rabbi Pinchas HaLevi Horovitz, they were also guilty of disloyalty to Moses as the Divinely chosen leader, which is considered like disloyalty to God. See *Panim Yafot* (B'nei B'rak, Israel: Mishor, 1990). This Hebrew work is paginated separately for each of the Five Books, and the idea cited here occurs on page 68 of the commentary on Deuteronomy in the second volume.

SUPPLEMENT to STAGES II AND III

Section 15
Supplement to the Test in Genesis

e saw in Section 6 that the Five Books of the Torah align in order with the five Shared Principles, with Genesis corresponding to Principle A (respecting Creation), Exodus to Principle B (loyalty to a primary relationship), etc. We also saw in Section 6 that Genesis itself divides into five Parts (A–E) in the same ordered alignment. Finally, Section 6 also showed that Part A, in turn, subdivides into five Subparts, fitting the pattern. That leaves the remaining Parts (B–E) to be subdivided into Subparts, which is the purpose of this section.

Subdivision of the remaining Parts will follow the same approach as in subdividing Part A. First, we begin reading *parshah* by *parshah* from the beginning of the Part. In line with the Shared Principles, the initial subtext in a given Part will reflect Principle A (respecting Creation) and begin Subpart A in that Part. Reading on, we should (if the pattern holds) find the *parshah* in the Part where themes first shift from Principle A to Principle B (loyalty to a primary relationship). With this shift, the new *parshah* begins Subpart B, while Subpart A ends just before it. We continue in the text to the first *parshah* that shifts to Principle C (limited access to spiritual/physical resources). That *parshah* begins Subpart C of the Part, and so on. (Recall that in Section 6 we already identified Subpart E of each Part in Genesis, except for Part E.)

i. Subdivision of Part B (Genesis 12:1–21:34)

We will proceed as in Part A by identifying each of the first four Subparts of Part B in succession, since Subpart E has already been identified as *parshah* 21:22–34. Here we start reading at the beginning of Part B, which would also be the beginning of Subpart A of Part B.

Subpart A (12:1–9): God's first revelation to Abraham and his travel to Canaan

In this single *parshah*, the revelation itself suggests Principle A (respecting Creation). As part of the revelation, Abraham, then called Abram, is given a blessing marking a special relationship with God, suggesting Principle B (loyalty to a primary relationship). In summary, the themes in this *parshah* align with either Principle A or Principle B. This alignment accords with the *parshah*'s belonging to Subpart A of Part B.

Subpart B (12:10–13:18): the abduction of Abraham's wife Sarah

This second *parshah* tells of the famine in the land of Canaan, which Abraham encounters when he moves there under God's direction. In order to obtain food, he and his wife Sarah (then called Sarai) travel to Egypt. There, as recorded in 12:15, she is abducted by Pharaoh but is then given back to her husband unmolested. This abduction, which occupies a substantial part of the *parshah*, brings a new theme linked to Principle B (loyalty to a primary relationship) and fits the designation of Subpart B of Part B.

Subpart C (14:1–17:27): the kidnap and rescue of Abraham's nephew Lot/ Covenant between the Parts/ strain in Abraham's marriage/ Ishmael's portended birth and thievery/ Covenant of Circumcision/ and name changes to Abraham and Sarah

In addition to recounting Sarah's abduction in Egypt, the previous *parshah* also included Lot parting from his uncle Abraham. What follows is the third *parshah* of Part B (this one), which describes Lot being kidnapped in a war (see 14:11). As kidnapping is related to Principle C (limited access to spiritual/physical resources), we note the shift from Principle B in the previous *parshah*. Following the kidnapping, Lot is rescued by Abraham, who in 14:23 refuses the spoils that are offered him, another action associated with Principle C.

Still in the same *parshah*, Chapter 15 primarily records the Covenant between the Parts in which God promises a special relationship with Abraham's descendants in the context of an animal sacrifice. This subtext thus relates to both Principle B (in the special relationship) and Principle C (in approaching God by following detailed instructions for the sacrifice). Likewise, Chapter 16 relates to both Principles B and C, with the strain in Abraham's marriage (Principle B) over his concubine Hagar in 16:5 and the use in 16:11 of God's name (Principle C) in the name Ishmael, the son of Abraham and Hagar. Ishmael's portended thievery (see 16:12) is also tied to Principle C.

Finally, the same holds as the *parshah* ends with the Covenant of Circumcision (Principle B) and name changes for Abraham and Sarah (Principle C) in Chapter 17. Thus, the themes of this *parshah* align with both Principle C (limited access to spiritual/physical resources) or Principle B (loyalty to a primary relationship), which identifies the *parshah* as Subpart C of Part B.

Subpart D (18:1–21:21): Abraham's hospitality to guests/ promise of child at appointed time/ Abraham's plea to save Sodom from impending destruction/ Lot's hospitality to guests whom the Sodomites wish to molest/ Lot's relations with his daughters/ Abimelekh's abduction of Sarah/ birth of Isaac/ expulsion of Ishmael

As we proceed into this *parshah*, we read of Abraham's hospitality to guests, a communal characteristic consonant with Principle D (duties of testimony/community). Further, in 18:14, God speaks to Abraham about the birth of a son to Sarah *la-moed* [at an appointed time]. By its use of that word, which shares its root with *edut* [testimony], the text suggests the event will testify to God's capacity to fulfill a promise, thus reflecting Principle D, as well.

The *parshah* then turns in 18:23–33 to Abraham's appeal to God not to destroy Sodom, a plea for the community (Principle D). This is followed by the account of the visitors to Sodom who warn Lot of its impending destruction. He provides hospitality in a place that was not only inhospitable (Principle D), but also wanted (see 19:5) to molest his guests (Principle B). After Lot's wife dies in the flight from Sodom, Lot's daughters, believing there were no more men left in the world (see 19:31), get their father drunk and have relations with him (Principle B). The *parshah* continues in Chapter 20 with another event linked with Principle B (loyalty to a primary relationship) — Abimelekh's abduction and subsequent return of Sarah. Finally in Chapter 21, we have the birth of Isaac *la-moed* and the expulsion of Ishmael from the community, both reflecting Shared Principle D. In sum, the themes in this *parshah* reflect Principles B and D.

We have already identified the next *parshah* 21:22–34, which recounts Abraham's treaty with the Philistines (involving the land and the future), as Subpart E. Notice that there are exactly five *parshiyot* in Part B, corresponding in order to Subparts A through E. In each case, the thematic associations line up with the Shared Principles, as projected in the pattern.

ii. Subdivision of Part C (Genesis 22:1–25:18)

Here, because Subpart E of Part C has already been found, we need to identify only Subparts A through D.

Subpart A (22:1–19): the Binding of Isaac

In this account, which occupies a single *parshah*, God tests Abraham by telling him to take Isaac and sacrifice him on an altar. Both this command (which is later countermanded in 22:12) and Abraham's actions toward its fulfillment reflect both Principle C (for instructions to approach God) and Principle A (respecting Creation) for planned homicide. The designation of Subpart A of part C conforms to this association with Principles A and C.

Subpart B (22:20–24): Abraham hears of his brother Nahor's offspring

This very brief *parshah* consists of just five verses, all involving Nahor's offspring. However, the *parshah* places its concluding stress on one of his grandchildren in particular, Rebecca, who would later become Isaac's wife. On its face (independent of any other part of the text), this *parshah*, in recording lineage, does not seem to shift from

Principle A (respecting Creation) in the previous *parshah* to any other Shared Principle. However, it is known soon afterwards that Rebecca would marry Isaac. In fact, the text in this *parshah* adds a key phrase in 22:20 that news of Milcah's children "was told to Abraham."[1] Thus, I would tentatively link this *parshah* with Principle B (loyalty to a primary relationship), but with less textual evidence than I would like. The designation of this *parshah* as Subpart B is by far the least straightforward point in all of Genesis for the fit of the pattern, as the analysis below will show.

Subpart C (23:1–24:67): Sarah's death and Abraham's negotiations for a burial place/ mission of Abraham's servant to find and bring home a wife for Isaac

The third *parshah* in Part C opens with Sarah's death and Abraham's extended negotiations (covering nearly all of Chapter 23) with the Hittites to buy her a burial place. These negotiations are aimed at gaining access to a plot and clearly reflect Principle C. The *parshah* then tells of Abraham sending his servant Eliezer to find Isaac a wife. This mission reflects Principle B (loyalty to a primary relationship), but intrinsic to the mission is the oath that Abraham requires Eliezer to take. This oath (using God's name) in 24:7 relates to Principle C (limited access to spiritual/physical resources), as does Eliezer's subsequent self-imposed oath in 24:12–14. As the *parshah* continues, Eliezer meets Rebecca at a well, where she gives access to water.

Eliezer then engages in lengthy negotiations with her and her family over her betrothal. The objective of these negotiations would still fit best with Principle B, though with a certain element of testimony (Principle D). Principle C also emerges in several ways, notably in Rebecca herself being asked to consent to leave immediately (against the initial wishes of her mother and brother) in 24:58 — thereby avoiding any residue of kidnapping (the most severe form of stealing). The *parshah* closes with Rebecca meeting Isaac, who, in 24:63, had gone into the field to pray (Principle C), and his taking her as a wife and loving her (Principle B).

Overall, this *parshah* seems most related to Principle C (limited access to spiritual/physical resources), but with substantial signs of

Principle B in the context of marriage and with a suggestion of Principle D through testimony. The designation of this *parshah* as Subpart C of Part C is therefore quite reasonable, even if it requires some subjective judgment.

Subpart D (25:1–12): the end of Abraham's life
Before Abraham dies, he sends away the children of his concubine Ketura with gifts (see 25:6), thus defining the main community in line with his legacy to Isaac. This action recalls Abraham's previous expulsion of Ishmael in Subpart D of Part B and clearly aligns with Principle D (duties of testimony/community). That alignment and the consequent designation of this *parshah* as Subpart D are straightforward.

We have already identified the fifth *parshah* 25:13–18, which involves fulfillment of the prophecy about Ishmael, as Subpart E. Thus, in viewing Part C, we have three Subparts (A, D, and E) that fit very well with the pattern in terms of the Subparts Claim. The association of the third *parshah* with Principle C (limited access to spiritual/physical resources), while taking some judgment, remains quite reasonable. However, the association of the second *parshah* with Principle B (loyalty to a primary relationship) is much less clear.

iii. Subdivision of Part D (Genesis 25:19–35:22)

Subpart A (25:19–36): prayer to God for Rebecca's childbearing/ God's revelation to her about difficult pregnancy/ Esau's sale of birthright to Jacob
Because this *parshah* initially involves both belief in God as well as revelation, the initial alignment goes with Principle A (respecting Creation). The reference in 25:23 to two nations in Rebecca's womb also touches on Principle D as a matter of communal definition. While the sale of the birthright (a primary relationship) suggests Principle B, the *parshah*'s overall content fits clearly with its designation as Subpart A of Part D.

Subpart B (26:1–32:3): concealment of Isaac and Rebecca's marriage from Abimelekh and the subsequent strife with the Philistines/ Jacob's deception in taking his brother Esau's blessing/ Jacob's flight to escape Esau's wrath/

Jacob's marriage to both Leah and Rachel after their father Laban switches them/ birth of Jacob's children/ Laban's trickery in compensating Jacob/ theft of Laban's idols when Jacob's family flees/ Jacob's truce with Laban grounded in marital conditions

This single *parshah*, which occupies more than six full chapters and the majority of Part D, is arguably the most complex *parshah* in Genesis. In light of the number and range of topics covered, a careful analysis of this *parshah* in relation to the Shared Principles requires greater length and detail than we have presented until now. Thus, I ask the reader's indulgence as we review the content of the individual chapters to check the proper designation of a Subpart.

The *parshah* opens in Chapter 26 with famine in the land of Canaan where Isaac and Rebecca are living. Recalling the special relationship with Abraham and his offspring, God tells Isaac he cannot leave Canaan. Isaac and Rebecca travel instead to the area of Canaan controlled by the Philistines. Like his father before him, Isaac hides his marriage from the leader of the Philistines, Abimelekh, who later expels him from the area, ushering in a period of strife with the Philistines. Chapter 26 ends with Isaac and Rebecca's grief from Esau's marriage to Canaanite women. In sum, the events of this chapter chiefly concern marriage and the special relationship of the prior covenants, thus aligning with Principle B (loyalty to a primary relationship). Isaac's expulsion by Abimelekh from his community also provides a sense of Principle D.

Chapter 27 begins with Jacob's deception in taking the blessing meant by his father Isaac for Esau, Jacob's older brother. The deception itself aligns both with Principle D (through false testimony) and with Principle C (through gaining access to earthly resources). Yet one might also link the blessing with Principle E (accepting one's place/status) in its focus on the future. Then we read of Esau's wrath and his plan for murder, a repeated theme in Genesis reflecting Principle A (respecting Creation). Sensing Esau's intent, Rebecca persuades Isaac to send Jacob to Haran, ostensibly to look for a wife, suggesting Principle B (loyalty to a primary relationship).

Next, in Chapter 28, Esau takes a new wife to placate his parents.

This development, which accords with Principle B, is followed by Jacob's vision of a ladder ascending to Heaven. His vision could link to Principle A (through revelation), to Principle B (as a continuation of the special relationship begun with Abraham), or to Principle C (in gaining access to sanctity). That brings us to Chapter 29, with Jacob's arrival in Haran. There, in return for seven years of work for Laban, Jacob is betrothed to Laban's daughter Rachel, whom Laban replaces on their wedding night with Rachel's sister Leah. Jacob is then forced to work another seven years for Rachel. Rachel is childless at first, while Leah gives birth to four sons. There is strain in the marriage as a result. The events of this chapter predominantly align with Principle B through the various marital issues, but with an element of Principle D through Laban's deception.

Chapter 30 continues with more marital strain as the maidservants of Rachel and Leah begin having children with Jacob. Rachel finally gives birth to her first child Joseph. Up to this point, the chapter reflects Principle B (loyalty to a primary relationship). However, the text turns to Laban's further deceit in changing Jacob's compensation for tending sheep, thus suggesting either Principle C (limits on spiritual/physical resources) or D (duties of testimony/community).

In Chapter 31, God directs Jacob to return to Canaan after he notices a change in Laban's disposition towards him. Most commentaries read this as a change for the worse, resulting from Laban's envy of Jacob's wealth (amassed despite Laban's deceit).[2] Leah and Rachel agree to leave their father, and Rachel takes his idols (Principle B) on the way out. Laban gives chase and overtakes Jacob's entourage, asking why Jacob has stolen (Principle C) his idols. Jacob responds with his own grievance over Laban's deceit (Principle D). Finally, a treaty signaled by a testimonial marker (Principle D) is reached with Laban's declaration of marital conditions (Principle B) in relation to his daughters.

The three verses in Chapter 32 explain the name *machanayim* [camps] for the place of the treaty involving community (Principle D). In the *parshah* as a whole, we see that Principles B and D predominate, consistent with the designation of the *parshah* as Subpart B of Part D.

Subpart C (32:4–34:31): Jacob prepares for his meeting with Esau/ Jacob's struggle with an angel who gives him another name/ the meeting and truce with Esau/ abduction of Dinah and the retaliatory destruction of Shechem

This too is a single *parshah*. It tells first of Jacob's preparations for his meeting with Esau. Some of these preparations involve gifts to placate the older brother whose blessing he took. These gifts are often understood to signal that while Jacob got the blessings for access to earthly resources, he would gladly share them with Esau and is not trying to compete with him. Thus we would link these gifts to Principle C. Meanwhile, the other preparations (in case Esau is not placated) are for war, a communal activity linked with Principle D. Chapter 32 ends with Jacob's successful struggle with an angel who gives him the name Israel. Since the name Israel includes God's name, this event corresponds to Principle C (limited access to spiritual/physical resources). Chapter 33 records Jacob and Esau's meeting and reconciliation. Esau wants the two communities to merge, but Jacob declines. This concern with community composition reflects Principle D. After parting from Esau, Jacob and his family settle in Shechem.

The abduction and violation of Jacob's unmarried daughter Dinah by the son of the Shechemite leader opens Chapter 34. The Shechemites want to intermarry with Jacob's family. This subtext marks both Principle B (loyalty to a primary relationship) and Principle C (limited access to spiritual/physical resources) through kidnapping. Jacob's sons tell the Shechemites that intermarriage would require circumcising the male Shechemites, to which they agree. In that weakened condition, Dinah is rescued, and two of her brothers exterminate the male population of Shechem. As Chapter 34 ends, Jacob rebukes the two brothers for exposing their family to likely attack by others in the area who will see the family as enemies. These further events suggest Principle D (duties of testimony/community) in involving deceit and war.

We have seen that this *parshah* mainly reflects Principles C and D, confirming its designation as Subpart C of Part D.

Subpart D (35:1–8): the journey of Jacob's camp from Shechem and the fear of other peoples of making war with them

This very brief *parshah* offers one event suggesting Principle B: the destruction of idols picked up along the way by Jacob's camp. Yet, as the previous *parshah* closed with Jacob's worry over attacks from other Canaanites, the focus in this *parshah* remains with those peoples not making war. This link with Principle D (duties of testimony/community) is reinforced by the first application in 35:6 of the word *am* [nation] to the Jewish people, as represented by Jacob's camp. Thus the designation of this *parshah* as Subpart D fits, but requires some judgment.

Subpart E of Part D was already identified in Section 6 of Stage II as the *parshah* 35:9–22, involving God's promise to Jacob for the future, Rachel's death giving birth to Benjamin (fulfilling Jacob's unintended curse in 31:32), and Reuben's disrespectful act toward his father following Rachel's death. This completes the analysis of the Subparts Claim for Part D, in which the alignment with the Shared Principles is quite strong overall. As with Part B (focusing on Abraham) and Part C (focusing on Isaac), Part D consists of exactly five *parshiyot*, so there is exactly one *parshah* for each Subpart.

iv. Subdividing Part E (Genesis 35:23–50:26)

Subpart A (35:28–37:36): Isaac's death and burial/ progeny of murderous Esau/ the planned murder of Joseph, the dreamer, who is instead sold into slavery

There are four *parshiyot* in this Section. The first, 35:23–29 pertains to Isaac's death and burial, while the next two deal with Esau's progeny. The fourth, 37:1–36, tells of Joseph's dreams, his brothers' plan to kill him, and his eventual sale into slavery. Section 6 of Stage II stressed how the listing of Esau's descendants connects to Principle A (respecting Creation). The burial of Isaac by Esau and Jacob suggests Principle E (accepting one's place/status) as a mark of respect for a parent. That leaves the fourth *parshah*, which involves Jacob's dreams of his destiny to rule (Principle E) and his brothers' plan for murder (Principle A). Altogether, these four *parshiyot* fit the designation of Subpart E of Part A.

Subpart B (38:1–39:23), Judah's unintended affair with his daughter-in-law Tamar/ the adulterous designs on Joseph by the wife of Potiphar, his Egyptian master

This single *parshah* begins with marital improprieties involving Judah's two older sons over which they die. Judah then denies the surviving daughter-in-law Tamar access to his last son. Tamar disguises herself as a prostitute and is intimate with Judah after his wife dies. When Tamar becomes pregnant, he admits his culpability, and two sons are born of the affair. This story, which constitutes all of Chapter 38, primarily involves Principle B in matters of intimacy. However, it also involves Principle E (accepting one's place/status) in the refusal of Judah's second son Onan to follow his father's wishes that he (Onan) consort with Tamar, his brother's widow. Finally, Principle D is also suggested in Tamar's deceit and in Judah's confession.

Chapter 39 returns to Joseph, then in Egypt after being sold into slavery. The wife of his master Potiphar makes adulterous advances on Joseph, which he refuses. When he flees as a result, she accuses him of the advances, and he is imprisoned. These events most clearly link to Principle B (loyalty to a primary relationship), though there is also deceit by Potiphar's wife (Principle D). On the whole, the designation of the *parshah* as Subpart B of Part E makes sense.

Subpart C (40:1–23): the dreams of Pharaoh's chief steward and baker and Joseph's interpretation of those dreams

This single *parshah* first describes the dreams of two former officials of Pharaoh who had been removed from their posts and imprisoned with Joseph. They both tell their dreams to him, and he interprets the dreams in terms of the steward's and baker's future access to Pharaoh. The notion of regaining access relates to Principle C (limited access to spiritual/physical resources), while the context of the future relates to Principle E (accepting one's place/status). Thus the designation of this *parshah* as Subpart C of Part E is straightforward.

Subpart D (41:1–47:31): Pharaoh's dreams and Joseph's interpretation involving communal resources /Joseph's elevation to oversee those resources/

hiding of Joseph's identity from his brothers when they come to Egypt to buy grain/ Simeon's imprisonment/ testimony of brothers and the test of their responsibility for Benjamin on returning to Egypt/ Joseph revealing himself to his brothers/ Jacob's family invited to Egypt and given separate area in Goshen by Pharaoh/ Joseph's setting of taxes

Although this single *parshah* fully covers seven chapters, it is easy to see, without going through each chapter, that its major events are very suggestive of Principles D and E. Principle D arises in all the events involving communal resources and responsibility, deceit, testimony, and imprisonment (separation from community). Principle E arises in Pharaoh's dreams (telling the future) and in Joseph's elevation (fulfilling his own dreams). Several events interweave both Principles. For example, in Chapter 44, Joseph tests the brothers' communal responsibility by having his own chalice planted in Benjamin's bag and making it appear stolen. Thus deceit joins communal responsibility (Principle D). When Joseph says he will hold Benjamin as a slave, the brothers offer themselves in his place, thus fulfilling Joseph's original dream (in Chapter 37) that his brothers would bow down to him. The fulfillment of a dream reflects Principle E.

Subpart E (48:1–50:26): recounting Jacob's blessing of Joseph's two sons and then Joseph's brothers/ Jacob's last command that he be buried in Canaan/ Jacob's death and burial following that command/ Joseph's will that he be reburied in Canaan and his death

This final subtext of Genesis includes seven *parshiyot*, spanning three chapters. The first *parshah* coincides with Chapter 48 and Jacob's blessing of Joseph's two sons, with the future context of blessing linked to Principle E (accepting one's place/status). Chapter 49 includes five *parshiyot* and part of a sixth and covers the blessings to Joseph's brothers, which describe their essential traits. It also covers Jacob's command to bury him in Canaan with his forefathers. Thus Chapter 49 also reflects Principle E through blessing and the connection with the land. Finally, Chapter 50 with the rest of the last *parshah* tells of Jacob's sons honoring their father's last command and of Joseph's will to be reburied in Canaan. This completes the association with Subpart E of Part E.

Summary

In Section 6, we saw that Part A of Genesis subdivided smoothly into five Subparts aligned with the Shared Principles. In this section, we smoothly subdivided Parts B, D, and E of Genesis. In Part C of Genesis, the only element of the subdivision that raised an issue was the identification of Subpart B with a *parshah* generally devoted to lineage. However, there was still some basis for the linkage to Principle B (loyalty to a primary relationship).

Section 16
Supplement to the Test in Exodus

In Section 8, we tested how well the Shared Principles fit Exodus, leaving until now some details of the Test of Alternate Partition (versus the Parts Claim) and the Test of Ambiguous Subdivision (versus the Subparts Claim). These details are now provided in the order below.

1. Test of Alternate Partition
2. Test of Ambiguous Subdivision for Part B
3. Test of Ambiguous Subdivision for Part C
4. Test of Ambiguous Subdivision for Part D
5. Test of Ambiguous Subdivision for Part E

i. Test of Alternate Partition

In Section 8, we divided Exodus according to the following alternate partition below that seemed to not fit the pattern.

DISPLAY 16.1: Alternate Partition of Exodus into a Sequence of Topics		
1. Enslavement of Jewish people	~Chapters 1–2	B (Loyalty)
2. Revelations of God to Moses and Aaron	~Chapters 3–5	A (Creation)
3. Liberation through Plagues, Splitting of Sea	~Chapters 6–17	B (Loyalty)
4. Ten Commandments and civil law	~Chapters 18–24	C (Limits)

5. Directions for making Tabernacle	~Chapters 25–31	D (Community)
6. Incident of Golden Calf	~Chapters 32–33	B (Loyalty)
7. Actual making of Tabernacle	~Chapters 34–40	D (Community) or E (Acceptance)

In particular, three of the topics (the first, sixth, and seventh) did not align clearly with a proper Shared Principle. Full details were given in analyzing the first (enslavement of Jewish people) at the opening of Exodus and in analyzing the seventh (actual making of Tabernacle) at the end of Exodus. Those details showed why the first topic truly fits Principle A (respecting Creation), and not B (loyalty to a primary relationship). Thus, the first topic could be combined with the second (revelations of God to Moses and Aaron), which was already clearly aligned with Principle A. This combination became the revised first topic (oppression and revelations). Likewise, the full details for the seventh topic showed why it fit Principle E (acceptance of one's place/status), and not D (duties of testimony/community).

However, some details were omitted in Section 8 in analyzing the sixth topic, the Incident of the Golden Calf. There we concluded that the Incident should be linked to Principle D in spite of its apparent connection to idolatry (and thus Principle B). That analysis did note several Principle D themes within the subtext of the Incident (e.g., the Sabbath, Aaron's testimony and Moses' appeal to God based on nationhood). At the same time, those themes did not appear (by themselves) to outweigh idolatry in assigning a Shared Principle — especially in the first two *parshiyot* of the four that make up the Golden Calf subtext.

The Word *Am* in the Incident of the Golden Calf

The critical factor beyond those themes in linking the subtext to community was the unusual use of the word *am* to refer to the Jewish people in that subtext. That is where additional details are needed. The word *am* carries a communal connotation, as opposed to that of the term *b'nei Yisrael* [children of Israel], which stresses ancestry and which is more commonly used elsewhere in Exodus. We recognize the stress on ancestry in *b'nei Yisrael* because Israel is the alternative name Jacob acquired after his encounter with the angel of Esau in Genesis 32:25–33. Thus "children of Israel" specifically refers to the descendants of Jacob.

In the 901 verses in Exodus prior to the Incident of the Golden Calf, the Jewish people are referred to almost exclusively by either *b'nei Yisrael* or *am*. As noted above, *b'nei Yisrael* (appearing 121 times in those 901 verses) stresses ancestry, while *am* (appearing 74 times) stresses community, since *am* is linguistically related to the Hebrew word *im* [with].[3] This means that before the Golden Calf, the word *am* (referring to the Jewish people) occurs in Exodus on average once every twelve verses. In contrast, within the subtext of the Golden Calf itself (which occupies fifty-two verses) there are twenty-eight such occurrences of *am*, more than once every two verses. Over the same subtext, the term *b'nei Yisrael* appears only three times.

This contrast is confirmed by what happens in the 256 verses of Exodus after the Golden Calf: eighteen occurrences of *b'nei Yisrael* and four of *am*. Overall in Exodus, the word *am* appears in reference to the Jewish people 106 times, with more than one quarter of these occurrences within the Incident of the Golden Calf, which comprises less than three percent of the verses in the whole book.

Consider the comparable effect in an English document. Suppose that within 97% of a document, a single noun with a marked connotation appears very infrequently since a different noun is used. In one excerpt, however, this "rare" noun appears roughly every other sentence. In other words, from the unusual and frequent use of *am* in the account of the Golden Calf, I had to concede that this episode seems at least to signal a communal theme.

Yet, before fully giving in, I looked for other places in Exodus where the term *am* is used as often. This review would help confirm or deny my sense of this word's effect. I found no other contiguous excerpts of subparagraphs with similar intensity of *am* that were sustained as much as the Golden Calf (twenty-eight occurrences in fifty-two verses). The closest other case occurs in the preparations for receiving the Torah in Chapter 19 with twelve occurrences of *am* in twenty-five verses.

That repeated use of *am* in Chapter 19 reflects the collective nature of preparations and willingness to accept the Torah. However, when *am* is the subject there, no verb of independent action appears (rather "answered" in 19:8 and "trembled" in 19:16). In fact, in all of Exodus, the subject *am* only places the Jewish people in a passive role, except in the first component of the Golden Calf. In that component, we find two verbs of independent action by the subject *am*: the mobbing of Aaron (in 32:1) and the removing of gold earrings (in 32:3). This evidence finally convinced me to combine the Incident of the Golden Calf (the sixth topic) with directions for making Tabernacle (the fifth topic), which was already aligned with Principle D. This merging of the fifth and six topics was then renamed "Tabernacle Directions and Golden Calf."

ii. Subdivision of Part B (Exodus 7:1–18:27)

In subdividing Part B of Exodus, a particular aspect of the Subpart D drew our attention, but we have waited until this point to discuss it in detail. Recall that in our earlier discussion in Section 8, we identified Subpart D as below:

Subpart D (14:1–17:16): communal Exodus from Egypt, the Splitting of the Sea, communal complaint, and the war with Amalek

Let us again review the three major events that take place within those verses:

1. the Exodus from Egypt;
2. the Splitting of the Sea; and
3. the war with Amalek.

Each of those events reflects a clear communal character (Principle D). This communal character, together with the underlying linkage to Principle B in escaping from Egyptian mastery, should be expected to describe the themes we would find in Subpart D of Part B.

Yet, as we went along from *parshah* to *parshah* in that Section, other themes sometimes emerged beyond Principles B and D. There was, most strikingly, the theme of access to food and water (Principle C), which emerged in the three *parshiyot* spanning 15:20–17:7. At first, I had congratulated myself on noting features to help challenge the Shared Principles. Yet with more thought, I realized these other themes did not truly ruin the alignment of Subpart D of Part B, but rather represented a further embedding of the pattern. This embedding involves subdividing this Subpart into five Segments as shown below.

DISPLAY 16.2: Subpart D of Part B Subdivided According to the Shared Principles

Segment	Verses	Features Related to Shared Principle
A (Creation)	14:1–31	Awareness of and belief in God brought by Splitting of the Sea
B (Loyalty)	15:1–19	Song of Sea as testimony to God's unique power (only one God)
C (Limits)	15:20–17:7	Communal complaint over perceived loss of access to food, water
D (Community)	17:8–13	War with Amalek
E (Acceptance)	17:14–16	Promise by God to erase Amalek's memory in the future

In support of this further subdivision, let us stress several specific points in aligning the individual Segments of Subpart D in order with the Shared Principles:

Segment A: While Segment A refers several times to awareness of and belief in God, the final verse of that segment is especially telling: "And Israel saw the great hand God inflicted upon Egypt; and the people revered God, and they believed in God and in Moses, his servant." This stress on belief reflects Principle A (respecting Creation).

Segment B: This Segment features verse 15:11 declaring God's uniqueness. Other verses in the Segment describe God's defeat of the Egyptians who claimed mastery over the Jewish people, thus suggesting Principle B (loyalty to a primary relationship).

Segment C: We noted above the repeated theme of access to food and water in this Segment, in accord with Principle C (limited access to spiritual/physical resources).

Segment D: The Battle with Amalek in Segment D marks communal action and thus Principle D.

Segment E: The promise for the future regarding Amalek defines this Segment in connection with Principle E (acceptance of one's place/status).

iii. Subdivision of Part C (Exodus 19:1–24:18)

Part C contains seven *parshiyot*, just two more than the minimum to subdivide into Subparts. Moving through these seven *parshiyot*, changes in the dominant theme could be identified clearly and allowed for a straightforward progression through the Shared Principles. Moreover, Principle C (limited access to spiritual/physical resources) played at least a material role in most of the Subparts — not just Subpart C. This role is consistent with the Subparts belonging to Part C. For example, Subpart A includes what the Jewish people had to do (cleanse themselves and refrain from marital relations for three days) before receiving the Torah. Subpart B addresses the allowable forms of altars, which involve spiritual access, while Subpart D presents laws, such as the ban on taking interest on loans, which limit access to resources. The actual subdivision was shown originally in Section 4 as Display 4.8 and is repeated below as Display 16.3.

DISPLAY 16.3: Part C of Exodus Subdivided According to the Shared Principles

Subpart	Verses	Features Related to Shared Principle
A (Creation)	19:1–20:14	Revelation in giving the Ten Commandments
B (Loyalty)	20:15–20:23	Banned images and altars revealing nakedness, i.e., illicit union
C (Limits)	21:1–22:12	Laws involving damages to persons and to property
D (Community)	22:13–23:19	Duty to support poor, not to oppress weak, or take false testimony/ holidays as testimonial occasions [*moadim*] and times to assemble
E (Acceptance)	23:20–24:18	Blessing of bread/ promise of military victory/ Moses' ascent without Elders (exclusivity of role)

In analyzing this subdivision, the following points emerge in aligning the Subparts in order with the Shared Principles:

Subpart A: This Subpart includes two *parshiyot*. The first describes preparations for and then the onset of the revelation at Sinai, along with the first three of the Ten Commandments. The second *parshah* presents the final seven Commandments, leading off with the Fourth (to observe the Sabbath), which identifies God with Creation. Clearly, this Subpart reflects Principle A (respecting Creation).

Subpart B: The short single *parshah* of Subpart B opens with the people shying away from the revelation but then forbids making images and making altars that reveal nakedness. Thus this *parshah* connects to Principle B (loyalty to a primary relationship) through idolatry and adultery.

Subpart C: The laws of damages relate to limited access to physical resources (Principle C) in the long single *parshah* that makes up this Subpart.

Subpart D: The previous Subpart focused on personal liability. In contrast, Subpart D, in its one *parshah*, mainly concerns two types of civil obligation: (1) personal obligation to others but without formal liability or (2) obligation on the whole community. In the first category, we have, for example, an individual's duty to support the poor, which involves preserving the community (Principle D) in a way that liability claims between two parties (in the previous *parshah*) do not. Of course, the testimonial occasions also reflect Principle D.

Subpart E: This Subpart consists of two *parshiyot*, with the first (23:20–33) keyed to the promised future — especially for the conquest of Canaan and for prosperity and healthy living therein. The second *parshah* (24:1–18) also reflects the theme of accepting one's place (Principle E) through the special mission of Moses to approach God, as opposed to the Elders and to Aaron and his family.

Odd Spacing in the Ten Commandments

While the pattern easily passed the Test of Ambiguous Subdivision in Part C, a striking feature surfaced in identifying the Subparts. That feature is the odd spacing within the Ten Commandments, which, as noted above, are split into two *parshiyot* of Subpart A. Specifically, the first *parshah* of Subpart A opens with a subparagraph (ending in a *s'tumah*) on preparations for the Sinai revelation. Then comes a subparagraph for the first two Commandments (also ending in a *s'tumah*) followed by a third subparagraph for the Third Commandment alone, which closes the first *parshah* of Subpart A and ends with a *p'tuchah*. In contrast, the second *parshah* of Subpart A consists of seven subparagraphs, one for each of the remaining Commandments, with a *s'tumah* between each two successive Commandments within those seven.

This placement of the *p'tuchah* (a stronger separation than a *s'tumah*) between the Third and Fourth Commandments seems at odds with the pairing of the Commandments by the Shared Principles. I would have expected a single *p'tuchah* within the Commandments to fall after the Fifth to emphasize the overall pairing of Commandments 1 through 5 with Commandments 6 through 10. Failing that placement, the next most logical position would be after the Second Commandment. While that position would not support the pattern directly, it would not actually conflict. Rather, it would reflect the tradition (see *Makkot* 24a) that God taught the first two Commandments directly to the people while the rest were taught through Moses. In fact, this tradition explains the lack of any spacing between the first two Commandments.

But the actual placement of a *p'tuchah* after the Third Commandment left me seeking a rationale. That search led to the third century Midrash *Tanna d'Vei Eliyahu* (26:14), which notes that taking God's name in vain cannot be forgiven (see Exodus 20:7). This brought the Midrash to equate breaking the Third Commandment with breaking both prior Commandments. That relationship would explain why the first three Commandments in Exodus are set apart from the rest by a *p'tuchah*. However, the spacing of the Commandments in Deuteronomy 5 muddies matters, since a *s'tumah* (not a *p'tuchah*) follows the Third Commandment there.

The spacing disparity between the two versions of the Commandments may be resolved with part of Ramban's approach to variation of laws given in earlier books versus their statements in Deuteronomy: the change responds to a transgression in the Wilderness.

In other words, did such a transgression require a closer relationship between the first Three Commandments and the Fourth? We need look no further than the last law in Deuteronomy before the second set of Commandments, the ban on adding or subtracting from any of the laws (see Deuteronomy 4:1–4).

That text clearly suggests the ban came from the Incident of Baal Peor (Numbers 25:1–3), in which idolatrous worship was enabled by intended denigration of an idol.[4] In other words, those intending denigration added to the Torah, according to their own ideas, in this case on the prohibition of idolatry and in doing so came to worship the idol. Intrinsic to this error is a presumption that one can claim the Torah's imprimatur to exceed the law if he is sure of its intent. In making that claim, he verges on taking God's name in vain — a violation of the Third Commandment.

However, as a practical matter, the ban on adding or subtracting typically applies to various laws of testimonial observance,[5] which derive from the Fourth Commandment (keeping the Sabbath). Thus, in Deuteronomy, the Fourth Commandment would connect to the Second and Third through the error with Baal Peor, which was not present in Exodus for the first set of Commandments. That error may explain the smaller separation of a *s'tumah* between the Third and Fourth Commandments in Deuteronomy.

iv. Subdivision of Part D (Exodus 25:1–33:23)

There are fourteen *parshiyot* in Part D. The grouping of those *parshiyot* into Subparts aligned with the Shared Principles did not raise any material difficulties, since the main issues involving the Incident of the Golden Calf were resolved earlier. Specifically, earlier analysis in this section and in Section 6 addressed the tendency to see the Golden Calf in terms of Principle B (loyalty to a primary relationship), on account of idolatry or something close to it. That analysis has shown that while it makes sense for idolatry or near-idolatry to happen in Exodus (aligned with Principle B), the Incident of the Golden Calf, as actually reported in the Torah, is more closely aligned with Principle D (duties of testimony/

community). The detailed subdivision of Part D into Subparts appears below in Display 16.4.

DISPLAY 16.4: Part D of Exodus Subdivided According to the Shared Principles

Subpart	Verses	Features Related to Shared Principle
A (Creation)	25:1–28:5	Instructions for building Tabernacle and for making its furnishings (corresponds to Creation of World and its elements)
B (Loyalty)	28:6–30:10	Instructions for making priestly garments and accessories (corresponds to special partnership)
C (Limits)	30:11–31:11	Instructions for actions in Tabernacle on behalf of entire people
D (Community)	31:12–33:11	Sabbath observance in relation to Tabernacle/ Incident of the Golden Calf/ Role of Ohel Moed [Tent of Meeting]/ Moses successfully pleads that people not be destroyed
E (Acceptance)	33:12–23	Moses asks God to remain with people (and not just refrain from annihilation) and to show His glory/ God's promise in response

In analyzing this subdivision, the following points emerge in aligning the Subparts in order with the Shared Principles:

Subpart A: This Subpart includes four *parshiyot*, which are focused on the materials and making of both the Tabernacle itself and the furnishings inside it, such as the altars. As stated in the endnote in the display, this description corresponds to the elements of Creation described during the first seven days of the world in Genesis 1:1–2:3 (which make up Subpart A of Part A of Genesis).

Subpart B: The two *parshiyot* in this Subpart describe the clothing and accessories of the priests. Their special relationship to God in the activity of the Tabernacle suggests the special relationship of Man to God in the activity of the world, as told in the Eden story in Subpart B of Part

A of Genesis (2:4–3:21). Clothes also play a notable role in the Eden story. Moreover, use of a distinctive verb for priestly service (*l'khahein*) supports the notion of special relationship.

Subpart C: This subpart includes in its three *parshiyot* several items that directly suggest access (Principle C). First among them is the condition for taking a census (that it must be done indirectly by counting half-shekels). Second is the required use of a laver (with directions for its construction) before service is performed in the Tabernacle (the inclusion of the laver here and not with the Tabernacle's other furnishings in Subpart A can be explained by its role in allowing access to service). Finally, there is the need to anoint Aaron and his sons before they can serve as priests.

Subpart D: The inclusion in Subpart D of the Sabbath's limitations on building the Tabernacle and the Tent of Meeting's role in communication come as no surprise in relation to Principle D (duties of testimony/community). Beyond the signs of testimony and community noted earlier for the Incident of the Golden Calf, another indication of Principle D deserves mention. That indication is the parallel with Subpart D of Part A of Genesis, the story of the Flood. In that story, Noah saves his family from the waters after the degradation of society, while here in Exodus Moses saves the people from destruction after the Golden Calf.

Subpart E: Subpart E consists of two short *parshiyot*, which recount Moses' plea that God stay with the people and reveal His glory. To the first of these requests for the future, reflecting Principle E (acceptance of one's place/status), God assents; to the second, He only partially agrees.

v. Subdivision of Part E (Exodus 34:1–40:38)

There are fifteen *parshiyot* in Part E, which describe the actual construction of the Tabernacle and its furnishings, mirroring the instructions for such construction in Part D. There were no material issues in the subdivision of Part E into Subparts as shown in Display 16.5.

DISPLAY 16.5: Part E of Exodus Subdivided According to the Shared Principles		
Subpart	Verses	Features Related to Shared Principle
A (Creation)	34:1–39:1	Revelation to Moses as promised/ construction of Tabernacle and furnishings
B (Loyalty)	39:2–32	Actual making of the priestly garments and accessories
C (Limits)	39:33–43	Tabernacle and its related objects brought to Moses
D (Community)	40:1–33	Moses erects Tabernacle and puts furnishings in proper locations
E (Acceptance)	40:34–38	Cloud of God's presence settles on Tabernacle, keeping promise

Subpart A: Consistent with Principle A (Creation), this Subpart with nine *parshiyot* begins with revelation in the context of the second Tablets. Then this section turns in Chapter 35 to the actual construction of the Tabernacle and its furnishings, which parallels the instructions for the construction in Subpart A of Part D.

Subpart B: In its three *parshiyot*, Subpart B continues the correspondence of actual construction relative to the instructions in Part D, this time in regard to the priestly garments and accessories. This section thus aligns with Principle B (Loyalty) in the priests' special relationship.

Subpart C: Subpart C consists of a single *parshah* that summarizes the completed construction in the previous two sections, Subparts A and B. While its summative tone marks a clear change from those Subparts, it does not correspond directly with the contents of Subpart C of Part D. At first blush, it seems to feature no reference to access (Principle C). On closer scrutiny, however, its last two verses (39:42–43) stress at great length that the completed work of the Tabernacle conformed to God's instructions. As Rashi explains, with the people's work now finished, they had to bring the final products to Moses for the erection of the Tabernacle. In other words, the people would not have the same access to the Tabernacle beyond this point for the erection (and operation) of the Tabernacle. Further signaling Principle C (Limits), the listed furnishings and clothing/accessories are precisely those sacred items forbidden for personal use (see Rashi on Leviticus 5:15).

Subpart D: Also a single *parshah*, this Subpart focuses on the placement of furnishings in the Ohel Moed [Tent of Meeting], which suggests a communal purpose in line with Principle D (Subpart D of Part D) that describes the role of the Ohel Moed.

Subpart E: Subpart E is identical with the last *parshah* in Exodus. Its five verses show the fulfillment of God's promise to Moses in the settling of the Cloud of Glory over the Tabernacle. In fulfilling this promise, Principle E (Acceptance) is suggested.

Section 17
Supplement on Matching Division Points

The Test of Point Disparity was one of the three tests used to challenge the pattern of Shared Principles. In this test, we compared our independent choices of division points between Parts with Rabbi Honigwachs' division points. Recall that each book divides into five Parts aligned in order with the pattern. The division points between Parts occur at *p'tuchot* [open spacing to the left margin in columns of text], and all *p'tuchot* are listed in Appendix a.

To confirm that a declared pattern is truly present in a certain environment, the pattern must be perceived in at least roughly the same way by different informed viewers — in this case, by Rabbi Honigwachs and me. Should substantial discrepancies recur in the outline of the pattern as seen by the different viewers, one must ask whether the pattern is sufficiently well-defined or whether it is so fungible as to be essentially meaningless. Of course, a key question is what level of closeness in points of division should constitute reasonable agreement.

The issues involved in setting the required level of closeness and the degree of matching are more technical and would have slowed our progress enormously had we dealt with them in our main development. We will now address these issues in the following order.

1. Odds against a substantial match;
2. Effect of other tests on matching;
3. Closeness for purpose of matching;
4. Level of failure permitted.

i. Odds Against a Substantial Match

As we have indicated earlier, the difficulty in getting a substantial match (enough to confirm some sense of validity) is framed by the number of *p'tuchot* in each of the first four Books. Not counting the enlarged spacing at the end of each Book, Genesis has 43 *p'tuchot*, Exodus 69, Leviticus 52, and Numbers 92. Thus, the odds of an exact match would be best in Genesis among the four because Genesis has the fewest *p'tuchot*.

In each Book, there are four points of division between Rabbi Honigwachs' successive Parts (i.e., between Parts A and B, between Parts B and C, between Parts C and D, and between Parts D and E). In addition, in each Book there are four points of division between my successive Parts. To calculate the odds of a full match of all four points of division, we would compute:

(the odds of matching the point between Parts A and B) x
(the odds of matching the point between Parts B and C) x
(the odds of matching the point between Parts C and D) x
(the odds of matching the point between Parts D and E).

In Genesis (which already has the fewest *p'tuchot*), the odds of matching Rabbi Honigwachs' four points with our independent selection would run even higher. This is because we began with the natural fivefold partition in Genesis: (1) universal history, (2) the life of Abraham, (3) the life of Isaac, (4) the life of Jacob, and (5) the lives of Joseph and his brothers. In other words, even though I had not looked at *The Unity of Torah* for more than two years (and did not remember Rabbi Honigwachs' points of division specifically), I did have in mind the general sense of the partition in Genesis.

This sense did confine the beginning of each Part. For example, Part C (focusing on the life of Isaac) could begin only as early as Isaac's birth and only as late as the first time he acted truly independently of his father Abraham. Thus, my identification of the first *parshah* in Part C could only be one of five *parshiyot*: 18:1–21:21 (with Isaac's birth), 21:22–34, 22:1–19, 22:20–24, and 23:1–24:67 (with Isaac's marriage to Rebecca). Since there are five possible beginnings for Part C, there are five possibilities for the point of division between Part B and Part C, and the odds of matching Rabbi Honigwachs are 1 in 5, or 20%.

The same method applies to choices for the points of division for Parts A and B, for Parts C and D, and for Parts D and E. Since each Part can begin only as early as the birth of the new key figure and only as late as his first action independent of his father, I see two choices for the first *parshah* in Abraham's life (odds of matching Rabbi Honigwachs 1 in 2), one choice for Jacob's life (odds of matching Rabbi Honigwachs 1 in 1), and eight choices for Joseph's life (odds of matching Rabbi Honigwachs 1 in 8).[6] Recalling the odds of matching Rabbi Honigwachs 1 in 5 for Isaac's life, the likelihood of matching all four of Rabbi Honigwachs' points of division would be:

1/2 x 1/5 x 1/1 x 1/8 = 1.25% (product of odds for Abraham, Isaac, Jacob, and Joseph).

In other words, on a purely mathematical level, the odds are stiff but not overwhelming. In fact, should we be satisfied with matching any three of the four points of division for Parts in Genesis, the odds rise from 1.25% to 16.25%. Outside Genesis, however, the odds become prohibitive without a natural fivefold partition that limits where a Part could begin. In Exodus, for example, with its sixty-nine *p'tuchot*, the odds are 4 in 69 of randomly choosing one of Rabbi Honigwachs' points of division for Parts. Assuming success on the first choice, there would be three more points among sixty-eight *p'tuchot* for odds of 3 in 68. Continuing in this way, we would find the odds for randomly choosing all four points as:

4/69 x 3/68 x 2/67 x 1/66 < 00012%.

Even dropping expectations to three or more matches raises the odds to only .03%. Extensive agreement seems a poor bet.

ii. Effect of Other Tests on Matching

As you will recall, there were two other tests used to challenge the pattern of Shared Principles, and each of them can affect the circumstances for matching division points. We discussed two ways to test the pattern in Exodus, Leviticus, and Numbers:

- The Test of Alternate Partition offered an alternative sequence of topics within a book that does not seem to align with the Shared Principles. We attempted to confirm this non-alignment through close review of the text and thereby document a failure of the Parts Claim (that each Book divides into five Parts aligned with the pattern).
- The Test of Ambiguous Subdivision challenged the Subparts Claim: the capacity of a Part (with at least five *parshiyot*) to subdivide into Subparts aligned with the pattern. Unlike Rabbi Honigwachs, who used the Standard Opening (of "God spoke to Moses saying") to recognize progression of one Subpart to another, we used only thematic changes to recognize such progression.

Let us now consider the effect of these strategies on how closely our division points might match those of Rabbi Honigwachs. Obviously, these two bulleted strategies would also reduce the likelihood that our respective points of division (whether between Parts or between Subparts) actually match. For points of division between Subparts, however, clear comparisons of mine with those of Rabbi Honigwachs are limited or hampered by several factors:

- Not all of the breakdowns of Parts into Subparts are presented in Rabbi Honigwachs' *The Unity of Torah*. Thus it is impossible to get a full comparison.
- Two Parts in Leviticus (Parts B and E) and one Part in Numbers (Part C) do not have enough *parshiyot* to allow for further subdivision. Shall we simply ignore these cases (reducing the pool for testing) or shall we give credit to the pattern by default?
- Suppose two of my successive division points exactly match those of Rabbi Honigwachs. Then there may not be much more than five paragraphs between those two points. Thus, if the resulting division points between Subparts match, that need not add much to the fit, since the matching of these division points was almost forced by the agreement of the division points between Parts.

- Suppose my division point between specific Parts does not match its counterpart from Rabbi Honigwachs. Then what allowance (if any) in the matching of Sections from those Parts should be given? This question would arise where, for example, I identify a certain point as dividing Part A from Part B, but Rabbi Honigwachs identifies the same point as dividing Subpart A of Part A from Subpart B of Part A.

For all these reasons, the most straightforward approach is to compare only division points between Parts and to set aside division points between Subparts in the context of the overall fit. As for points of division between Parts, we must set stiff enough standards for the comparison in two respects. How close must a specific pair of respective points of division (one mine and one from Rabbi Honigwachs) fall to be considered matching, and how many must match in order to view the Parts divisions as reflecting a similar pattern?

iii. Closeness for Purpose of Matching

The most basic question regarding the standard of closeness is why not simply require our respective points separating two specific Parts to be exactly the same. The answer is twofold. First, visual recognition of a pattern does not require an exact fit, and second, we often draw inferences from data without absolute certainty. Most frequently, such inferences about a statistic are drawn from random sampling with 95% confidence with a particular range of uncertainty (plus or minus a particular quantity). While our task of comparing points of division does not actually involve random sampling, it is still natural to set standards in terms of the most common form of statistical inference, as described below.

For our statistic, we might count the number of *p'tuchot* that separate each of my points of division from the corresponding ones of Rabbi Honigwachs. To make this idea more precise, let us say that in one of the Books, my division point [x] between Parts A and B occurs at the eleventh *p'tuchah* in the Book, while his corresponding point [y] occurs at the eighth. Then $x-y = 3$ would be the count in question. Note that for the opposite choice of *p'tuchot*, x–y would be −3. In any event, if the pattern were valid, then we would require two things. First, we would want the average of x—y to be zero. Second, under the conditions of random sampling, we would also demand that the range of uncertainty be small with 95% confidence. A natural "small" range would be plus or minus one *p'tuchah*.

I promised earlier not to get involved with high-powered mathematics, and I intend to keep that promise. The question we must answer here is what maximum distance between each of our respective points fits this standard, i.e., an average difference of zero with a 95% confidence range of plus or minus one *p'tuchah*. Alternatively, assume our respective points differ in each case by the same number [n] of *p'tuchot*; what's the largest value of [n] that retains an overall mean of 0, with a confidence level of 95% for a range of plus or minus one *p'tuchah*?

Intuitively, you might say that since the positions −1 and 1 are two units apart, the maximum value of [n] must be two. And as a matter of fact you would be correct, though a basic statistical calculation (which I have done) is needed to reach that conclusion. Even without those details, one can take comfort in this standard by noting that of the first four Books, Genesis has the fewest *p'tuchot* (43). Thus, a limitation of two *p'tuchot* for the distance between respective points amounts to less than 5% of the total *p'tuchot* in any book, i.e., 2 < 5% of 43.

iv. Level of Failure Permitted

With this standard of closeness in hand, I could now count how many times the standard must be applied in the first four Books. This count would be the total number of pairs of respective points (one Rabbi Honigwachs' and one mine) of division that would be tested accordingly. The points of division between Parts in any single Book would be as follows: between Parts A and B, between Parts B and C, between Parts C and D, and between Parts D and E. (We don't need to worry about the point of division between Part E of one Book and the succeeding Part A of the next Book because there are several rows of *p'tuchot* at that point that mark it clearly.) Thus, there are four points of division in any single Book, and 16=4x4 in the first four Books. This means testing the closeness of sixteen pairs of division points for Parts.

The next task was to decide how many of these sixteen tests could fail before tossing out the pattern as not having enough matching in points of division for Parts. This decision would require some subjectivity, no matter what lengths I took to avoid it. In the end, two different approaches seemed to make the most sense.

The first and simplest approach again relies on the convention of a 95% level, but this time applied to the sixteen pairs of division points being tested to see whether they are close enough to be considered matching. We would say then that we want at least 95% to match, and .95x16=15.2, which rounds to fifteen. Accordingly, if there were more than one failure to match, I would view the pattern as not being adequately replicated.

The second and more sophisticated approach relies on the statistical concept of independent events. We calculate the odds of a series of separate independent events occurring as the product of the odds of each of them separately. Thus, if A and B are independent events, the odds of both of them occurring would be calculated as the odds of A times the odds of B. And if the event C is also independent of both A and B, then the odds of all three occurring would be the odds of A times the odds of B times the odds of C, and so on.

In particular, consider the event in a given Book of no more than one of the four pairs of points of division failing to match. That event is independent of the same event occurring in another Book. This independence thus guides the calculation of the odds that none of the first four Books will have no more than one pair failing to match. Keep in mind that failing to match means being three or *p'tuchot* apart. That calculation is the product of the odds in each Book of that event: {odds of the event in Genesis} x {odds of the event in Exodus} x {odds of the event in Leviticus} x {odds of the event in Numbers}.

As we noted earlier, Genesis has much better odds for matching identically than any of the three subsequent Books. This same relationship holds when we are talking about the division points being within two *p'tuchot* of each other. In particular, when we consider the number of *p'tuchot* between Abraham's birth and his first independent action, we find that any choice of the *p'tuchah* with which to start the focus on Abraham will be within two *p'tuchot* of any other choice. The same thing is true for the focus on Jacob. In other words, only for the focus on Isaac and for the focus on Joseph is there enough range not to be forced into a match.

For the focus on Isaac, there are a total of five choices of *p'tuchot*, of which three occupy positions that would be considered to match. For Joseph, there are eight choices of which three occupy positions that would be considered to match. This means the odds of all four division points matching is 3/5x3/8, just under 25%. To match on Isaac but miss on Joseph, the odds would be 3/5x5/8, just under 40%; and to miss on Isaac and match on Joseph, the odds are 2/5x3/8=15%. Thus, the odds for at least three matches (not necessarily identical) in the highly constrained environment of Genesis are 80%.

Let us adjust the odds in the other Books only for the relative increase in *p'tuchot* over Genesis, which requires squaring in line with our calculations above. Here we do not try to take any account of the differences resulting from the natural fivefold division of Genesis, and we obtain the following odds for at least three matches in Exodus, Leviticus, and Numbers:

Exodus: $80\% \times (43/69)^2 = 31.069\%$
Leviticus: $80\% \times (43/52)^2 = 54.704\%$
Numbers: $80\% \times (43/92)^2 = 17.476\%$

With the odds in Genesis at 80%, the odds of at least three matches in each of the first four Books would be

$80\% \times 31.069\% \times 54.704\% \times 17.476\% < 3\%$

Thus, the second approach, which would allow as many as four failures among the sixteen pairs (up to one in each Book), would cut the pattern more slack than the first, which would only allow at most one failure. At the same time, I did not see my task as cutting the pattern more slack. Even if the second approach was justified, it meant there could be a failure in more than half the first four Books. Thus I would allow the pattern at most two failures. Since the test for fit would now apply only to Parts, the most logical point for that test would be immediately after the test of the Parts Claim.

Notes

1. The insertion of the phrase that Abraham was told about Milcah's children suggests that he had an interest in them, and, indeed, he sends his servant Eliezer soon after to their place to find a wife for Isaac.
2. The account of Laban's face not looking the same to Jacob as before is generally read to mean that Laban's attitude (though it was already marked by deceipt) had changed for the worse. However, some read this account to mean that Jacob realized his own gradual accommodation of Laban's materialistic values. In other words, while Laban's face (representing his values) once repulsed him, it now looked acceptable. Accordingly, Jacob chose to flee Laban before he (Jacob) became even more assimilated. This interpretation appears in P. Peli, *Torah Today* (Washington, DC: B'nai Brith Books, 1987), pp. 29–32, but I recall encountering it long ago in a much earlier source that I cannot find.
3. There is another view of the word *am* popularized in the eighteenth century commentary *Or HaChaiyim*, in which *am* specifically includes the "mixed multitude" (see Exodus 12:38) that left Egypt with the Jewish people. According to this view (see the *Or HaChaiyim* on 13:17 and on 32:4), the heavy use of the word *am* in the account of the Golden Calf signals that the mixed multitude instigated the incident — though others were guilty of joining in later or perhaps of not stopping it at the outset. Although this view puts a different cast on the account, it does not materially change the focus on communal dysfunction.
4. According to *Sanhedrin* 106a, the people defecated on the idol intending to denigrate it, even though that act was the designated form of worship.
5. See Rashi on Numbers 4:2 for specific examples of what is banned. Each involves testimonial observance.
6. For the lives of each of Abraham, Jacob, and Joseph, possible choices for the beginning the respective Subparts are as follows:
Abraham: 11:1–32 (birth), 12:1–9 (first independent action);
Jacob: 25:19–34 (birth and first independent action);
Joseph: 26:1–32:3 (birth), 32:4–34:31, 35:1–8, 35:9–22; 35:22–29, 36:1–30, 36:31–43, 37:1–36 (first independent action).
Note that there is a *p'tuchah* in the middle of the verse 35:22.

APPENDICES

Appendix A
Location of *P'tuchot* in the Five Books of Moses

The paragraph structure on a Torah scroll is delineated through *p'tuchot* [blank spaces open to the left side of a column of text]. Specifically, each of the Torah's 295 *parshiyot* [paragraphs] ends with a *p'tuchah*. According to Jewish tradition, these *p'tuchot* were included in the Torah from Sinai, with their accuracy maintained through the generations using specially annotated manuscripts. Within this chain of transmission, the tenth century Aleppo Codex became the source for Maimonides' authoritative listing of all the Torah's *p'tuchot* in his code *Mishneh Torah*, which guides today's Torah scrolls. That listing appears in Chapter 8 of the section titled *Hilchot Sefer Torah* (Laws of a Torah Scroll).[1] There the location of each *p'tuchah* is identified by providing a few words of the text that follows immediately after the *p'tuchah* — without an indication of chapter and verse.

To make the present listing more accessible, we use the chapter and verse that precedes the *p'tuchah* to identify its location. In other words, the *p'tuchah* generally marks the end of a *parshah* [paragraph] whose last verse is identified. There are two cases, however, in which a *p'tuchah* occurs in the middle of a verse, and these cases are marked with asterisks. In those two cases, the verse indicated is the one within which the *p'tuchah* occurs. Because Maimonides did not count the open spacing before a Book's first verse, the number of *parshiyot* in a Book actually exceeds the total number of *p'tuchot* in that Book by one.

Genesis: (1:5), (1:8), (1:13), (1:19), (1:23), (1:31), (2:3), (3:21), (6:4), (6:8), (9:17), (9:29), (10:32), (11:9), (11:32), (12:9), (13:18), (17:27), (21:21), (21:34), (22:19), (22:24), (25:67), (25:10), (25:18), (25:34), (32:2), (34:31), (35:8), (35:22)*, (35:29), (36:30), (36:43), (37:36), (39:23), (40:23), (47:31), (48:23), (49:4), (49:7), (49:12), (49:13), (49:26). 43 *p'tuchot* total.

* The first word after the *p'tuchah* is *va-yiyu* [and they were].

Exodus: (1:7), (1:22), (2:22), (4:17), (4:26), (6:9), (6:12), (6:30), (7:7), (7:25), (8:28), (9:7), (9:21), (9:35), (10:20), (10:29), (12:20), (12:36), (12:42), (12:51), (13:10), (13:22), (14:14), (14:25), (14:31), (15:19), (16:10), (16:36), (17:7), (17:13), (17:16), (18:27), (20:7), (20:14), (20:23), (21:27), (22:12), (22:23), (23:19), (23:33), (24:18), (25:21), (25:30), (26:14), (28:5), (29:46), (30:10), (30:16), (30:21), (31:11), (32:6), (32:14), (33:11), (33:16), (33:23), (34:26), (35:3), (35:28), (36:13), (36:38), (37:9), (37:16), (37:24), (39:1), (39:7), (39:21), (39:32), (39:43), (40:33). 69 *p'tuchot* total.

Leviticus: (1:13), (2:16), (3:5), (3:11), (3:17), (4:12), (4:20), (4:26), (4:31), (4:35), (5:16), (5:18), (5:26), (6:11), (6:16), (6:23), (7:10), (7:27), (7:38), (10:7), (10:11), (10:20), (11:47), (12:8), (13:8), (13:17), (13:28), (13:59), (14:32), (14:57), (15:18), (15:33), (16:34), (17:16), (18:30), (19:22), (19:37), (20:27), (21:24), (22:16), (22:33), (23:3), (23:8), (23:22), (23:32), (23:44), (24:4), (24:12), (24:23), (26:2), (26:13), (26:46). 52 *p'tuchot* total.

Numbers: (1:21), (1:23), (1:25), (1:27), (1:29), (1:31), (1:33), (1:35), (1:37), (1:39), (1:41), (1:43), (1:47), (2:31), (2:34), (3:4), (3:10), (3:13), (3:43), (3:51), (4:16), (4:20), (4:49), (5:4), (5:10), (5:31), (6:21), (7:17), (7:23), (7:29), (7:35), (7:41), (7:47), (7:53), (7:59), (7:65), (7:71), (7:77), (7:83), (7:89), (8:4), (8:26), (9:8), (9:23), (10:10), (10:36), (11:15), (11:22), (11:35), (12:13), (12:16), (14:10), (14:25), (14:45), (15:16), (15:31), (15:36), (15:41), (17:5), (17:15), (17:24), (17:26), (18:7), (18:24), (18:32), (19:22), (20:6), (20:21), (21:3), (21:20), (24:25), (25:9), (25:15), (26:1)**, (26:51), (27:5), (27:11), (27:23), (28:8), (28:10), (28:31), (30:1), (30:17), (31:54), (32:19), (32:42), (33:56), (34:15), (34:29), (35:8), (35:34). 92 *p'tuchot* total.

** The first word after the *p'tuchah* is *va-yomer* [and He said].

Deuteronomy: (3:29), (4:24), (4:40), (4:49), (6:3), (7:11), (7:26), (8:18), (8:20), (9:29), (10:11), (13:1), (14:21), (15:18), (15:23), (16:12), (17:7), (19:10), (20:20), (22:5), (25:16), (25:19), (26:19), (27:26), (28:14), (28:69), (29:8), (30:20), (31:13), (31:30), (32:44), (32:47), (32:52), (33:7). 34 *p'tuchot* total.

Appendix B
Spelling and Spacing Differences in Torah Scrolls

Although the Torah dates back well over three millennia, the level of agreement in its text — and not just in the location of *p'tuchot* [open spacing] — is striking. One would expect even more variation than found in pre-Gutenberg (i.e., handwritten) versions of the Christian New Testament, which originated over 1,000 years later. Scholars of that document count thousands of discrepancies (with a modest number substantially affecting meaning) in Greek manuscripts from which printed versions were ultimately produced.[2] That degree of variation resulted from the repeated copying by hand, without the control present in the Jewish Masoretic tradition.

In contrast, there is only one difference between Ashkenazic and Sephardic scrolls. It involves the fourth word in Deuteronomy 23:2. Ashkenazic scrolls spell it as the three-letter sequence *dalet-caf-hei*, while Sephardic scrolls have *dalet-caf-alef*. In both traditions the word is pronounced identically as *dakkah* and understood to mean "crushed." This is the only difference in spelling, and there are no spacing differences in Ashkenazic and Sephardic scrolls, which account for the vast majority of scrolls.

Yemenite scrolls agree with the Sephardic spelling in Deuteronomy 23:2. In addition, there are twelve spelling and spacing differences between Ashkenazic/Sephardic scrolls (A/S) and those of the Yemenites (Y) as shown below:[3]

Genesis 4:13, last word *mi-n'so* [than can be carried]: A/S includes silent *vav* as next to last letter, while Y omits it.

Genesis 7:11, sixth from last word *may'not* [fountains]: Same difference as in Item 1 above.

Genesis 9:29, first word: A/S has *va-hi* [and it was], while Y has *va-yiyu* [and they were]. The Y version includes a *vav* as the last letter, while the A/S version does not.

Genesis 41:45, twelfth/thirteenth word: A/S has two words for the proper name *Poti Fera*, while Y combines them.

Exodus 25:31, sixth word, *teiaseh* [you shall make]: A/S includes silent *yud* as second letter, while Y omits it.

Exodus 28:26, next to last word *ha-eifod* [the tunic]: Same difference as in Item 1 above.

Leviticus 7:22 and 7:28: A/S has a *p'tuchah* before 7:28, while Y has it before 7:22.

Numbers 1:17, last word *b'sheimot* [by name]: Same difference as in Item 1 above.

Numbers 10:10, fifth word *chadsheikhem* [your months]: A/S includes silent *yud* as fourth letter, while Y omits it.

Numbers 22:5, sixth word, proper name *B'or*: Same difference as in Item 1 above.

Numbers 25:12, last word *shalom* [peace]: In A/S the third letter (a *vav*) is cut into a top and bottom part, while it appears normally in Y.

Deuteronomy 32:1–43. These verses appear on seventy lines in A/S but on sixty-seven lines in Y.

Appendix C
List of Remaining Parts in First Four Books Subdivided into Subparts

Genesis: The subdivision of Part E into Subparts appeared in Section 4 of Stage I. The sub-divisions of the remaining Parts of Genesis are shown below.

Part A: Universal History

Part A of Genesis Subdivided According to Shared Principles		
Subpart	Verses	Features Related to Shared Principle
A (Creation)	1:1–2:3	Seven days of Creation
B (Loyalty)	2:1–3:21	Woman created from Man/ their relation formed in Garden of Eden
C (Limits)	3:22–6:8	Adam and Eve expelled from (no longer had access to) the Garden of Eden/ Cain and Abel's sacrifices, with Abel's preferred/ leads to murder and degradation of Mankind
D (Community)	6:9–9:17	Noah builds Ark and takes responsibility for limited community during Flood/ rainbow as sign of no further flood in future
E (Acceptance)	9:18–11:32	Ham disgraces his father Noah and is cursed forever/ Tower of Babel built, defying command to disperse and attempting to be on God's level

Part B: Focus on Abraham

Part B of Genesis Subdivided According to Shared Principles		
Subpart	Verses	Features Related to Shared Principle
A (Creation)	12:1–9	Initial revelation of God to Abraham (then Abram) and command to travel to Land of Canaan
B (Loyalty)	12:10–13:18	Famine in Canaan drives Abram and Sarah (then Sarai) to Egypt, where Pharaoh takes but releases her after God's intervention
C (Limits)	14:1–17:27	Abram's nephew Lot kidnapped by warring kings but saved by Abram, who refuses booty/ Covenant between the Parts made by animal sacrifice/ Ishmael, son of concubine Hagar, portended as thief/ names changed to Abraham and Sarah
D (Community)	18:1–21:21	Birth of child to Abraham and Sarah promised *lamoed* [at witnessed time]/ Abraham pleads to save community of Sodom/ inhospitable Sodom destroyed/ Ishmael sent away from Abraham's community after Isaac born to Abraham and Sarah
E (Acceptance)	21:22–34	Covenant with Abimelech for future involving the land

Part C: Focus on Isaac

Part C of Genesis Subdivided According to Shared Principles		
Subpart	Verses	Features Related to Shared Principle
A (Creation)	22:1–19	Binding of Isaac to altar (revelation and potential homicide)
B (Loyalty)	22:20–24	Abraham told of Nahor's offspring, with stress on Rebecca who is destined to marry Isaac
C (Limits)	23:1–24:67	Sarah dies and Abraham negotiates for access to burial place/ Eliezer's two oaths in mission to find wife for Isaac/ Rebecca's consent to go at once for marriage needed so as not to kidnap
D (Community)	25:1–11	Abraham sends away his progeny from his concubine Ketura, thus limiting the communal legacy to Isaac and his descendants
E (Acceptance)	25:12–18	Fulfillment of prophecy for Ishmael given in Genesis 16:12

Part D: Focus on Jacob

Part D of Genesis Subdivided According to Shared Principles		
Subpart	Verses	Features Related to Shared Principle
A (Creation)	25:19–36	Prayers to God for Jacob's wife Rebecca to conceive/ revelation to her about cause of hard pregnancy
B (Loyalty)	26:1–32:2	Jacob's brother Esau sells birthright/ Jacob impersonates Esau to get father's blessing and flees Canaan from Esau's vengeance/ Jacob weds both Leah and Rachel through their father Laban's deceit/ their competition during birth of twelve sons (tribes) and a daughter
C (Limits)	32:3–34:31	Jacob renamed Israel after struggle with angel/ encounter with Esau in return to Canaan/ Jacob's daughter Dinah abducted

D (Community)	35:1–8	Jacob and entourage are referred to as *am* [nation] for first time
E (Acceptance)	35:9–22	God's promise to Jacob for future/ Rachel dies in childbirth and fulfills Jacob's unintended curse (from Genesis 31:32)/ Reuben shows disrespect to his father Jacob

Exodus: The subdivision of Part C into Subparts appeared in Section 4 of Stage I. The sub-divisions of the remaining Parts of Exodus are shown below.

Part A: Oppression of Jewish People and Divine Revelations to Moses and Aaron

Part A of Exodus Subdivided According to Shared Principles		
Subpart	Verses	Features Related to Shared Principle
A (Creation)	1:1–1:22	Oppression of Jewish people culminating in infanticide/ midwives' belief in God
B (Loyalty)	2:1–2:22	Moses' father takes wife/ Moses born, brought to Pharaoh's court/ Moses kills Egyptian beating Jew, flees to Midian where he weds
C (Limits)	2:23–4:17	Burning Bush revelation where Moses must remove shoes and where he asks for God's name
D (Community)	4:18–6:9	Moses' return to Egypt as communal leader/ first approach to Pharaoh fails, with people now required to gather straw for bricks
E (Acceptance)	6:10–30	Moses attributes initial failure to his own unrefined lips

Part B: Plagues, Passover, and the Splitting of the Sea

Part B of Exodus Subdivided According to the Shared Principles		
Subpart	Verses	Features Related to Shared Principle
A (Creation)	7:1–7	Moses told that goal of plagues is making Egypt recognize God
B (Loyalty)	7:8–10:29	First nine plagues asserting Jews' freedom from human masters
C (Limits)	11:1–14:10	Laws of Passover with Tenth Plague in between/ firstborn sanctified
D (Community)	14:11–17:16	Communal Exodus/ Splitting of Sea/ communal complaint/ war with Amalek
E (Acceptance)	18:1–27	Judicial hierarchy set as proposed by Moses' father-in-law Jethro

Part D: Instructions for the Tabernacle and Related Objects/ Incident of the Golden Calf

Part D of Exodus Subdivided According to the Shared Principles		
Subpart	Verses	Features Related to Shared Principle
A (Creation)	25:1–28:5	Instructions for building Tabernacle and for making its furnishings (corresponds to Creation of World and its elements)
B (Loyalty)	28:6–30:10	Instructions for making priestly garments and accessories (corresponds to special partnership)
C (Limits)	30:11–31:11	Instructions for actions in Tabernacle on behalf of entire people
D (Community)	31:12–33:11	Sabbath observance in relation to Tabernacle/ Incident of the Golden Calf/ Role of *Ohel Moed* [Tent of Meeting]/ Moses successfully pleads that people not be destroyed
E (Acceptance)	33:12–23	Moses asks God to remain with people (and not just refrain from annihilation) and to show His glory/ God's promise in response

Part E: Actual Construction of the Tabernacle and Making of Related Objects

Part E of Exodus Subdivided According to the Shared Principles		
Subpart	Verses	Features Related to Shared Principle
A (Creation)	34:1–39:1	Revelation to Moses as promised/ construction of Tabernacle and furnishings
B (Loyalty)	39:2–32	Actual making of the priestly garments and accessories
C (Limits)	39:33–43	Tabernacle and its related objects brought to Moses
D (Community)	40:1–33	Moses erects Tabernacle and puts furnishings in proper locations
E (Acceptance)	40:34–38	Cloud of God's presence settles on Tabernacle, keeping promise

Leviticus: The subdivision of Parts A and C into Subparts appeared in Section 4 of Stage I. Parts B and E of Leviticus have only three *parshiyot* each and therefore cannot be subdivided into Subparts (since such a subdivision requires at least five *parshiyot*). Thus, only Part D remains to be subdivided as shown below.

Part D: Disqualification of Sacrifices, Days of Holiness, and Years of the Sabbatical and Jubilee

Part D of Leviticus Subdivided According to the Shared Principles		
Subpart	Verses	Features Related to Shared Principle
A (Creation)	22:1–22:16	Sacrifices disqualified by contact with death, other ritual impurity
B (Loyalty)	22:17–22:33	Other sacrifices disqualified as violating relationship with God
C (Limits)	23:1–24:12	Sabbath, holidays as calls to holiness/ God's name cursed
D (Community)	24:13–24:33	Blasphemer taken outside camp for communal stoning

| E (Acceptance) | 25:1–26:2 | Effect of Sabbatical, Jubilee on land/ redeeming slaves/ valuation |

Numbers: The subdivision of Parts A and E into Subparts appeared in Section 4 of Stage I. Part C of Numbers has only one *parshah* and therefore cannot be subdivided into Subparts (since such a subdivision requires at least five *parshiyot*). Thus, only Parts B and D can be subdivided.

Part B: Desire for Meat, Criticism of Moses' Marital Separation, Spies, Korach's Rebellion

Part B of Numbers Subdivided According to the Shared Principles		
Subpart	Verses	Features Related to Shared Principle
A (Creation)	11:1–15	People craving for meat and doubting God's power to provide it
B (Loyalty)	11:16–22	Special relationship of seventy elders in assisting Moses with people
C (Limits)	11:23–12:16	Access of elders to prophecy and people to quail/ Miriam questions Moses' access to God as reason for him separating from his wife
D (Community)	13:1–15:41	Incident of Spies and related ritual law/ case of Sabbath violation
E (Acceptance)	16:1–18:32	Mutiny of Korach/ selection of Aaron as High Priest confirmed

Part D: Transgressions in Fortieth Year of Wandering

Part D of Numbers Subdivided According to the Shared Principles		
Subpart	Verses	Features Related to Shared Principle
A (Creation)	20:1–21:3	God doubted after Miriam dies/ Aaron and Moses fail to promote belief at rock/ Aaron dies/ God's help sought against Arad
B (Loyalty)	21:4–20	Complaints over quality of food and punishment with serpents
C (Limits)	21:21–24:25	Passage through Emorite land denied/ Balaam's failed effort to use God's name to curse the Jewish people
D (Community)	25:1–25:9	Public immorality with Midianite women/ communal judgment fails/ Phineas kills offenders and stops deadly plague
E (Acceptance)	25:10–26:1	Covenant of peace and priestly status for Phineas for his actions

Appendix D
Glossary

Please note an asterisk (*) follows some words in the explanations. This means that the word in question is also explained in this glossary.

Aleppo Codex	a tenth century manuscript of the Torah, on which current Torah scrolls are based; oldest such manuscript in existence.
Alternate Partition	name of test used in this book to challenge the Parts Claim.*
Ambiguous Subdivision	name of test used in this book to challenge the Subparts Claim.*
Aseret HaDibrot	Hebrew for Ten Commandments.
Ashkenazi/Ashkenazic	of or pertaining to customary practices of northern European Jews.
baal korei	one who reads the Torah publicly on behalf of a congregation.
Babylonian Talmud	Sixty-three-volume analysis of Oral Law* compiled in Babylonia by the end of the fifth century.

baraita	legal pronouncement contemporaneous with but not included in original redaction of the Oral Law* in the second century.
Biblical Criticism	the literary approach to understanding the Five Books that is generally taught at colleges; adherents known as Bible Critics.
b'nei Yisrael	literally, the offspring of Yisrael (known in English as Israel or Jacob), the most common Torah name for the Jewish people.
Chiastic sequences (of text)	see symmetric sequences (of text).
Consistency challenge	a perceived case of textual inconsistency that Source Criticism* uses to challenge single authorship of the Torah.
Dead Sea Scrolls	ancient manuscripts, including versions of Biblical texts, found in eleven arid caves in 1946–56 CE; manuscripts thought to date back to the first three centuries before the Common Era.
Decalogue	Greek name for the Ten Commandments.
Documentary Hypothesis	any theory that the Torah was compiled from multiple sources over time.
Doublet	a pair of Torah narratives with certain similarities that Source Criticism* regards as evidence of different authors.
E-Name	five-letter Hebrew name for God that stresses His more distant role as Creator and Judge.
edah	Hebrew word for an assembly.

edut	Hebrew word for testimony; its shared root with *edah* (see above) gives testimony a connotation of communal responsibility.
Essenes	"End of Days" sect that left the Jewish community in Israel in the last centuries of Common Era; commonly thought to have lived in Qumran* and to have written the Dead Sea Scrolls.*
gematria	the numerical value of a Hebrew word, which is the sum of the values of the individual letters in the word.
Hertz Pentateuch	printed Torah text with English translation and commentary by Rabbi Joseph Hertz, Chief Rabbi of British Empire from 1913 to 1946 and stalwart opponent of Source Criticism.
Hobbes, Thomas	seventeenth century philosopher who raised questions on certain Torah passages while accepting single authorship for the balance.
Honigwachs, Rabbi Yehoshua	author of the 1991 work *The Unity of Torah*, which introduced the idea that the Torah is structured by five shared principles in the Ten Commandments.
Ibn Ezra, Rabbi Avraham	important eleventh century Torah commentator whose comments were reinterpreted by Spinoza* to support his view of multiple authorship of the Torah.

J-Name	four-letter name for God beginning with the Hebrew letter *yud* (commonly transliterated as "j"); also known as Tetragrammaton.
korban (plural: *korbanot*)	Hebrew word for offerings or sacrifices; shares root with verb to come close, thus reflecting belief in God.
Langton, Stephen	Archbishop of Canterbury (d. 1228) who devised the system of chapters and verses used today in locating Biblical passages.
Maimonides	Rabbi Moshe ben Maimon (acronym of Rambam), twelfth century philosopher and codifier of Jewish law; his code *Mishneh Torah* lists all *p'tuchot** and *s'tumot** in the Torah.
Masoretes	scribes who dedicated themselves to faithful textual transmission of the original Five Books of Moses in the centuries following completion of the Babylonian Talmud*; Masoretic notations preserved the ends of verses, spellings, and melodic cues for chanting the Torah.
Mekhilta	standard law-related *Midrash* on Exodus; contains the framework of five principles shared by pairs of adjacent Commandments on the two Tablets (1st and 6th, 2nd and 7th, etc.)

Midrash	an explanation or illustrative story contemporaneous with but not included in original redaction of the Oral Law in second century.
Oral Law	Jewish legal tradition handed down by word of mouth from Sinai along with written Torah; first written down in second century.
Order Challenge	term used in this book for a perceived case of textual disorder that Source Critics use to challenge the Torah's single authorship.
p'tuchah (plural: *p'tuchot*)	Hebrew for open spacing on a Torah scroll (open fully to left column); marks the end of a *parshah*.*
Parallel sequences (of text)	sequences of subtexts whose respective themes repeat in the same order such as the eight-fold sequence A-B-C-D-A-B-C-D or the fifteen-fold sequence A-B-C-A-B-C-A-B-C-A-B-C-A-B-C.
parshah (plural: *parshiyot*)	Hebrew word for paragraph on a Torah scroll (of which there are 295), whose end is marked by a *p'tuchah*.*
Parts Claim	term used in this book for the claim made by Rabbi Honigwachs* that each of the Five Books can be divided into five Parts that align in order with the Shared Principles.*
Pentateuch	Greek name for the Five Books of Moses.

Point Disparity	test used in this book to challenge the replication of the pattern by different trained observers.
Qumran	site where the Dead Sea Scrolls* were found.
Ramban	Hebrew acronym for Rabbi Moshe ben Nachman, the standard thirteenth century Torah commentator, also known as Nachmanides; often deals with larger structural issues in the text.
Rashi	Hebrew acronym for Rabbi Sh'lomo ben Yitzchak, the standard eleventh century Torah commentator; often deals with troubling transitions between apparently unrelated topics in the text.
s'tumah (plural: *s'tumot*)	closed spacing on one line in Torah scroll (with text on both sides); marks the end of a subparagraph.
Segment	one of five subtexts into which a Subpart with five or more *parshiyot** can be subdivided in alignment with the Shared Principles* in the first four books.
Separation of Church, State	term used for bar in First Amendment to the U.S. Constitution on "legislation respecting an establishment of religion."
Sephardi/Sephardic	of or pertaining to the customary practices of the Jews of Mediterranean countries.

Shared Principles	term used in this book for five principles shared by pairs of adjacent Commandments on the two Tablets; first identified by the *Mekhilta*.*
Source Criticism	the dominant strain of Biblical Criticism, which embraces the Documentary Hypothesis*; adherents known as Source Critics.
Spinoza, Benedict	seventeenth century philosopher and father of Source Criticism,* who totally rejected single authorship of the Torah.
Standard opening	term used in this book for the phrase "And God said to Moses, saying," which opens many *parshiyot** of law.
Subparts Claim	term used in this book for Rabbi Honigwachs' claim that all Parts* in the first four books with at least five *parshiyot* subdivide into five Subparts* aligned in order with the Shared Principles.*
Symmetric sequences (of text)	sequences of subtext whose respective themes occur in a symmetric pattern, such as the six-fold sequence A-B-C-C-B-A or the seven-fold sequence A-B-C-D-C-B-A.
Wellhausen Hypothesis	theory popularized by the nineteenth century German academic Julius Wellhausen that the Torah was compiled over time from four source documents (J, E, D, P) by different authors.

Notes

1. The actual listing can be found in Volume 7 of Rabbi Eliyahu Touger's annotated translation of *Mishneh Torah*, Moznaim Publishing Corporation, 1990, pp. 157–164.
2. B. Ehrman, *The Orthodox Corruption of Scripture: The Effect of Early Christological Controversies on the Text of the New Testament* (New York: Oxford University Press, 1993). Professor Ehrman writes that the extent of variation was not widely recognized until 1707 when a study by a scholar named John Mill showed some 30,000 discrepancies among 100 New Testament manuscripts.
3. Based on A. Korah, *Saarot Teiman* (Jerusalem: Mosad haRav Kook, 1954), pp. 103–105.

About the Author

Dr. Robert Appleson was born in Memphis, Tennessee, and was taught in his youth by Rabbi Ephraim Greenblatt, *zt"l*, to whom this work is dedicated. He is a trained mathematician (Ph.D., Vanderbilt 1975), who retired in 2014 after many years as a vice president for the Higher Learning Commission, an accrediting body for colleges and universities in nineteen states. Now spending most of his time studying at the Illinois Center for Jewish Studies, he and his wife are blessed with three married children and their spouses, each with children of their own. He has published articles in the fields of mathematics, educational policy, and Jewish studies.